God Today

God's Message
to
Everyone
for
the End
of
the World

God Today

God's Message to Everyone for the End of the World

John C. Sun
God Today Ministries

Printed in the United States of America

Packaged by WinePress Publishing, PO Box 428, Enumclaw, WA 98022. The views expressed or implied in this work do not necessarily reflect those of WinePress Publishing. Ultimate design, content, and editorial accuracy of this work are the responsibilities of the author.

ISBN 1-57921-271-9
Library of Congress Catalog Card Number: 99-68647

Contents

Chapter Two: Who Is Jesus?

Chapter Four: Ears Can Hear, Eyes Can See

Chapter Seven: The Eternal Life

Chapter Eight: Defeat Satan

Chapter Nine: Love

Chapter Ten: Sin

Chapter Eleven: Pray

Chapter Twelve: Spread the Gospel

Preface

Not long ago, a wealthy Christian friend, a retired doctor of medicine, died after a short period of serious illness. Before he passed away, my mother and I preached the Gospel to him many times hoping that he would follow Jesus more closely. He liked us to pray for him, because he believed in God's miracle healing. The first thing that came to my mind when I heard about his death was a question: "Will he receive eternal life?" I also questioned: Am I saved?

Around A.D. 1040, my forefather, a Diaspora Jew, migrated to Kaifeng, in Henan Province, China. He changed his last name to Sun. Around A.D. 1500 two brothers of the Sun family moved to Laiyang, Shandong Province, China. About 110 years ago, my great-grandfather was scorched to death for being a Christian. I am a fourth-generation Christian. My mother had been a teacher and part-time preacher. One of my elder sisters gave up her profession as a doctor of medicine and became a full-time preacher more than 20 years ago. One of my younger brothers had been a part-time preacher.

I, however, refused to go to church, because I believed that most of the people who went to church spent their time on something other than preaching or studying the Word of God. I seldom read the Holy Bible. Instead, I pursued what the world could offer me in its endless temptations. I devoted myself to my career in banking and finance. For 30 years I worked very hard, averaging more than 12 hours every day. Then I took an early retirement from being the CEO of an international merchant/commercial bank in Hong Kong.

I had thought of serving God full time in my 40s; however, I believed that I had committed too much sin in my younger days and God might not accept me. In 1990, my wife and I prayed that God would give us our last child. We decided to dedicate this future child—if God would grant us one—to Him for His service. About one year later, God granted us a baby boy, whom we named Jonathan. We taught him Bible stories every night and sent him to a Christian school. My wife and I have been encouraging him to become a preacher when he grows up.

But God had a plan for me. In 1995, my wife, Jonathan and I had been participating in miracle healing services in Orlando, Florida. During those services, we prayed for others as well as for ourselves that God would heal sickness. At that time, I had been advised by my primary care doctor that I had a hernia. The surgeon he recommended told me I had an urachal cyst. Although we had seen many healing miracles, they had happened to others, not to me.

Things changed the morning of January 27, 1996. I had burning pain from my navel to my upper abdomen. I had a fever, and felt weak. So I was rushed to a nearby hospital's emergency room and underwent surgery. Following the surgery, the pain in my upper abdomen still existed, but both my urologist and surgeon said the pain could have been caused by the surgery and would therefore go away after a few weeks.

On February 7, 1996, my surgeon told me that my pathology report showed that I had a rare and dangerous cancer. When I heard the news, I instantly lost interest in everything. All my plans for my family, especially for the four-year-old Jonathan, seemed no longer valid in a matter of seconds. Our friend, the retired doctor of medicine, whom I mentioned earlier, was very worried about me. He contacted my surgeon and many other doctors before he gave me his advice: "Make a will."

My urologist, who was also a fishing partner of mine, advised me that he had already made an appointment for me to visit a famous Jewish professor, an experienced urologist, oncologist, and surgeon on the following Tuesday, February 13, 1996 for a second opinion. That same evening, my sister's family came to our house for a prayer meeting. We also asked my preacher sister to join us via a long-distance conference call. When it was my turn to pray, I was so desperate I shouted: "Jesus, Jesus why have You forsaken me? Please, hear my prayer, I have cancer! I need Your healing!" Immediately, we felt the presence of the Holy Spirit among us.

Our prayers were answered. Not only did Jesus save my life from terminal cancer, He also revealed Himself to me many times, and those revelations have changed my life.

February 15, 1996, during my second surgery, I saw a tall man with white clothes standing in front of me while I was lying down. I tried my best to look at his face, but I could see only his collar. It was round, similar to the collar of a T-shirt, and was made of a light material like linen.

He spoke to me in English: "John, you lived half of your life for yourself. The remaining half, you will live for Me!"

The first thing that came to my mind was that the man implied that since I was 51 at that time, I would live to 102.

I asked myself: Who was the tall man with white clothes? He must be Jesus!

Later I asked my surgeons and anesthetists whether I might have been dreaming during the surgery. They all told me it was not possible. The surgeon who conducted my second surgery, a Jewish professor, told me that it was my spirit who had seen and heard this message. He also told me that he had heard about other patients having similar experiences.

Ever since that incident, I have felt that my old self died and the new self sprang to life by the grace of God. And, as if hearing from Jesus were not enough, I also received confirmation that I was miraculously healed prior to my second operation.

My second surgery, to remove part of my bladder and my navel, was intended to rectify any missing steps from my first surgery. The surgeon conducting my first surgery was not aware I had an urachal cancer. In my second surgery, in addition to the originally proposed scope of operation, the doctor removed three additional parts from my body. I asked him if he removed them because the cancer had spread. He told me he did it as a preventive measure, because he did not have proof at the time of surgery. I explained that I had asked because I wanted to know whether Jesus healed me as we prayed, before I went to the second surgery. He answered, "For this reason, the answer to your question is positive."

Based on his expertise, the cancer could have spread, but four days after the second surgery, the pathology report confirmed that no malignancy was present. This was truly a miracle!

The second time Jesus spoke to me was about three months after my second surgery. It was a Sunday morning, and I was listening to a pastor's preaching at Lake Park Baptist Church. A clear voice came to my right ear. Speaking in Mandarin, my native language, the voice announced. "You must stay alert and pray in order not to fall into temptation. Peter denied Me three times because he did not stay alert and pray." I shouted: "Jesus!"

The third time I heard from Jesus was also when I was listening to a pastor's preaching. This happened to me at the Christ Fellowship Church on November 9, 1997. The pastor was preaching about the request the mother of James and John made to Jesus. The voice spoke to me in two parts. The second part stated: "Write down in the book that this book should not sit on the bookshelf. After one has read it, it should be passed onto another. I shall bless the person who passes this book to another."

Clearly, God wants everyone who can read, to read this book.

Since salvation came through the Jews to the Gentiles over thousands of years (see John 4:22), the Gentiles (especially Christians) now have an excellent opportunity to reciprocate by helping the Jews find their Messiah through God's words, as found in this book:

> Pray for the peace of Jerusalem. May all who love this city prosper. (Psalm 122:6)

> Messenger of good news, shout to Zion from the mountaintops! Shout louder to Jerusalem—do not be afraid. Tell the towns of Judah, "Your God is coming!" Yes, the Sovereign Lord is coming in all his glorious power. He will rule with awesome strength. See, He brings His reward with Him as He comes. (Isaiah 40:9–10)

The Jews should encourage each other to find their Messiah in this book:

> Let the ruins of Jerusalem break into joyful song, for the Lord has comforted His people. He has redeemed Jerusalem. The Lord will demonstrate His holy power before the eyes of all the

> nations. The ends of the earth will see the salvation of our God. (Isaiah 52:9–10)

> The Lord says, Shout and rejoice, O Jerusalem, for I am coming to live among you. Many nations will join themselves to the Lord on that day, and they, too, will be my people. I will live among you, and you will know that the Lord Almighty sent me to you. (Zechariah 2:10–11)

The fourth time Jesus talked to me was on Sunday morning, February 21, 1999. About five minutes before the start of morning service at Christ Fellowship Church I prayed to thank God, not because He healed my mother's bad cough, but for listening to my prayer. I heard a voice say: "Yes, I heard each and every word of your prayers."

What an awesome God!

Each time Jesus spoke to me it was so clear. Unlike dreams, which I always forgot when I woke up, it was spirit talking to spirit with thorough understanding and no distortion.

Jesus said: "Blessed are those who have not seen and yet have believed" (John 20:29 NKJV). Due to different backgrounds, each person has his or her own preconceived ideas when reading a new book, especially a book involving God and man. These preconceived ideas are known as "human filters." In order to remove all the obstacles and barriers between God and man, I suggest that you keep your mind completely open when reading this book. Pay particular attention when reading God's words quoted in the text.

This book was initiated by God Himself and written under His instructions. It reveals many of God's own secrets. Every reader may find his or her Messiah or Savior in this book. It serves as a "banner" and a "whistle" to the Jews (see Isaiah 5:26, 11:11–12, and Zechariah 10:8). To Gentiles, it acts as a "key" to the door (see John 10:9). And I urge you to hurry, since I believe this door may close very soon. This book is intended to serve as a forerunner of Jesus' return and a compass to guide the reader to eternal life. It was written not by human wisdom but under the guidance and inspiration of the Holy Spirit.

In early January 2000, when this book was in its editing stage, the Holy Spirit told me to read the Book of Isaiah. As I had just completed reading the first 45 chapters of Isaiah, the Holy Spirit instructed me to go back to the beginning. At that moment, I had already taken many notes on Isaiah 18:3–4; 32:1–3; 40:9–10; and 44:6, 23. The Holy Spirit then led me to Isaiah 29:18, "In that day deaf people will hear words read from a book and blind people will see through the gloom and darkness." Did Isaiah prophesy about this book 2700 years ago?

While I was writing this book, Satan tried all his tricks to interfere. Fortunately, whenever I asked for God's help, He gave me the help I asked for. I was not in the battle with Satan alone. My best companion, the Holy Spirit, who stayed with me. Together, we defeated Satan.

Sometimes I wonder why Jesus gave such an important delegation to a broken vessel like me. Certainly my words cannot lead anyone to God. Only God's own words can lead His believers to the destination He promised. God's words contained herein have been selected from both the Old and New Testaments. In order to minimize readers' efforts, I've quoted a total of 1686 verses of the Holy Bible. All these quoted verses are used to form twelve topics, one topic per chapter. There are no deviations and omissions from the Holy Bible. The quoted Bible verses are taken mainly from the New Living Translation, with a smaller portion from the New King James Version. No matter what the translation, though, God is always the same from the beginning to the end. He does not change His ways today from yesterday. Nor will He change tomorrow. He said: "I am the Lord, and I do not change.

That is why you descendants of Jacob are not already completely destroyed." (Malachi 3:6; see also Psalm 102:27, Hebrews 1:12, and James 1:17)

As He always has, God chooses today to heal His people by replacing their hardened hearts with softened hearts. Today He also heals His people by removing all obstacles so they can hear and see clearly. (see Psalm 95:7–8, Isaiah 6:9–10, John 12:40, and Hebrews 3:7–8)

Those who wish to move closer to God and be rewarded with eternal life can find God's "secret" instructions herein. (see Isaiah 40:10; 62:11 ; Matthew 7:14, 21; John 6:37–40; and Revelation 22:12) Only the Holy Spirit can reveal God's own secrets. There are many secrets explained in this book. They seem to be ancient treasures just being discovered. On June 29, 1999, the Holy Spirit gave me a message regarding two different Promised Lands, one in the Old Covenant and the other in the New Covenant. Details can be found later in this book.

If you have already decided to follow Jesus, I wish to share with you scriptures fundamental to my faith: "But those who endure to the end will be saved" (Matthew 24:13), and "Remain faithful even when facing death, and I will give you the crown of life." (Revelation 2:10)

God always lets us make our own choices. However, if you haven't accepted Jesus as your Savior or Messiah, you owe it to yourself to read this book. Although we are approaching the time of the Second Coming of Jesus (also known as "the end of the world"), no one knows the exact date and time except God Himself. On the other hand, no one knows the date and time of his or her own death. In order to be awarded with the eternal life rather than to be cast into everlasting hell, "the lake of fire," it is only logical and wise to make preparations today before the door closes.

As I said, we never know when the door will close. My urologist died suddenly in a car accident. March 3, 1999, at the age of 48.

I was very sad at his funeral service. It was not simply because I'd lost a friend, but because I had asked him many times to follow Jesus, but he never gave a positive response. The last time I asked him was about 10 days before his death. He again declined, telling me: "I still enjoy my sinful life. When I feel ready in the future, I'll go to the church with you and read the Holy Bible." He assumed that he had plenty of time to make his decision. He didn't!

I wish my friend had embraced the example of my faithful Christian mother. She led me closer to God every minute for more than six years. Even in her last days, when she was suffering from severe pain and agony due to a gastric cancer, she did not fail to spread the Gospel to friends and members of the younger generation. Her faithful endurance gave glory to God. She asked the younger generations: "Must Jesus bear the cross alone?" She also reminded us to prepare ourselves for eternal life: "Stop loving this evil world and all that it offers you, for when you love the world, you show that you do not have the love of the Father in you. For the world offers only the lust for physical pleasure, the lust for everything we see, and pride in our possessions. These are not from the Father. They are from this evil world. And this world is fading away, along with everything it craves. But if you do the will of God, you will live forever." (1 John 2:15–17)

About 930 years before Christ, the wisest, richest and the most influential king of Israel, Solomon, documented the following:

> For there is no more remembrance of the wise than of the fool forever, since all that now is will be forgotten in the days to come. And how does a wise man die? As the fool! (Ecclesiastes 2:16 NKJV)

For the living know that they will die; but the dead know nothing. And they have no more reward, for the memory of them is forgotten. (Ecclesiastes 9:5 NKJV)

Whatever your hand finds to do, do it with your might; for there is no work or device or knowledge or wisdom in the grave where you are going. (Ecclesiastes 9:10 NKJV)

Jesus said: "And how do you benefit if you gain the whole world but lose your own soul in the process? Is anything worth more than your soul?" (Matthew 16:26)

JOHN C. SUN
AUGUST, 2000

chapter one

Jesus' Return and the End of the World

MANY PEOPLE WISH TO SEE JESUS' SECOND COMING. THEY HOPE it will happen as soon as possible, preferably in their life time. However, the vast majority of people either don't believe in the Second Coming or they prefer to stay as long as possible in their present life. They do not wish to see the end of the world or the Second Coming of Jesus. They are satisfied with this present life and choose to ignore the truth that God has given us in His word. They assume that since it hasn't happened yet, it won't happen. Unfortunately, that's not what God says. For sure, Jesus is returning, and He is returning soon.

Although no one can tell the date and the time except God Himself, Jesus did tell His disciples the relevant generation and signs of His Second Coming. Only in God's own words we may rely on the signs of the last days.

The apostle Paul told Timothy, a young pastor of a church in Ephesus, precisely what to watch out for:

> That in the last days there will be very difficult times. For people will love only themselves and their money. They will be boastful and proud, scoffing at God, disobedient to their parents, and ungrateful. They will consider nothing sacred. They will be unloving and unforgiving; they will slander others and have no self-control; they will be cruel and have no interest in what is good. They will betray their friends, be reckless, be puffed up with pride, and love pleasure rather than God. They will act as if they are religious, but they will reject the power that could make them godly. (2 Timothy 3:1–5)

Although these words were written nearly 2,000 years ago, they seem to be right out of today's headlines. Based on those signs, we are already situated in the last days.

The Last Days?

Referring to the last days, Jesus told His disciples that the Gospel would reach the entire world during the last days. "And the Good News about the Kingdom will be preached throughout the whole world, so that all nations will hear it; and then, finally, the end will come." (Matthew 24:14)

Advances in satellite technology and aggressive missionary efforts have truly brought the Gospel to all the world, and the world has responded. In recent years, millions of people have decided to follow Jesus in Africa, Asia, Eastern Europe and many other areas of the world. One evangelist reported more than 300,000 attended each of his evening preaching services in India, and more than 30,000 decided to follow Jesus. Similar or larger numbers were also recorded in 1999 in New Guinea and 2000 in the Philippines.

Today, the Holy Bible can be printed officially in China, where the Gospel had been suppressed for five decades. In the Philippines, thousands are filled with the Holy Spirit through preaching services and daily television broadcasts. In Eastern Europe, the

Gospel is being spread to the people who had lived for decades under communist rule. In Zambia, the president led millions of his people to accept Jesus as their Savior. Thousands of Africans are coming to Jesus every day.

Today there is an overall hunger for the Gospel and Jesus Christ throughout the world. Until about ten years ago, no one would have predicted or believed that the present situation would come about within such a short period of time. But the words Jesus spoke to His disciples 2,000 years ago on the Mount of Olive are being fulfilled. Even in the Gospel-saturated United States, people are responding to the Good News more than ever before. Some 48,000 New Yorkers made decisions to follow Christ in a series of meetings in Madison Square Garden in 1999.

The End of the World—God's Own Words

I have been preaching the Gospel of Jesus Christ to the Jews on an informal basis since 1995. For the first two years, I met with no success at all. Since early 1997, however, the situation has changed dramatically. Many Jews have begun to show keen interest in knowing more about Jesus as their Messiah. When I suggested they read verses in both the Old and New Testaments of the Holy Bible regarding Jesus, most of them accepted my suggestions! Many of them were well educated and well known in the local community.

Why is this happening now? This change was certainly not due to any improvement of my preaching. It is the work of the Holy Spirit, who is causing the barriers between Jews and Jesus to be diminished every day.

God's timetable for all the Jews accepting Jesus as their Messiah has already begun. The "spiritual touch" to open the ears and the eyes of each and every Jew is now in the hands of the Holy Spirit.

One afternoon in early 1997, the Holy Spirit guided me to Matthew 24: "As Jesus was leaving the Temple grounds . . . Later,

Jesus sat on the slopes of the Mount of Olives. His disciples came to him privately and asked, 'When will all this take place? And will there be any sign ahead of time to signal your return and the end of the world?'" (v. 3)

Among other things, Jesus said the following to His disciples, while He sat on the slope of the Mount of Olives:

> Now learn a lesson from the fig tree. When its buds become tender and its leaves begin to sprout, you know without being told that summer is near. Just so, when you see the events I've described beginning to happen, you can know his return is very near, right at the door. I assure you, this generation will not pass from the scene before all these things take place. Heaven and earth will disappear, but my words will remain forever.
>
> However, no one knows the day or the hour when these things will happen, not even the angels in heaven or the Son himself. Only the Father knows. (Matthew 24:32–36)

This is a very important clue Jesus gives us. The message appears three times in the Holy Bible: Matthew 24, Mark 13:28–32, and Luke 21:29–36. "This generation" refers to the generation alive when the above scene takes place. A generation normally represents a period between 20 and 40 years.

Immediately after I read this message in Matthew 24:32–36, the Holy Spirit guided me to Jeremiah 24. In that chapter God used figs to symbolize the Jews. God sees the two baskets of figs representing all the Jews (also refer to Isaiah 27:6, Jeremiah 29:17). The message filled in my mind was that the time of Jesus' Second Coming has a direct link to the Jews' accepting Jesus as their Messiah.

The fig tree in Matthew 24:32 refers to the Jews. "When its buds become tender and its leaves begin to sprout" signals a time when Jews in unprecedented numbers accept Jesus as their Messiah; and more and more Gentiles accept Jesus as their Savior. Then, in that generation, Jesus will return.

This is the generation Jesus referred to!

God's Condition for Jesus' Return

After I finished reading Jeremiah 24, the Holy Spirit guided me to the book of Matthew again:

> O Jerusalem, Jerusalem, the city that kills the prophets and stones God's messengers! How often I have wanted to gather your children together as a hen protects her chicks beneath her wings, but you wouldn't let me. And now look, your house is left to you, empty and desolate. For I tell you this, you will never see me again until you say, "Bless the one who comes in the name of the Lord!" (Matthew 23:37–39; see also Luke 13:34–35, John 12:13, and Psalms 118:26)

"Jerusalem, Jerusalem, the city" refers to the Jews. Jesus spread the Gospel to the Jews, His own people, but they refused to accept Him (see John 1:11).

"Bless the one who comes in the name of the Lord." This had also been spoken by God about 1,000 years before Jesus was born (Psalms 118:26). The statement refers to no one else but Jesus. By adding the word "bless," it bears the meaning that all the Jews will accept Jesus as their Messiah. "I will leave none of my people behind." (Ezekiel 39:28; also see Jeremiah 23:3–4; John 6:39) This is the promise made by God Himself.

"You will never see me again until. . . ." Jesus gave the Jews His own words that His Second Coming will take place only after all the Jews have accepted Him as their Messiah. All the Jews will see Jesus in His Second Coming, including the ones who pierced Him (see Zechariah 12:10; John 19:34,37, Revelation 1:7, and Romans 11:25–27).

There is no doubt that Jesus will come again and the world will come to an end. No one and nothing can prevent it from happening. Jesus said: "I am the one who is, who always was, and who is still to come, the almighty one." (Revelation 1:8)

God Heals the Jews

Although most Jews do not believe Jesus is their Messiah, once the Jews do believe they will be saved.

But despite all the miraculous signs Jesus did among the Jews, most of the people did not believe in Him. This is exactly what Isaiah the prophet had predicted: "Lord, who has believed our message? To whom will the Lord reveal his saving power?"

But the people couldn't believe, for as Isaiah also said: "The Lord has blinded their eyes and hardened their hearts—so their eyes cannot see, and their hearts cannot understand, and they cannot turn to me and let me heal them."

Isaiah was referring to Jesus when he made this prediction, because he was given a vision of the Messiah's glory.

Many people, including some of the Jewish leaders, believed in Jesus. But they wouldn't admit it to anyone, because of their fear that the Pharisees would expel them from the synagogue. For they loved human praise more than the praise of God. (see John 12:37–43, also refer to Isaiah 53:1 and 6:9–10)

The time has come, and it is today. God will let His people see and hear clearly. God will also soften the hearts of His people and write His words in them. All the Jews will realize that the praise of God is far more important than the praise of men. They will also realize that "all who believe in God's Son have eternal life. Those who don't obey the Son will never experience eternal life, but the wrath of God remains upon them." (John 3:36)

"They cannot turn and let me heal them" means as soon as the Jews accept Jesus as their Messiah, they are promised by God that they will have eternal life—"to return to their own land." The words of Jesus will be fulfilled and remain forever (see Matthew 24:35).

A Great Rebellion Against God

The apostle Paul warned about rebellion against God in his second letter to the church in Thessalonica:

> And now, brothers and sisters, let us tell you about the coming again of our Lord Jesus Christ and how we will be gathered together to meet him. Please don't be so easily shaken and troubled by those who say that the day of the Lord has already begun. Even if they claim to have had a vision, a revelation, or a letter supposedly from us, don't believe them. Don't be fooled by what they say.
>
> For that day will not come until there is a great rebellion against God and the man of lawlessness is revealed—the one who brings destruction. He will exalt himself and defy every god there is and tear down every object of adoration and worship. He will position himself in the temple of God, claiming that he himself is God. Don't you remember that I told you this when I was with you? And you know what is holding him back, for he can be revealed only when his time comes.
>
> For this lawlessness is already at work secretly, and it will remain secret until the one who is holding it back steps out of the way. Then the man of lawlessness will be revealed, whom the Lord Jesus will consume with the breath of his mouth and destroy by the splendor of his coming. This evil man will come to do the work of Satan with counterfeit power and signs and miracles. He will use every kind of wicked deception to fool those who are on their way to destruction because they refuse to believe the truth that would save them. So God will send great deception upon them, and they will believe all these lies. Then

> they will be condemned for not believing the truth and for enjoying the evil they do. (2 Thessalonians 2:1–12)

Get Ready!

A simple way to get ready is to ask ourselves as frequently as necessary whether we are ready to meet Jesus in His Second Coming. How can our sins be forgiven? Did we obey the words of God and accept that Jesus is the Son of God, the Savior, and the Redeemer? The answers can be found in this book.

In His Sermon on the Mount of Olives, Jesus also told His disciples:

> Know this: A homeowner who knew exactly when a burglar was coming would stay alert and not permit the house to be broken into. You also must be ready all the time. For the son of man will come when least expected.
>
> Who is a faithful, sensible servant, to whom the master can give the responsibility of managing his household and feeding his family? If the master returns and finds that the servant has done a good job, there will be a reward. I assure you, the master will put that servant in charge of all he owns. But if the servant is evil and thinks, 'My master won't be back for while,' and begins oppressing the other servants, partying, and getting drunk—well, the master will return unannounced and unexpected. He will tear the servant apart and banish him with the hypocrites. In that place there will be weeping and gnashing of teeth. (Matthew 24:43–51)

A servant who is doing a good job is a Christian who obeys the will of God and helps others to accept Jesus as the Savior or the Messiah. We must be ready all the time, since no one knows the exact date and time of the Second Coming of Jesus or the exact date and time for his/her own death. Jesus told His disciples that watchful waiting and preparation is necessary:

> The Kingdom of Heaven can be illustrated by the story of ten bridesmaids who took their lamps and went to meet the bridegroom. Five of them were foolish, and five were wise. The five who were foolish took no oil for their lamps, but the other five were wise enough to take along extra oil. When the bridegroom was delayed, they all lay down and slept. At midnight they were roused by the shout, "Look, the bridegroom is coming! Come out and welcome him!"
>
> All the bridesmaids got up and prepared their lamps. Then the five foolish ones asked the others, "Please give us some of your oil because our lamps are going out." But the others replied, "We don't have enough for all of us. Go to a shop and buy some for yourselves."
>
> But while they were gone to buy oil, the bridegroom came, and those who were ready went in with him to the marriage feast, and the door was locked. Later, when the other five bridesmaids returned, they stood outside, calling, "Sir, open the door for us!" But he called back, "I don't know you!"
>
> So stay awake and be prepared, because you do not know the day or hour of my return." (Matthew 25:1–13)

There are four minimum steps by which Christians can stay awake and be prepared:

1. Read the Holy Bible regularly, preferably every day. Live within the guidelines of God's Word and avoid deliberate sins.

2. Confess sins (as the sins occur, or at least once every day) to God, and ask Him to wash away our sins by means of the blood of Jesus.
3. Always pray and invite the Holy Spirit to live inside us to guide and strengthen us so that we may stand against temptations from Satan.
4. Love others as God loves us.

Time Is Running Out! Wake Up!

The apostle Paul reminded the Christians in Rome of the need to stay alert, and he gave them specific directions on how to be ready for Jesus' return:

> Another reason for right living is that you know how late it is; time is running out. Wake up, for the coming of our salvation is nearer now than when we first believed. The night is almost gone; the day of salvation will soon be here. So don't live in darkness. Get rid of your evil deeds. Shed them like dirty clothes. Clothe yourselves with the armor of right living, as those who live in the light. We should be decent and true in everything we do, so that everyone can approve of our behavior. Don't participate in wild parties and getting drunk, or in adultery and immoral living, or in fighting and jealousy. But let the Lord Jesus Christ take control of you, and don't think of ways to indulge your evil desires. (Romans 13:11–14)

In many cases, Bible passages have more than one meaning. When Paul said "time is running out," he was referring to the Second Coming of Jesus, but the expression also refers to the limit to the days of our lives. We do not know the date and time of our own death. Jesus will accompany us only when we have invited His representative, the Holy Spirit, to live inside us and to take control. The Holy Spirit can remind us the words of Jesus as and when we are in need.

The apostle Peter also wrote of this coming day in a letter to all believers in Christ:

> But the day of the Lord will come as unexpectedly as a thief. Then the heavens will pass away with a terrible noise, and everything in them will disappear in fire, and the earth and everything on it will exposed to judgment. Since everything around us is going to melt away, what holy, godly lives you should be living! You should look forward to that day and hurry it along—the day when God will set the heavens on fire and the elements will melt away in the flames. But we are looking forward to the new heavens and new earth he has promised, a world where everyone is right with God. (2 Peter 3:10–13, also see Isaiah 65:17–19, 66:22; John 14:2–4; Revelation 21)

When Jesus Comes Again

"When Jesus comes again" bears the same meaning as "the Return of Jesus" or the "Second Coming of Jesus." Based on God's own words, He will return and judge the world. About 1,000 years before Christ, God disclosed information about His return:

> For the Lord is coming! He is coming to judge the earth. He will judge the world with righteousness and all the nations with his truth. (Psalm 96:13; also see Psalm 98:9)

Around A.D. 32, Jesus told the Jewish leaders about this coming judgment: "And the Father leaves all judgement to his Son, so that everyone will honor the Son, just as they honor the Father. But if you refuse to honor the Son, then you are certainly not honoring the Father who sent him." (John 5:22–23)

Around A.D. 96, the Resurrected Jesus revealed more of this coming judgment to His apostle John in a vision on the Island of Patmos: "See, I am coming soon, and my reward is with me, to repay all according to their deeds. I am the Alpha and the Omega, the First and the Last, the Beginning and the End." (Revelation 22:12–13; also see Isaiah 40:10, 62:11)

Describing the events leading up to His return, Jesus also told His disciples:

> When the Son of Man returns, it will be like it was in Noah's day. In those days before the Flood, the people were enjoying banquets and parties and weddings right up the time Noah entered his boat. People did not realize what was going to happen until the Flood came and swept them all away. That is the way it will be when the Son of Man comes.
>
> Two men will be working together in the field; one will be taken, the other left. Two women will be grinding flour at the mill; one will be taken, the other left. So be prepared, because you don't know what day your Lord is coming. (Matthew 24:37–42)

Because God loves us, He does not want us to be surprised by the return of Jesus. Although Jesus did not notify us the exact day and time of His Return, He did give us the signs, hints, and warnings so that His believers may be saved.

Not all who witness Jesus' Second Coming will rejoice. Jesus described the reaction of some of those upon the earth who see Him return:

> For as the lightning comes from the east and flashes to the west, so also will the coming of the Son of Man be. Then the sign of the Son of Man will appear in heaven, and then all the tribes of the earth will mourn, and they will see the Son of Man coming on the clouds of heaven with power and great glory. And He will send His angels with a great sound of a trumpet, and they will gather together His elect from the four winds, from one end of heaven to the other." (Matthew 24:27, 30–31 NKJV)

Why will all the tribes of earth mourn His return? Because they will realize for the first time that Jesus, the Son of God, was despised, persecuted, and crucified by man, and that He who had no sin acted as the High Priest using His own blood to cleanse sins of all mankind. Unlike the first time Jesus came to the world from heaven and humbled Himself as a son of man, at the Second Coming, Jesus will bring with Him power and great glory, with His original authority and more. The Resurrected Jesus told His disciples: "All authority has been given to Me in heaven and on earth." He will be the King of kings and the Lord of lords—and every knee shall bow and every tongue shall confess that fact. (see Isaiah 45:21–23)

Stages of Jesus' Second Coming

There will be three stages of Jesus' Second Coming.

In the first stage, Jesus will bring with Him the Christians resurrected from the dead, together with all Christians who are still alive. They will meet with Him in the clouds. It will be the First Resurrection. The Christians resurrected from the dead will be only those who were beheaded for their testimony about Jesus, for proclaiming the Word of God, and those true Christians who obeyed the will of the Father in heaven.

In the apostle Paul's first letter to the church in Thessalonica, the capital and a seaport of the Roman province of Macedonia, he described the event known as the Rapture:

> And now, brothers and sisters, I want you to know what will happen to the Christians who have died so you will not be full of sorrow like people who have no hope. For since we believe that Jesus died and was raised to life again, we also believe that when Jesus comes, God will bring back with Jesus all the Christians who have died.
>
> I can tell you this directly from the Lord: We who are still living when the Lord returns will not rise to meet him ahead of those

> who are in their graves. For the Lord himself will come down from heaven with a commanding shout, with the call of the arch-angel, and with the trumpet call of God. First, all the Christians who have died will rise from their graves. Then, together with them, we who are still alive and remain on the earth will be caught up in the clouds to meet the Lord in the air and remain with him forever. (1 Thessalonians 4:13–17; also see Isaiah 52:8–9)

Those true Christians who are still alive will be transformed from perishable, earthly bodies to heavenly bodies that will never die. (see 1 Corinthians 15:50–54)

In the second stage, Jesus will bring all the resurrected and transformed Christians to reign with Him for 1,000 years, a period called the Millennium. Satan, the Devil, will be bound in chains for this period. This will happen following the period of Tribulation. (see Revelation 20:4–6)

The third stage will see Satan temporarily released after 1,000 years of imprisonment. Satan will deceive the nations. He will then be cast into the lake of fire, where he will stay and suffer forever. All the remaining people who died but were not resurrected during the First Resurrection will also be resurrected. This will be the Second Resurrection or the final resurrection. All those resurrected in the Second Resurrection will be subject to judgment for their individual deeds. Death and Hades will also be cast into the lake of fire together with those whose names cannot be found in the Book of Life. It will also be the end of the world and the beginning of the New Jerusalem. (see Revelation 20:7–15)

The New Jerusalem: The Place for Eternal Life

Through the visions and symbols of the resurrected Christ, the apostle John envisioned the arrival of a new heaven and a new earth at the return of Jesus. He wrote:

> Then I [John] saw a new heaven and a new earth, for the old heaven and the old earth had disappeared. And the sea was also gone. And I saw the holy city, the New Jerusalem, coming down from God out of heaven like a beautiful bride prepared for her husband. (Revelation 21:1–2)

The New Jerusalem is the unique eternal destination for all Christians when Jesus returns, both for the Jews and the Gentiles, as described in Isaiah 35:10, 65:17–19, 66:18–22; John 14:2–4; Hebrews 4:1–11, 12:22 and 2 Peter 3:13. It is the land God promised the Jews in the New Covenant. It is also the eternal home for Christians after the world we live in fades away and disappears. It is also God's own home and Resting Place. (refer to Genesis 28:10–13; John 1:51)

Transformed Bodies

In his first letter to the church in Corinth, the apostle Paul wrote about the transformed bodies that will never die:

> What I am saying, dear brothers and sisters, is that flesh and blood cannot inherit the Kingdom of God. These perishable bodies of ours are not able to live forever. But let me tell you a wonderful secret God has revealed to us. Not all of us will die, but we will all be transformed. It will happen in a moment, in the blinking of an eye, when the last trumpet is blown. For when the trumpet sounds, the Christians who have died will be raised with transformed bodies. And then we who are living will be transformed so that we will never die. For our perishable earthly bodies must be transformed into heavenly bodies that will never die. When this happens—when our perishable earthly bodies have been transformed into heavenly bodies that will never die—then at last the Scriptures will come true: 'Death is swallowed up in victory. (1 Corinthians 15:50–54)

Anyone who has sin cannot enter into the Kingdom of God. Satan was thrown out of Heaven because he sinned. We can hardly avoid sin completely when we are still carrying our earthly bodies. Only the transformed heavenly bodies may stay away from sin. The blood of Jesus is the only source of cleansing for our sins and the only way that we may be made whole.

Death is the penalty for sin. Mankind has committed sin since the first generation, Adam and Eve. Therefore everyone must die. On the Judgment Day, those whose names are not registered in the Book of Life will be cast permanently into hell —the lake of fire— together with Satan. The lake of fire is also known as the second death. Since there will be no more sin, death will have no reason to exist. Therefore, the death and grave will also be cast into the lake of fire. It will be a great victory for our God in Trinity and His believers on that day!

Rewards and Punishments

At judgment, God will decide who should be rewarded and who should be punished. The rules God established for man are mentioned many times in both the Old Testament and the New Testament. God is love. He knows man cannot keep all the laws of the Old Covenant. He therefore gave us the New Covenant through Jesus Christ. Those who believe in Him will not be judged, because God has already promised them eternal life.

No matter whether he is involved in a test, a race, a game or a competition, each participant is looking forward to the rewards instead of the punishments. Let us first focus on the generous rewards God gives, and then His punishments, with an eye on how to avoid punishments and to earn the rewards:

> Yes, the Sovereign Lord is coming in all his glorious power. He will rule with awesome strength. See, he brings his reward with him as he comes. (Isaiah 40:10, see also 62:11)

> I, the Lord, search all hearts and examine secret motives. I give all people their due rewards, according to what their actions deserve. (Jeremiah 17:10)

Consider these wonderful rewards promised by the Resurrected Jesus for those who believe on Him and trust in Him for salvation:

> Everyone who is victorious will eat from the tree of life in the paradise of God. (Revelation 2:7)

> Remain faithful even when facing death, and I will give you the crown of life. (Revelation 2:10)

> Everyone who is victorious will eat of the manna that has been hidden away in heaven. (Revelation 2:17)

> To all who are victorious, who obey me to the very end, I will give authority over all the nations. They will rule the nations with an iron rod and smash them like clay pots. They will have the same authority I received from my Father, and I will also give them the morning star! (Revelation 2:26–28)

> All who are victorious will be clothed in white. I will never erase their names from the Book of Life, but I will announce before my Father and his angels that they are mine. (Revelation 3:5)

> Look, I am coming quickly. Hold on to what you have, so that no one will take away your crown. All who are victorious will become pillars in the Temple of my God, and they will never have to leave it. And I will write my God's name on them, and they will be citizens in the city of my God—the new Jerusalem that comes down from heaven from my God. And they will have my new name inscribed upon them. (Revelation 3:11–12)

> I will invite everyone who is victorious to sit with me on my throne, just as I was victorious and sat with my Father on his throne. (Revelation 3:21)
>
> See, I am coming soon, and my reward is with me, to repay all according to their deeds. I am the Alpha and the Omega, the First and the Last, the Beginning and the End. (Revelation 22:12–13)

God's Criteria for Judgment

We are cautioned against being useless servants. Jesus told this story about the Kingdom of Heaven to underscore the importance of using everything we are and everything we have for His kingdom:

> Again, the Kingdom of Heaven can be illustrated by the story of a man going on a trip. He called together his servants and gave them money to invest for him while he was gone. He gave five bags of gold to one, two bags of gold to another, and one bag of gold to the last—dividing it in proportion to their abilities—and then left on his trip. The servant who received the five bags of gold began immediately to invest the money and soon doubled it. The servant with two bags of gold also went right to work and doubled the money. But the servant who received the one bag of gold dug a hole in the ground and hid the master's money for safekeeping.
>
> After a long time their master returned from his trip and called them to give an account of how they had used his money. The servant to whom he had entrusted the five bags of gold said, "Sir, you gave me five bags of gold to invest, and I have doubled the amount." The master was full of praise. "Well done, my good and faithful servant. You have been faithful in handling this small amount, so now I will give you many more responsibilities. Let's celebrate together!"

> Next came the servant who had received the two bags of gold, with the report, "Sir, you gave me two bags of gold to invest, and I have doubled the amount." The master said, "Well done, my good and faithful servant. You have been faithful in handling this small amount, so now I will give you many more responsibilities. Let's celebrate together!"
>
> Then the servant with the one bag of gold came and said, "Sir, I know you are a hard man, harvesting crops you didn't plant and gathering crops you didn't cultivate. I was afraid I would lose your money, so I hid it in the earth and here it is."
>
> But the master replied, "You wicked and lazy servant! You think I'm a hard man, do you, harvesting crops I didn't plant and gathering crops I didn't cultivate? Well, you should at least have put my money into the bank so I could have some interest. Take the money from this servant and give it to the one with the ten bags of gold. To those who use well what they are given, even more will be given, and they will have an abundance. But from those who are unfaithful, even what little they have will be taken away. Now throw this useless servant into outer darkness, where there will be weeping and gnashing of teeth." (Matthew 25:14–30)

Everything we have belongs to God—not merely our personal assets but also our loved ones and even our own life. God is not interested in how much profit we can make in monetary terms. Instead, He gives us His wisdom—the words of Jesus—as the capital. God wishes to see how we can increase the assets He gave us. He will be happy when His children use their abilities to bring in new believers, to find His lost sheep, and to strengthen those Christians who are weak physically or spiritually.

He will also be happy when He finds that we have listened to Him and live according to His words. Jesus told His disciples the important criteria God will use in the Judgment:

> But when the Son of Man comes in his glory, and all the angels with him, then he will sit upon his glorious throne. All the nations will be gathered in his presence, and he will separate them as a shepherd separates the sheep from the goats. He will place the sheep at his right hand and the goats at his left. Then the King will say to those on the right, "Come, you who are blessed by my Father, inherit the Kingdom prepared for you from the foundation of the world. For I was hungry, and you fed me. I was thirsty, and you gave me a drink. I was a stranger, and you invited me into your home. I was naked, and you gave me clothing. I was sick, and you cared for me. I was in prison, and you visited me."
>
> Then these righteous ones will reply, "Lord, when did we ever see you hungry and feed you? Or thirsty and give you something to drink? Or a stranger and show you hospitality? Or naked and give you clothing? When did we ever see you sick or in prison, and visit you?" And the King will tell them, "I assure you, when you did it to one of the least of these my brothers and sisters, you were doing it to me!"
>
> Then the King will turn to those on the left and say, "Away with you, you cursed ones, into the eternal fire prepared for the Devil and his demons! For I was hungry, and you didn't feed me. I was thirsty, and you didn't give me anything to drink. I was a stranger, and you didn't invite me into your home. I was naked, and you gave me no clothing. I was sick and in prison, and you didn't visit me."

> Then they will reply, "Lord, when did we ever see you hungry or thirsty or a stranger or naked or sick or in prison, and not help you?" And he will answer, "I assure you, when you refused to help the least of these my brothers and sisters, you were refusing to help me." And they will go away into eternal punishment, but the righteous will go into eternal life. (Matthew 25:31–46)

There is no judgment pending for those who accepted Jesus as their Savior or Messiah (refer to John 3:18; Roman 8:1). Love comes from God. It is important for us to love each other (refer to Matthew 22:37–40 and Galatians 5:14). Unbelievers and those who did not obey the will of God will subject to judgment, to be judged by the words of Jesus.

There are only two destinations. The first one is the New Jerusalem, where God will live among His people. The other is the everlasting lake of fire.

The apostle Paul described this judgment of unbelievers to the church in Thessalonica:

> But God will use this persecution to show his justice. For he will make you worthy of his Kingdom, for which you are suffering, and in his justice he will punish those who persecute you. And God will provide rest for you who are being persecuted and also for us when the Lord Jesus appears from heaven. He will come with his mighty angels, in flaming fire, bringing judgment on those who don't know God and on those who refuse to obey the Good News of our Lord Jesus. They will be punished with everlasting destruction, forever separated from the Lord and from his glorious power when he comes to receive glory and praise from his holy people. And you will be among those praising him on that day, for you believed what we testified about him. (2 Thessalonians 1:5–10)

The Good News is also known as:

- the Word of God
- the Gospel of Christ
- the New Covenant
- the New Testament
- the Bread of Life

The apostle Peter also wrote warning of the fate of non-believers:

> First, I want to remind you that in the last days there will be scoffers who will laugh at the truth and do every evil thing they desire. This will be their argument: "Jesus promised to come back, did he? Then where is he? Why, as far back as anyone can remember, everything has remained exactly the same since the world was first created."
>
> They deliberately forget that God made the heavens by the word of his command, and he brought the earth up from the water and surrounded it with water. Then he used the water to destroy the world with a mighty flood. And God has also commanded that the heavens and the earth will be consumed by fire on the day of judgement, when ungodly people will perish. (2 Peter 3:3–7)

The Book of Life

A vision that the Resurrected Jesus gave the apostle John dealing with the end of the world reveals how vital it is that our name appears in the Book of Life:

> And I saw a great white throne, and I saw the one who was sitting on it. The earth and sky fled from his presence, but they

found no place to hide. I saw the dead, both great and small, standing before God's throne. And the books were opened, including the Book of Life. And the dead were judged according to the things written in the books, according to what they had done. The sea gave up the dead in it, and death and the grave gave up the dead in them. They were all judged according to their deeds. And death and the grave were thrown into the lake of fire. This is the second death—the lake of fire. And anyone whose name was not found recorded in the Book of Life was thrown into the lake of fire. (Revelation 20:11–15)

"Father, thank you for the Alarm, we can wake up NOW on time!"

chapter two

Who Is Jesus?

Many people, including myself before 1990, have believed that Jesus was simply a man born about 2,000 years ago. They may believe He was a teacher, a good man, and maybe even a prophet. While those thoughts are correct, they are insufficient. Jesus was the Son of God, born of a virgin, who died for our sins and was resurrected on the third day. He was God made mediator so that man can be reconciled with God. When we know Him better, we may have more faith in Him. We need to know Him well as He can be our best friend in addition to our Savior/ Messiah.

Based on the Holy Bible (both the Old and New Testaments), we find that there are no fewer than 222 titles for Jesus. He knows us better than we know ourselves. However, how much we know about Him is more important to us. The following is a list of selected verses of the Holy Bible that help reveal the attributes and titles of Jesus:

The Son of Man

When Jesus was born in this world about 2,000 years ago, He was 100 percent man. The only exception was that He inherited no sin nature from His father the Holy Spirit, nor did He ever sin in His 33 years on earth. He was the only man who gave a name to Himself before He was born. Let us see the following witnesses in the Holy Bible about Him before He was born as a man:

About 1900 before Christ, the Hebrew patriarch Jacob gave blessings to his children. Jacob, the forefather of all the Jewish people, also bore the name of Israel. He blessed his son Judah in a unique way:

> And Jacob called his sons and said, "Gather together, that I may tell you what shall befall you in the last days: . . . Judah, you are he whom your brothers shall praise; Your hand shall be on the neck of your enemies; your father's children shall bow down before you. Judah is a lion's whelp; from the prey, my son, you have gone up. He bows down, he lies down as a lion; And as a lion, who shall rouse him? The scepter shall not depart from Judah, nor a lawgiver from between his feet, until Shiloh comes; and to Him shall be the obedience of the people. Binding his donkey to the vine, and his donkey's colt to the choice vine, he washed his garments in wine, and his clothes in the blood of grapes. His eyes are darker than wine, and his teeth whiter than milk." (Genesis 49:1, 8–12 NKJV)

This scripture is an early prophecy concerning Jesus in the Old Testament. In Matthew 1:1–17, we can see Judah was one of Jesus' forefathers. When Jacob prophesied, "Your father's children shall bow down before you," he was indicating that all the Jews will worship Jesus one day.

The term "lion" also refers to Jesus. In Revelation 5:5 "The Lion of the tribe of Judah, the Root of David, has prevailed to open the scroll and to loose its seven seals."

When Jacob prophesied that "the scepter shall not depart from Judah," he was referring to the kingship of Jesus, not to the temporary rules of King David or King Solomon. Only Jesus is the King of kings and the Lord of lords forever.

The reference to a donkey and a donkey's colt, also mentioned in Zechariah, Matthew, and John, prophesies the entry of Jesus into Jerusalem on a donkey. More details can be found in Chapter Four.

All You Descendants of Jacob, Glorify Him

Many verses of Psalm 22 written by King David prophesied about Jesus as David was being guided by the Holy Spirit. Those relevant verses are highlighted below:

> My God, my God! Why have you forsaken me? (v. 1)
>
> Is this the one who relies on the Lord? Then let the Lord save him! If the Lord loves him so much, let the Lord rescue him! (v. 8)
>
> They have pierced my hands and feet. (v. 16)
>
> They divide my clothes among themselves and throw dice for my garments. (v. 18)
>
> You who fear the Lord, praise him! All you descendants of Jacob, glorify him, and fear him, all you offspring of Israel! (v. 23)
>
> The poor will eat and be satisfied. All who seek the Lord will praise him. Their hearts will rejoice with everlasting joy. (v. 26)

All these verses from Psalm 22, except verse 23, were fulfilled during the lifetime of Jesus, as described in the New Testament. The fulfillment of verse 23 has just begun. "All you descendants of Jacob glorify him" means "all the Jews or all the people of Israel glorify Jesus."

King David also wrote: "He guards all his bones; not one of them is broken." (Psalms 34:20 NKJV). This prophecy was fulfilled in John 19:36. When Jesus was crucified, none of His bones were broken.

Asaph, a priest of music composed the following verses more than 600 years before Christ:

> Let Your hand be upon the man of Your right hand, upon the son of man whom You made strong for Yourself. Then we will not turn back from you; revive us, and we will call upon Your name. (Psalms 80:17–18 NKJV)

"The Man of Your right hand" and "son of man" both refer to Jesus. Jesus was called the Son of man, and only Jesus can revive the Jews.

Conceived by the Holy Spirit

About 700 years before Christ, the prophet Isaiah uttered many prophecies about Jesus. All of these prophecies have been fulfilled. One such prophecy concerned Jesus' birth: "Therefore the Lord Himself will give you a sign: 'Behold, the virgin shall conceive and bear a Son, and shall call His name Immanuel.'" (Isaiah 7:14 NKJV, also refer to Matthew 1:23, Luke 1:31–33)

"Immanuel" means "God is with us", and Jesus was born of a virgin.

Matthew, a tax collector who answered the call from Jesus and became one of His apostles, documented what he knew about the birth of Jesus:

> Now this is how Jesus the Messiah was born. His mother, Mary, was engaged to be married to Joseph. But while she was still a virgin, she became pregnant by the Holy Spirit. Joseph, her fiance, being a just man, decided to break the engagement quietly, so as not to disgrace her publicly.

> As he considered this, he fell asleep, and an angel of the Lord appeared to him in a dream. "Joseph, son of David," the angel said, "do not be afraid to go ahead with your marriage to Mary. For the child within her has been conceived by the Holy Spirit. And she will have a son, and you are to name him Jesus, for he will save his people from their sins." (Matthew 1:18–21)

The difference between Jesus and every other man was that Mary conceived Jesus by the Holy Spirit instead of a man with flesh and blood. Therefore, Jesus had no sin inherited from His Father. Adam's sin, which caused man to become a slave of Satan, did not apply to Jesus.

About thirty years following the resurrection of Jesus, the apostle Paul wrote to a young pastor, Timothy, describing the birth of Jesus:

> And without controversy great is the mystery of godliness: God was manifested in the flesh, justified in the Spirit, seen by angels, preached among the Gentiles, believed on in the world, received up in glory. (1 Timothy 3:16 NKJV)

The Priest

Jesus was born as a man and died as a man so that He completed His duty as a "one-time priest." Subsequent to the crucifixion of Jesus, there was no need of any priest to offer the blood of animals as a sacrifice for sin, because Jesus offered His own blood to wash away sins of all man once for all. He also acted as a lamb in a sacrifice offering to God (see Isaiah 53). Jesus is known as the cornerstone many hundred years before He was born as a man.

In Psalm 110, King David made many important prophecies about Jesus:

> The Lord said to my Lord, "Sit in honor at my right hand until I humble your enemies, making them a footstool under your feet."

> The Lord will extend your powerful dominion from Jerusalem; you will rule over your enemies.
>
> In that day of battle, your people will serve you willingly. "Arrayed in holy garments, Your vigor will be renewed each day like the morning dew."
>
> The Lord has taken an oath and will not break his vow: "You are a priest forever in the line of Melchizedek."
>
> The Lord stands at your right hand to protect you. He will strike down many kings in the day of his anger.
>
> He will punish the nations and fill them with their dead; he will shatter heads over the whole earth.
>
> But he himself will be refreshed from brooks along the way.
>
> He will be victorious. (Psalm 110:1–7)

In the first verse, "The Lord" refers to God the Father and "my Lord" refers to Jesus. Although there is only one God, because God is a spirit, He can act severally or collectively. We should not imagine that God only acts as a man because His power is far beyond our imagination.

"He himself will be refreshed" means that Jesus would become a man, acting completely on the instructions of God the Father. Jesus defeated Satan as a man, giving the God the Father the victory and glory.

"For He Will Bear All Their Sins"

Now comes one of the most obvious prophecies of Jesus in the Old Testament. No one can deny that this prophecy was prophesied about Jesus 700 years before He was born as a man. Most

Jews have not believed in Jesus as their Messiah, because they missed the meaning of this prophecy over the past 2,000 years. All the following prophecies made by Isaiah were fulfilled after approximately 700 years; and the same prophecy will last until the Second Coming of Jesus:

> Who has believed our message? To whom will the Lord reveal his saving power? My servant grew up in the Lord's presence like a tender green shoot, sprouting from a root in dry and sterile ground. There was nothing beautiful or majestic about his appearance, nothing to attract us to him. He was despised and rejected—a man of sorrows, acquainted with bitterest grief. We turned our backs on him and looked the other way when he went by. He was despised, and we did not care.
>
> Yet it was our weaknesses he carried; it was our sorrows that weighed him down. And we thought his troubles were a punishment from God for his own sins! But he was wounded and crushed for our sins. He was beaten that we might have peace. He was whipped, and we were healed! All of us have strayed away like sheep. We have left God's paths to follow our own. Yet the Lord laid on him the guilt and sins of us all.
>
> He was oppressed and treated harshly, yet he never said a word. He was led as a lamb to the slaughter. And as a sheep is silent before the shearers, he did not open his mouth. From prison and trial they led him away to his death. But who among the people realized that he was dying for their sins— that he was suffering their punishment? He had done no wrong, and he never deceived anyone. But he was buried like a criminal; he was put in a rich man's grave.
>
> But it was the Lord's good plan to crush him and fill him with grief. Yet when his life is made an offering for sin, he will have a

> multitude of children, many heirs. He will enjoy a long life, and the Lord's plan will prosper in his hands. When he sees all that is accomplished by his anguish, he will be satisfied. And because of what he has experienced, my righteous servant will make it possible for many to be counted righteous, for he will bear all their sins. I will give him the honors of one who is mighty and great, because he exposed himself to death. He was counted among those who were sinners. He bore the sins of many and interceded for sinners. (Isaiah 53:1–12; also refer to Matthew 8:17; 26:63; 27:38, 57–60; Mark 15:4–5; 15:24, 15:32; Luke 22:37; 23:1–25, 34; John 1:10–11, 29; 12:38; Romans 4:25; 5:18–19; 10:16; 1 Corinthians 15:3; Hebrews 9:28; 1 Peter 2:24–25; and Revelation 6:12–13)

"My servant" refers to no other than Jesus.

"A root in dry and sterile ground" refers to the sinful nature of human beings, which causes them to die as a plant's root placed in dry and sterile ground. Without Jesus, there was no hope of eternal life, especially when the people of Israel could not keep up with the Old Covenant.

"A tender green shoot" refers to Jesus, who was sent by God to this world as a man to carry away all the sins of His believers. Only through Jesus do we have life, and we may also have eternal life!

"He was led as a lamb to the slaughter." This was the source of Jesus being called the "Lamb of God."

"It was the Lord's good plan to crush him" refers to the death of Jesus as a man to defeat Satan and death. Only as a man could He die. It was the means God used to save His people. Since Jesus was resurrected on the third day, all His believers will also be resurrected and receive eternal life in the same way as Jesus, when He comes again.

"I will give him the honors of one who is mighty and great." This prophecy was fulfilled when the Resurrected Jesus told His disciples: "I have been given complete authority in heaven and on earth." (Matthew 28:18)

The Branch

About 520 years before Christ, Zechariah prophesied about Jesus:

> Tell him that the Lord Almighty says: Here is the man called the Branch. He will branch out where he is and build the Temple of the Lord. He will build the Lord's Temple, and he will receive royal honor and will rule as king from his throne. He will also serve as priest from his throne, and there will be perfect harmony between the two.
>
> The crown will be a memorial in the Temple of the Lord to honor those who gave it—Heldai, Tobijah, Jedaiah, and Josiah son of Zephaniah. Many will come from distant lands to rebuild the Temple of the Lord. And when this happens, you will know my messages have been from the Lord Almighty. (Zechariah 6:12–15)

Jesus is the Branch. He is also the priest and the king of kings. The Temple to be rebuilt is not a building. See more details on rebuilding God's Temple in Chapter Six. The body of Jesus and also Christians' bodies are the temple of God!

"They Will Grieve Bitterly for Him"

The Spirit of God also spoke through the prophet Zechariah about a sign related to the Second Coming of Jesus:

> Then I will pour out a spirit of grace and prayer on the family of David and on all the people of Jerusalem. They will look on me whom they have pierced and mourn for him as for an only son.

> They will grieve bitterly for him as for a firstborn son who has died. The sorrow and mourning in Jerusalem on that day will be like the grievous mourning of Hadad-rimmon in the valley of Megiddo. (Zechariah 12:10–11; also read Jeremiah 50:4–5, John 19:33–37, and Revelation 1:7)

"I," "Me" and "Him" all refer to Jesus. The term, "family of David," denotes that as a man, Jesus came out of the family of David. "Whom they have pierced" refers to the fact that Jesus was pierced on the day of His crucifixion.

This passage prophesies that one day, all the Jews will realize Jesus is their Messiah. At that moment, they will grieve bitterly for:

- The only way of salvation—God Himself—came to this world as a man in the name of Jesus, and
- The sin of their ancestors, when they crucified Him as a man, and
- The Holy Spirit reminds them of the words of God and their own sins, since they could not keep the Old Covenant.

"Just As You and I Are One"

This is one of the most important prayers Jesus prayed in the night before his crucifixion. Perhaps John was the only apostle who did not fall into sleep at that moment, and he recorded the entire prayer. No one would pray without speaking the truth. There was no exception for Jesus when He was a man. This prayer clearly shows the exact relationship between Jesus and God the Father, exposing the complete obedience in Jesus, as a man performing God's instructions fully. It also tells us who Jesus is:

> Father, the time has come. Glorify your Son so he can give glory back to you. For you have given him authority over everyone in all the earth. He gives eternal life to each one you have given

him. And this is the way to have eternal life—to know you, the only true God, and Jesus Christ, the one you sent to earth. I brought glory to you here on earth by doing everything you told me to do. And now, Father, bring me into the glory we shared before the world began.

I have told these men about you. They were in the world, but then you gave them to me. Actually, they were always yours, and you gave them to me; and they have kept your word. Now they know that everything I have is a gift from you, for I have passed on to them the words you gave me; and they accepted them and know that I came from you, and they believe you sent me.

My prayer is not for the world, but for those you have given me, because they belong to you. And all of them, since they are mine, belong to you; and you have given them back to me, so they are my glory! Now I am departing the world; I am leaving them behind and coming to you. Holy Father, keep them and care for them—all those you have given me—so that they will be united just as we are. During my time here, I have kept them safe. I guarded them so that not one was lost, except the one headed for destruction, as the Scriptures foretold.

And now I am coming to you. I have told them many things while I was with them so they would be filled with my joy. I have given them your word. And the world hates them because they do not belong to the world, just as I do not. I'm not asking you to take them out of the world, but to keep them safe from the evil one. They are not part of this world any more than I am. Make them pure and holy by teaching them your words of truth. As you sent me into the world, I am sending them into the world. And I give myself entirely to you so they also might be entirely yours.

I am praying not only for these disciples but also for all who will ever believe in me because of their testimony. My prayer

> for all of them is that they will be one, just as you and I are one, Father—that just as you are in me and I am in you, so they will be in us, and the world will believe you sent me.
>
> I have given them the glory you gave me, so that they may be one, as we are—I in them and you in me, all being perfected into one. Then the world will know that you sent me and will understand that you love them as much as you love me. Father, I want these whom you've given me to be with me, so they can see my glory. You gave me the glory because you loved me even before the world began!
>
> O righteous Father, the world doesn't know you, but I do; and these disciples know you sent me. And I have revealed you to them and will keep on revealing you. I will do this so that your love for me may be in them and I in them. (John 17:1–26)

Jesus mentioned three times "Your word" in this prayer. In fact, Jesus is the Word of God incarnate: He was clothed with a robe dipped in blood, and His name is called The Word of God. (Revelation 19:13 NKJV)

> For he is sent by God, He speaks God's words, for God's Spirit is upon him without measure or limit. (John 3:34)
>
> It is the Spirit who gives eternal life. Human effort accomplishes nothing. And the very words I [Jesus] have spoken to you are spirit and life. (John 6:63)

From the beginning to the end, there is only one God. Jesus was God before He was born as a man. During the period when Jesus lived in this world as a man, He was also God—100 percent man and 100 percent God. God is a Spirit. He can act both in singular and plural in numbers, individually and collectively. That is why Jesus, being God and yet born as a man, still ruled as God in the spirit form.

Without the presence and the guidance of the Holy Spirit, man can hardly understand God:

> No one really knows the Son except the Father, and no one really knows the Father except the Son and those to whom the Son chooses to reveal him. (Matthew 11:27)

> But we know these things because God has revealed them to us by his Spirit, and his Spirit searches out everything and shows us even God's deep secrets. (1 Corinthians 2:10)

It would be foolish for man to try to understand God and His Word by means of human wisdom. Imagine it—God can speak to each and every person in the world at the same time, using different words, if He chooses to do so. What an awesome God!

The Lamb of God

No man may stay in this world forever. Not only must every man die, the world will be completely destroyed one day. That is why God sent Jesus to this world so that all Christians may have eternal life as Jesus did—in the Kingdom of God—the New Jerusalem.

In the hope that more Jews would accept Jesus as their Messiah, the apostle Paul wrote the book of Hebrews 30 years after the resurrection of Jesus. One of the most important statements made by Paul was that Jesus offered Himself as a one-time priest—forever. Only in this way, He offered salvation to all mankind. Only those who believe in God's Son have eternal life (see John 3:36).

> So Christ has now become the High Priest over all the good things that have come. He has entered that great, perfect sanctuary in heaven, not made by human hands and not part of this created world. Once for all time he took blood into that Most Holy Place, but not the blood of goats and calves. He took his own blood, and with it he secured our salvation forever. (Hebrews 9:11–12)
>
> Under the old covenant, the priest stands before the altar day after day, offering sacrifices that can never take away sins. But our high priest offered himself to God as one sacrifice for sins, good for all time. Then he sat down at the place of highest honor at God's right hand. There he waits until his enemies are humbled as a footstool under his feet. For by that one offering he perfected forever all those whom he is making holy. (Hebrews 10:11–14)

The apostle John encountered this vision of Jesus as the Lamb of God on the island of Patmos:

> But one of the twenty-four elders said to me, "Stop weeping! Look, the Lion of the tribe of Judah, the heir to David's throne, has conquered. He is worthy to open the scroll and break its seven seals."
>
> I looked and I saw a Lamb that had been killed but was now standing between the throne and the four living beings and among the twenty-four elders. He had seven horns and seven eyes, which are the seven spirits of God that are sent out into every part of the earth. He stepped forward and took the scroll from the right hand of the one sitting on the throne. And as he took the scroll, the four living beings and the twenty-four elders fell down before the Lamb. Each one had a harp, and they held gold bowls filled with incense—the prayers of God's people!

And they sang a new song with these words:

> 'You are worthy to take the scroll and break its seals and open it. For you were killed, and your blood has ransomed people for God from every tribe and language and people and nation. And you have caused them to become God's kingdom and his priests. And they will reign on the earth.'
>
> Then I looked again, and I heard the singing of thousands and millions of angels around the throne and the living beings and the elders. And they sang in a mighty chorus:
>
> 'The Lamb is worthy—the Lamb who was killed. He is worthy to receive power and riches and wisdom and strength and honor and glory and blessing.'
>
> And then I heard every creature in heaven and on earth and under the earth and in the sea. They also sang: 'Blessing and honor and glory and power belong to the one sitting on the throne and to the Lamb forever and ever.'
>
> And the four living beings said, 'Amen!' And the twenty-four elders fell down and worshiped God and the Lamb. (Revelation 5:5–14)

The main reason Jesus was named as the Lamb of God was that He had no sin Himself, but was sent to die as an offering to God taking away the sins of all the sinners:

> He was oppressed and treated harshly, yet he never said a word. He was led as a lamb to the slaughter. And as a sheep is silent before the shearers, he did not open his mouth. From prison and trial they led him away to his death. But who among the

people realized that he was dying for their sins—that he was suffering their punishment. (Isaiah 53:7–8)

The next day John saw Jesus coming toward him, and said, "Look! There is the Lamb of God who takes away the sin of the world." (John 1:29; see also 1 Peter 1:19; Revelation 5:11–13; 7:14; 12:11; 17:14; 21:14; 22, 27; and 22:1–4)

The Cornerstone

The construction of a building cannot be complete in the absence of a cornerstone. Man cannot be made whole without Jesus. Jesus has been known as the Cornerstone for thousands of years: The stone rejected by the builders has now become the cornerstone (Psalm 118:22).

Therefore, this is what the Sovereign Lord says: "Look! I am placing a foundation stone in Jerusalem. It is firm, a tested and precious cornerstone that is safe to build on. Whoever believes need never run away again." (Isaiah 28:16)

Listen to me, O Jeshua the high priest, and all you other priests. You are symbols of the good things to come. Soon I am going to bring my servant, the Branch. Now look at the jewel I have set before Jeshua, a single stone with seven facets. I will engrave an inscription on it, says the Lord Almighty, and I will remove the sins of this land in a single day." (Zechariah 3:8–9)

Then Jesus asked them [Jewish religious leaders], "Didn't you ever read this in the Scriptures? 'The stone rejected by the builders has now become the cornerstone. This is the Lord's doing, and it is marvelous to see.'

"What I mean is that the Kingdom of God will be taken away from you and given to a nation that will produce the proper fruit. Anyone who stumbles over that stone will be broken to pieces, and it will crush anyone on whom it falls." (Matthew 21:42–44)

Let me clearly state to you and to all the people of Israel that he was healed in the name and power of Jesus Christ from Nazareth, the man you crucified, but whom God raised from the dead. For Jesus is the one referred to in the Scriptures, where it says, "The stone that you builders rejected has now become the cornerstone." (Acts 4:10–11)

We are his house, built on the foundation of the apostles and the prophets. And the cornerstone is Christ Jesus himself. (Ephesians 2:20)

Come to Christ, who is the living cornerstone of God's temple. He was rejected by the people, but he is precious to God who chose him. And now God is building you, as living stones, into his spiritual temple. What's more, you are God's holy priests, who offer the spiritual sacrifices that please him because of Jesus Christ. As the Scriptures express it, "I am placing a stone in Jerusalem, a chosen cornerstone, and anyone who believes in him will never be disappointed." Yes, he is very precious to you who believe. But for those who reject him, "The stone that was rejected by the builders has now become the cornerstone." And the Scriptures also say, "He is the stone that makes people stumble, the rock that will make them fall." They stumble because they do not listen to God's word or obey it, and so they meet the fate that has been planned for them. (1 Peter 2:4–8)

The Shepherd, the Servant of God

God refers to Himself as the Shepherd. He also raised a Shepherd for His people from the family of King David. In fact, there is only one God and there is also only one Shepherd.

About 600 years before Christ, Jeremiah prophesied about Jesus, the righteous Branch:

> "For the time is coming," says the Lord, "when I will place a righteous Branch on King David's throne. He will be a King who rules with wisdom. He will do what is just and right throughout the land. And this is his name: The Lord is our Righteousness. In that day Judah will be saved, and Israel will live in safety.
>
> "In that day," says the Lord, "when people are taking an oath, they will no longer say, 'As surely as the Lord lives, who rescued the people of Israel from the land of Egypt'. Instead, they will say, 'As surely as the Lord lives, who brought the people of Israel back to their own land from the land of the north and from all the countries to which he had exiled them.' Then they will live in their own land." (Jeremiah 23:5–8; also refer to Matthew 1:1, 21–23)

"A righteous Branch on King David's throne" refers to Jesus. He is also our Righteousness. Only when the Jews accept Jesus as their Messiah, they will be saved.

The phrase, "who brought the people of Israel back to their own land," has a special meaning that is not obvious at first glance. As the Jews could not keep the Old Covenant, God gave them the New Covenant through Jesus Christ. In the New Covenant (after the crucifixion and the resurrection of Jesus), this phrase means that as soon as the Jews accept Jesus as their Messiah they will be considered as going back to their own land, the land promised by God. When God referred to "their own land," He was not referring to the geographic location of the land of Israel, as it was only the Promised Land under the Old Covenant when Moses led the Jews out of Egypt to Canaan. Instead, He was referring to the New Jerusalem, as described in Revelation 21 and 22. More details can be found in Chapter Four: "Where is the People of Israel's Own Land?"

About 700 years before Jesus was born as a man, Isaiah spoke what God told him to prophesy about Jesus as God's chosen servant:

> Look at my servant, whom I strengthen. He is my chosen one, and I am pleased with him. I have put my spirit upon him. He will reveal justice to the nations. He will be gentle—he will not shout or raise his voice in public. He will not crush those who are weak or quench the smallest hope. He will bring full justice to all who have been wronged. He will not stop until truth and righteousness prevail throughout the earth. Even distant lands beyond the sea will wait for his instruction. (Isaiah 42:1–4)

About 520 years before Christ, Zechariah also prophesied about Jesus as God's servant:

> Listen to me, O Jeshua the high priest, and all you other priests. You are symbols of the good things to come. Soon I am going to bring my servant, the Branch. Now look at the jewel I have set before Jeshua, a single stone with seven facets. I will engrave an inscription on it, says the Lord Almighty, and I will remove the sins of this land in a single day. (Zechariah 3:8–9)

Later, some 430 years before Christ, the prophet Malachi also prophesied about the role of Jesus:

> "Look, I [the LORD] am sending my messenger, and he will prepare the way before me. Then the Lord you are seeking will suddenly come to his Temple. The messenger of the covenant, whom you look for so eagerly, is surely coming," says the Lord Almighty. (Malachi 3:1)

By the way, the covenant spoken of by Malachi is the "New Covenant." The New Covenant was brought to man by Jesus as God's messenger.

Two Different Shepherds?

About 570 before Christ, Ezekiel prophesied about Jesus in Babylon:

> For this is what the Sovereign Lord says: I myself will search and find my sheep. I will be like a shepherd looking for his scattered flock. I will find my sheep and rescue them from all the places to which they were scattered on that dark and cloudy day. I will bring them back home to their own land of Israel from among the peoples and nations. I will feed them on the mountains of Israel and by the rivers in all the places where people live. (Ezekiel 34:11–12)

> And I will set one shepherd over them, even my servant David. He will feed them and be a shepherd to them. And I, the Lord, will be their God, and my servant David will be a prince among my people. I, the Lord, have spoken. (Ezekiel 34:23–24)

Did God change His mind by appointing His servant David to be the Shepherd instead of Himself within a short period of time? No, God did not change His mind. The shepherd is the same. King David died about 400 years before Ezekiel's prophecy. "David" represents Jesus. The Resurrected Jesus who told Apostle John: "I, Jesus, have sent my angel to give you this message for the churches. I am both the source of David and the heir to his throne. I am the bright morning star." (Revelation 22:16)

Jesus preached when He was a man: "I am the good shepherd; I know my own sheep, and they know me." (John 10:14) "I have other sheep, too, that are not in this sheepfold. I must bring them also, and they will listen to my voice; and there will be one flock with one shepherd." (John 10:16)

Jesus is God. There is only one God. Jesus was Jehovah and the Spirit of God before He was born as a man. Then He became the Son of God in human form. God the Father is still in control all the time. God's main purpose in sending Jesus to become a man was to provide man with a way back to Himself. Only one way leads to eternal life: to follow and obey the Words of God given to man through Jesus.

When Jesus was a man, He carried with Him the Words of God as a messenger and He acted completely upon the instructions of God the Father. He was, therefore, being referred to as God's servant.

The Gate

In addition to His role as servant and messenger, Jesus preached to the Jews, including many Pharisees, that He was not only the Good Shepherd, He was the Gate through which the sheep must pass to reach safety:

> "I [Jesus] assure you, I am the gate for the sheep," he said. "All others who came before me were thieves and robbers. But the true sheep did not listen to them. Yes, I am the gate. Those who come in through me will be saved. Wherever they go, they will find green pastures. The thief's purpose is to steal and kill and destroy. My purpose is to give life in all its fullness.
>
> I am the good shepherd. The good shepherd lays down his life for the sheep." (John 10:6–11)

The Savior and the Redeemer

The Old Testament prophets made it clear that the coming Messiah would be a savior who would break the chains that bound

God's people. More than 700 years before Jesus was born, Isaiah prophesied this about Jesus, the Messiah:

> But there will be a time in the future when Galilee of the Gentiles, which lies along the road that runs between the Jordan and the sea, will be filled with glory. The people who walk in darkness will see a great light—a light that will shine on all who live in the land where death casts its shadow. Israel will again be great, and its people will rejoice as people rejoice at harvest time. They will shout with joy like warriors dividing the plunder. For God will break the chains that bind his people and the whip that scourges them, just as he did when he destroyed the army of Midian with Gideon's little band. In that day of peace, battle gear will no longer be issued. Never again will uniforms be bloodstained by war. All such equipment will be burned.
>
> For a child is born to us, a son is given to us. And the government will rest on his shoulders. These will be his royal titles: Wonderful, Counselor, Mighty God, Everlasting Father, Prince of Peace. His ever expanding, peaceful government will never end. He will rule forever with fairness and justice from the throne of his ancestor David. The passionate commitment of the Lord Almighty will guarantee this! (Isaiah 9:1–7, also refer to Luke 1:32–33)

"For God will break the chains that bind his people and the whip that scourges them" means that God will save His people from being the slaves of Satan, breaking the "chains" of sicknesses, depressions, addiction to drugs, alcohol and any other bondage.

"In that day of peace" refers to the day of Jesus' return.

"Never again will uniforms be bloodstained by war" refers to the fact that only in the New Jerusalem will bloodstains be avoided permanently, as there is no more temptation and greed in the minds of the people. Satan can no longer go there, because he has been cast into the lake of fire by then.

"For a child is born to us, a son is given to us" means God sent Jesus to this world as a man to die for the sins of all mankind so they may be made whole if they choose to follow Jesus.

"Wonderful, Counselor, Mighty God, Everlasting Father, Prince of Peace" are all titles for Jesus. This prophecy was announced by God Himself regarding God in Trinity. It also tells us that Jesus is the Messiah, God the Father, and the Holy Spirit. Before His crucifixion, Jesus mentioned many times about the importance of the Holy Spirit in the role of Counselor to His disciples (see John 14:16–17, 26 and 16:7–15).

"His government shall never end" means precisely what it says. Jesus is the Alpha and the Omega, the Beginning and the End (see Isaiah 41:4; 44:6–8; 48:12; Revelation 1:8, 17–18; 2:8; 21:6 and 22:13).

A Banner of Salvation to All the World

Isaiah also prophesied a banner of salvation to all the world. It will come from Jesus, the heir to King David's throne. He will gather the scattered people of Judah from the ends of the earth.

> Out of the stump of David's family will grow a shoot—yes, a new branch bearing fruit from the old root. And the Spirit of the Lord will rest on him—the Spirit of wisdom and understanding, the Spirit of counsel and might, the Spirit of knowledge and the fear of the Lord. He will delight in obeying the Lord. He will never judge by appearance, false evidence, or hearsay. He will defend the poor and the exploited. He will rule against the wicked and destroy them with the breath of his mouth. He will be clothed with fairness and truth.

> In that day the wolf and the lamb will live together; the leopard and the goat will be at peace. Calves and yearlings will be safe among lions, and a little child will lead them all. The cattle will graze among bears. Cubs and calves will lie down together. And lions will eat grass as the livestock do. Babies will crawl safely among poisonous snakes. Yes, a little child will put its hand in a nest of deadly snakes and pull it out unharmed. Nothing will hurt or destroy in all my holy mountain. And as the waters fill the sea, so the earth will be filled with people who know the Lord.
>
> In that day the heir to David's throne will be a banner of salvation to all the world. The nations will rally to him, for the land where he lives will be a glorious place. In that day the Lord will bring back a remnant of his people for the second time, returning them to the land of Israel from Assyria, Lower Egypt, Upper Egypt, Ethiopia, Elam, Babylonia, Hamath and all the distant coastlands.
>
> He will raise a flag among the nations for Israel to rally around. He will gather the scattered people of Judah from the ends of the earth." (Isaiah 11:1–12)

"Branch" refers to Jesus, a man born without sin. His Father is the Holy Spirit instead of a man. (refer to Matthew 1:20–21 and Luke 1:30–35)

"Breath of his mouth" refers to the words of Jesus that will judge the non-believers in the last day, as per John 12:48. No judgment will be pending for believers (see John 3:18 and Romans 8:1).

"Old root" refers to the sinful nature of human beings carried over from the days of Adam and Eve. Jesus was born as a man. His mother was Mary, one of the descendants of King David.

The second paragraph above describes events that will take place during the period of millennium. (refer to Revelation 20:4–6)

"A glorious place" refers to the New Jerusalem described in Revelation 21. There is no glorious place in this world. Only the Resting Place of God is a glorious place. (refer to Genesis 28:13)

"A remnant of his people" refers to those Jews who are still alive when Jesus returns. They will hear and see the words of God. They will all accept Jesus as their Messiah. (refer to Jeremiah 23:3–6 and Ezekiel 39:28) They will be considered as returned to the land of Israel (the New Jerusalem) once they have accepted Jesus as their Messiah. (refer to Romans 11:25–27 and Jeremiah 31:17)

"The second time" refers to the fact that Jesus will bring Jews to the New Jerusalem, not the geographic location of the country of Israel. The first time God instructed Moses to bring the Jews out of Egypt to the land of today's Israel. God gave the Ten Commandments, the Old Covenant (see Exodus 20:1–17), to His people. God then decided to give His people a New Covenant (see Matthew 26:27 and Luke 22:20) because they could not keep the Old Covenant. This was mentioned clearly in Jeremiah 31:31–34, Ezekiel 36:26–27, and 37:26. The second time, God will bring His people to the New Jerusalem as described in Isaiah 11:11, 65:17–19, 66:18–22; Revelation 21, Hebrews 12:22, and 2 Peter 3:9–13.

"The land of Israel" refers to the New Jerusalem. This is the everlasting land God promised to His people under the New Covenant. In the Old Covenant, God's Promised Land to the Jews was for them to settle in their present land until the New Covenant was brought into this world.

Jesus brought the New Covenant with Him when He was born as a man. In the New Covenant, God promises His people eternal life. The world we live is not a permanent place, since it will be destroyed and fade away. (refer to 1 John 2:17, John 6:37–40, John 14:2–4, and Revelation 21:1.)

About 700 years before Jesus was born as a man, the prophet Isaiah prophesied about John the Baptist, the man who witnessed about the coming of Jesus (see John 1:7–8):

> Listen! I hear the voice of someone shouting, "Make a highway for the Lord through the wilderness. Make a straight, smooth road through the desert for our God. Fill the valleys and level the hills. Straighten out the curves and smooth off the rough spots. Then the glory of the Lord will be revealed, and all people will see it together." The Lord has spoken! (Isaiah 40:3–5, also see Matthew 3:1–3; Luke 1:76; and 3:1–6)

His Kingdom Will Never Be Destroyed

While Israel was held captive in Babylon some 550 years before Christ, a young Jew named Daniel became famous and authoritative, because he alone could interpret the dream of Nebuchadnezzar, the King of Babylon. In those days, dreams played an important role in people's lives. Daniel recorded his own dream about Jesus:

> As my vision continued that night, I saw someone who looked like a man coming with the clouds of heaven. He approached the Ancient One and was led into his presence. He was given authority, honor and royal power over all the nations of the world, so that people of every race and nation and language would obey him. His rule is eternal—it will never end. His kingdom will never be destroyed. (Daniel 7:13–14)

About 550 years after Daniel's vision, an important event happened that confirmed his prophecy. It was recorded by a physician, a family doctor, named Luke. He became the apostle Paul's associate and traveling companion. Luke conducted detailed investigations about the testimonies of eyewitnesses of Jesus, and he wrote the Gospel of Luke:

> In the sixth month of Elizabeth's pregnancy, God sent the angel Gabriel to Nazareth, a village in Galilee, to a virgin named Mary.

> She was engaged to be married to a man named Joseph, a descendant of King David. Gabriel appeared to her and said, "Greetings, favored woman! The Lord is with you!"
>
> Confused and disturbed, Mary tried to think what the angel could mean. "Don't be frightened, Mary," the angel told her, "for God has decided to bless you! You will become pregnant and have a son, and you are to name him Jesus! He will be very great and will be called the Son of the Most High. And the Lord God will give him the throne of his Ancestor David. And he will reign over Israel forever; his Kingdom will never end!" (Luke 1:26–33)

The following words came from Jesus' beloved young disciple, the apostle John. It further strengthened Daniel's statement made about 630 years before: "His rule is eternal—it will never end:"

> For he is sent by God. He speaks God's words, for God's Spirit is upon him without measure or limit. The Father loves his Son, and he has given him authority over everything. And all who believe in God's son have eternal life. Those who don't obey the Son will never experience eternal life, but the wrath of God remains upon them. (John 3:34–36)

"The Covenant I Made With You, Sealed with Blood"

About 530 years before Jesus entered Jerusalem riding on a donkey's colt, Zechariah prophesied the following:

> Rejoice greatly, O people of Zion! Shout in triumph, O people of Jerusalem! Look, your king is coming to you. He is righteous and victorious, yet he is humble, riding on a donkey—even on a donkey's colt. I will remove the battle chariots from Israel and the warhorses from Jerusalem, and I will destroy all

> the weapons used in battle. Your king will bring peace to the nations. His realm will stretch from sea to sea and from the Euphrates River to the ends of the earth.
>
> Because of the covenant I made with you, sealed with blood, I will free your prisoners from death in a waterless dungeon. Come back to the place of safety, all you prisoners, for there is yet hope! I promise this very day that I will repay you two mercies for each of your woes! (Zechariah 9:9–12; also refer to Jeremiah 31:31 and Luke 22:20)

The contents and the meaning of Zechariah 9:10–12 are quite similar to those of Isaiah 9:3–5, which was prophesied about 200 years before Zechariah.

"The Messiah, the Son of the Living God"

From a prison cell, John the Baptist heard about all the Messiah was doing. So he sent his disciples to ask Jesus, "Are you really the Messiah we've been waiting for, or should we keep looking for someone else?"

Jesus told them, "Go back to John and tell him about what you have heard and seen—the blind see, the lame walk, the lepers are cured, the deaf hear, the dead are raised to life and the Good News is being preached to the poor. And tell him: God blesses those who are not offended by me." (Matthew 11:2–6)

In fact, John the Baptist knew Jesus the Messiah very well. Their mothers had discussed their future sons during their pregnancies. John even baptized Jesus. John might have believed that Jesus could have saved him from prison in view of so many miracles Jesus was performing at that time. It was a weakness of flesh and blood in John. It became a spiritual weakness later on. This kind of weakness can only be overcome by borrowing power from the Holy Spirit—through prayers.

Identifying Jesus as the prophesied Messiah was a matter of spiritual discernment, as evidenced by this conversation between Jesus and His disciples:

> When Jesus came to the region of Caesarea Philippi, He asked His disciples, "Who do people say that the Son of Man is?"
>
> "Well," they replied, "some say John the Baptist, some say Elijah, and others say Jeremiah or one of the other prophets."
>
> Then He asked them, "Who do you say I am?"
>
> Simon Peter answered, "You are the Messiah, the son of the living God."
>
> Jesus replied, "You are blessed, Simon son of John, because my Father in heaven has revealed this to you. You did not learn this from any human being. Now I say to you that you are Peter, and upon this rock I will build my church, and all the powers of hell will not conquer it. And I will give you the keys of the Kingdom of Heaven." (Matthew 16:13–19)

Sometimes Jesus made it clear who He truly was, as He did in a conversation with a Samaritan woman:

> "Believe me, the time is coming when it will no longer matter whether you worship the Father here or in Jerusalem. You Samaritans know so little about the one you worship, while we Jews know all about him, for salvation comes through the Jews. But the time is coming and is already here when true worshipers will worship the Father in spirit and in truth. The Father is looking for anyone who will worship him that way. For God is Spirit, so those who worship him must worship in spirit and in truth."

> The woman said, "I know the Messiah will come—the one who is called Christ. When he comes, he will explain everything to us."
>
> Then Jesus told her, "I am the Messiah." (John 4:21–26)

On another occasion, Jesus told His disciples: "I tell you this now, so that when it happens you will believe I am the Messiah." (John 13:19)

After Jesus was arrested at the request of the leading priests, the teachers of religious law and other leaders, He further identified Himself:

> Then the high priest stood up before the others and asked Jesus, "Well, aren't you going to answer these charges? What do you have to say for yourself?" Jesus made no reply. Then the high priest asked him, "Are you the Messiah, the Son of the blessed God?" Jesus said, "I AM, and you will see me, the Son of Man, sitting at God's right hand in the place of power and coming back on the clouds of heaven." (Mark 14:60–62)

As Messiah, Jesus also confirmed that He is both "the source of David and the heir to his throne." About sixty years after Jesus' resurrection, John, the beloved disciple of Jesus, saw and heard from the resurrected Messiah in his visions: "I, Jesus have sent my angel to give you this message for the churches. I am both the source of David and the heir to his throne. I am the bright morning star." (Revelation 22:16)

Because Jesus was Messiah, the source of David and heir to his throne, He told the Pharisees: "I, the Son of Man, am master even of the Sabbath." (Luke 6:5) Jesus said that everything was created by Him, and that the Sabbath was made by Him for His rest. (see John 1:3, Genesis 1)

The Way, the Truth, and the Life

Jesus told the people, "I am the light of the world. If you follow me, you won't be stumbling through the darkness, because you will have the light that leads to life." (John 8:12) Also, He said, "I have come as a light to shine in this dark world, so that all who put their trust in me will no longer remain in the darkness." (John 12:46)

Jesus answered a question raised by one of His apostles—Thomas: "I am the way, the truth, and the life. No one can come to the Father except through me. If you had known who I am, then you would have known who my Father is. From now on you know him and have seen him." (John 14:6–7, also see Isaiah 35:8–10, Colossians 1:15)

Notice that Jesus said that He was the way, not a way. There is only one way to reach heaven, and that is through Jesus! Because there is no other way one may be saved, the word "religion" has lost its meaning. Since there is only one God, every Christian has one unique relationship with God.

It is important to maintain a close and cordial relationship with God. Jesus said: "I know all the things you do, that you are neither hot nor cold. I wish you were one or the other! But since you are like lukewarm water, I will spit you out of my mouth." (Revelation 3:15–16)

Three years ago, two persons told me the same story. They said they believed that all different religions are worshiping the same God. All roads led to the same place. They asked me why I thought it was important to believe in Jesus and also the God Jewish people worship. I told them, "There is only one God. It is written clearly in Exodus 20:3 as the First Commandment. Only Jesus (God in Trinity) can give us eternal life. The Jewish people were punished every now and then for forty years in the wilderness as they worshiped idols rather than the real God, the God who guided them out of Egypt through Moses."

The New Covenant

The people of Israel could not keep the Old Covenant that God gave them through Moses. They gradually departed away from God for one reason or another, so God made a better arrangement for them through the New Covenant:

> For by power of eternal Spirit, Christ offered himself to God as a perfect sacrifice for our sins. That is why he is the one who mediates the New Covenant between God and people, so that all who are invited can receive the eternal inheritance God has promised them. (Hebrews 9:14–15)

There is nothing more powerful than the Word of God, the Holy Bible. At the very beginning of the Holy Bible, in Genesis Chapter 1, we learn that God created everything by His Word. At the end of the Holy Bible, in Revelation 19:13, we see that Jesus is the Word of God. God gave His New Covenant to His people by means of His Word. His Word, therefore, should be read and stored in the heart of every Christian just as man needs food, (bread) every day.

The night before Jesus was to be crucified as a man, He referred many times about God's Word in His prayer:

> I have told these men about you. They were in the world, but then you gave them to me. Actually, they were always yours, and you gave them to me; and they have kept your word. Now they know that everything I have is a gift from you, for I have passed on to them the words you gave me, and they accepted them and know that I came from you, and they believe you sent me. (John 17:6–8)

> I have given them your word. And the world hates them because they do not belong to the world, just I do not. (John 17:14)

> Make them pure and holy by teaching them your words of truth. (John 17:17)

About thirty years after the resurrection of Jesus, the apostle Peter preached:

> For you have been born again. Your new life did not come from your earthly parents because the life they gave you will end in death. But this new life will last forever because it comes from the eternal, living word of God. As the prophet says, "People are like grass that dies away; their beauty fades as quickly as the beauty of wildflowers. The grass withers, and the flower fall away. But the word of the Lord will last forever." And that word is the Good News that was preached to you. (1 Peter 1:23–25)

A Light to Guide All Nations to God

Laying the groundwork for the New Covenant that Jesus would establish, Isaiah prophesied what God told him about Jesus, the coming Messiah:

> LOOK at my servant, whom I strengthen. He is my chosen one, and I am pleased with him. I have put my spirit upon him. He will reveal justice to the nations. He will be gentle—he will not shout or raise his voice in public. He will not crush those who are weak or quench the smallest hope. He will bring full justice to all who have been wronged. He will not stop until truth and righteousness prevail throughout the earth. Even distant lands beyond the sea will wait for his instruction.

> God, the Lord, created the heavens and stretched them out. He created the earth and everything in it. He gives breath and life to

> everyone in all the world. And it is he who says, 'I, the Lord, have called you to demonstrate my righteousness. I will guard and support you, for I have given you to my people as the personal confirmation of my covenant with them. And you will be a light to guide all nations to me. You will open the eyes of the blind and free the captives from prison. You will release those who sit in dark dungeons.
>
> I am the Lord; that is my name! I will not give my glory to anyone else. I will not share my praise with carved idols. Everything I prophesied has come true, and now I will prophesy again. I will tell you the future before it happens. (Isaiah 42:1–9, also refer to Matthew 12:18–21 and Luke 2:32)

"My servant" refers to Jesus as God's servant, meaning He spoke and acted completely on the instructions given to him by God the Father when He was a man. He did nothing on His own.

"He is my chosen one" refers to Jesus, who was born to establish the New Covenant about 700 years after this prophecy.

"I have given you to my people" refers to the crucifixion of Jesus by the Jews (God's selected people). The New Covenant is sealed with the blood of Jesus. (see Luke 22:20)

"My covenant with them" refers to the New Covenant which God uses to fulfill the Old Covenant. Salvation was brought to man only by the New Covenant, the words of Jesus.

"I will not give my glory to anyone else" clearly indicates that Jesus is not "anyone else." Jesus is God Himself!

After about 100 years of Isaiah's prophecy of Jesus as the New Covenant, Jeremiah also prophesied about Jesus:

> "This is the new covenant I will make with the people of Israel on that day," says the Lord. "I will put my laws in their minds, and I will write them on their hearts. I will be their God, and they will be my people. And they will not need to teach their

> neighbors, nor will they need to teach their family, saying, 'You should know the Lord.' For everyone, from the least to the greatest, will already know me," says the Lord. "And I will forgive their wickedness and will never again remember their sins." (Jeremiah 31:33–34)

About 660 years later, Jesus brought this prophecy to pass when He told His disciples at the Last Supper: "This wine is the token of God's new covenant to save you—an agreement sealed with the blood I will pour out for you." (Luke 22:20)

Every Jew knows the Old Testament well. Once the Jews realize that Jesus is their Messiah and their God, they will need no further introduction. They will come running to accept Jesus. (see Zechariah 10:8)

"The Lord Is Our Righteousness"

Unlike the Old Covenant, which proved to be impossible to keep, it is not difficult to keep the New Covenant. Jesus said: "For My yoke is easy and My burden is light." (Matthew 11:30 NKJV)

Describing the way the New Covenant is kept, the apostle John wrote:

> Loving God means keeping his commandments, and really, that isn't difficult. For every child of God defeats this evil world by trusting Christ to give the victory. And the ones who win this battle against the world are the ones who believe that Jesus is the Son of God. (1 John 5:3–5)

In the New Covenant, when we repent of our sins and believe in Jesus as our Savior/Messiah, all our sins are forgiven. Only with the presence of the Holy Spirit in our hearts, sent to us by the Resurrected Jesus Christ, may we be made strong. We may always unload our burdens, both physical and spiritual, to Jesus, Who said: "Come to me, all of you who are weary and carry heavy burdens, and I will give you rest." (Matthew 11:28)

Jeremiah continued to prophecy about Jesus, revealing another aspect of our Messiah: He is our righteousness.

> "The day will come," says the Lord, "when I will do for Israel and Judah all the good I have promised them. At that time I will bring to the throne of David a righteous descendant, and he will do what is just and right throughout the land. In that day Judah will be saved, and Jerusalem will live in safety. And their motto will be 'the Lord is our righteousness!'" (Jeremiah 33:14–16)

"A righteous descendant" and "the Lord is our righteousness" both refer to no other than Jesus. (Read Revelation 22:16)

Complete Authority in Heaven and on Earth

The Resurrected Jesus gave His disciples the most important responsibility—that of obedience to His commands:

> Jesus came and told his disciples, "I have been given complete authority in heaven and on earth. Therefore, go and make disciples of all the nations baptizing them in the name of the Father and the Son and the Holy Spirit. Teach these new disciples to obey all the commands I have given you. And be sure of this: I am with you always, even to the end of the age." (Matthew 28:18–20)

To follow Jesus, we must obey the commands He has given us in His Word. Jesus has complete authority in heaven and on earth, and we have no hope unless we follow Him in obedience. We must thank the disciples of Jesus. If the disciples did not teach obedience to His word, the Gospel would not have been carried on to us today.

Spirit and Life

In speaking of the importance of obedience to His words, Jesus said to his disciples: "It is the Spirit who gives eternal life. Human effort accomplishes nothing. And the very words I have spoken to you are spirit and life." (John 6:63)

The best explanations to the above statement are:

1. The answer Jesus gave to Judas (not Iscariot): "All those who love me will do what I say. My Father will love them, and we will come to them and live with them. Anyone who doesn't love me will not do what I say. And remember, my words are not my own. This message is from the Father who sent me." (John 14:23–24)
2. The answer Jesus gave to the devil when He was tempted by him: "People need more than bread for their life; they must feed on every word of God." (Matthew 4:4)
3. Hundreds of years before Jesus was born as a man, He had already been worshiped: "This is my comfort in my affliction, for your word has given me life." (Psalms 119:50)

The teachings of Jesus are focused on the "spiritual life." He told us this world is not a permanent place for us, since the main duty given to Him by the Father was to give His believers eternal life. (see John 6:37–40, 12:25, 15:19, 17:14 and Matthew 16:25)

The Word of God

The apostle John saw the Resurrected Jesus in his visions on the island of Patmos, and gave us a better understanding of the relationship of Jesus to His title, "the Word of God":

> Then I saw heaven opened, and a white horse was standing there. And the one sitting on the horse was named Faithful and True.

> For he judges fairly and then goes to war. His eyes were bright like flames of fire, and on his head were many crowns. A name was written on him, and only he knew what it meant. He was clothed with a robe dipped in blood, and his title was the Word of God. The armies of heaven, dressed in pure white linen, followed him on white horses. From his mouth came a sharp sword, and with it he struck down the nations. He ruled them with an iron rod, and he trod the wine-press of the fierce wrath of almighty God. On his robe and thigh was written this title: King of kings and Lord of lords. (Revelation 19:11–16)

"Word of God" and "King of kings and Lord of lords" both refer to Jesus. In the last day, the word of Jesus will judge even the kings who are non-believers. (refer to John 12:47–48)

The apostle Paul also described the power of the Word of God as being sharp and powerful as a sword. In a letter he wrote to the Christian Jews he said:

> For the Word of God is living and powerful, and sharper than any two-edged sword, piercing even to the division of soul and spirit, and of joints and marrow, and is a discerner of the thoughts and intents of the heart. (Hebrews 4:12)

Thirty years later, the apostle John also described the words of Jesus as a sharp sword:

> He held seven stars in his right hand, and a sharp two-edged sword came from his mouth. (Revelation 1:16)

> Write this letter to the angel of the church in Pergamum. This is the message from the one who has a sharp two-edged sword. (Revelation 2:12)

> Repent, or I will come to you suddenly and fight against them with the sword of my mouth. (Revelation 2:16)

> Their entire army was killed by the sharp sword that came out of the mouth of the one riding the white horse. (Revelation 19:21)

Concerning His Word as a sword of judgement, Jesus taught the Jews:

> And if anyone hears my words and does not believe, I do not judge him; for I did not come to judge the world but to save the world. He who rejects Me and does not receive my words, has that which judges him "the word that I have spoken will judge him in the last day." (John 12:46–48)

Jesus also said: "For judgment I have come into this world." (John 9:39)

Judgment was mentioned in the Old Testament many times. God the Father delegated this duty to Jesus. Jesus is the Word of God. He was born as a man so that He could teach man face to face so that God's Words can be easily understood and kept in our hearts. Only by following Jesus, can man receive eternal life and avoid judgement on the last day. There is no judgment pending for those who repent and act in obedience on their belief in Jesus.

The Bread of Life

Expanding on His titles of the Word of God and the Bread of Life, Jesus preached this to the Jews:

> I assure you, anyone who believes in me already has eternal life. Yes, I am the Bread of Life! Your ancestors ate manna in the wilderness, but they all died. However, the bread from heaven gives eternal life to everyone who eats it. I am the living bread that came down out of heaven. Anyone who eats this bread will live forever; this bread is my flesh, offered so the world may live. (John 6:47–51)

Indeed, we need the Living Bread, the Word of God through Jesus, who has come down out of Heaven so that we may have eternal life.

More than 50 years after the resurrection of Jesus, the apostle John wished to further strengthen the faith among the Christians. He wrote:

> The one who existed from the beginning is the one we have heard and seen. We saw him with our own eyes and touched him with our own hands. He is Jesus Christ, the Word of life. (1 John 1:1)

It is a straightforward promise that once a person believes in Jesus, that person has eternal life, no matter whether this person will be resurrected from the dead or goes to meet Jesus alive. Jesus is the Bread of Life. When we eat the Bread of Life, we learn the Word of God spoken by Jesus. In order to have this bread "digested" we need the Holy Spirit. We also need the Holy Spirit to guide and strengthen us so that we may understand, keep, and obey the Words of God.

The Son of God

Not only is Jesus the Word of God, the Bread of Life, as Son of man, Jesus is also the Son of God:

> Now this is how Jesus the Messiah was born. His mother, Mary, was engaged to be married to Joseph. But while she was still a virgin, she became pregnant by the Holy Spirit. (Matthew 1:18)

Although Jesus' mother was a woman, His Father was the Holy Spirit. The angel announced that Jesus would be the Son of God:

> "Don't be frightened, Mary," the angel told her, "for God has decided to bless you! You will become pregnant and have a son,

> and you are to name him Jesus. He will be very great and will be called the Son of the Most High. And the Lord God will give him the throne of his ancestor David. And he will reign over Israel forever; his kingdom will never end!"
>
> Mary asked the angel, "But how can I have a baby? I am a virgin."
>
> The angel replied, "The Holy Spirit will come upon you, and the power of the Most High will overshadow you. So the baby born to you will be holy, and he will be called the Son of God." (Luke 1:30–35)

This event was prophesied a thousand years before Christ, when Nathan the prophet told King David what God told him:

> And now I declare that the Lord will build a house for you—a dynasty of kings! For when you die, I will raise up one of your sons, and I will make his kingdom strong. He is the one who will build a house—a temple—for me. And I will establish his throne forever. I will be his father, and he will be my son. I will not take my unfailing love from him as I took it from Saul, who ruled before you. I will establish him over my dynasty and my kingdom for all time, and his throne will be secure forever. (1 Chronicles 17:10–14; also see Luke 1:30–33, Acts 2:30 & Hebrews 1:5)

"One of your sons" refers to Jesus, not King Solomon.

"He is the one who will build a house—a temple—for me." The body of Jesus (also bodies of Christians) is the House and the Temple of God.

"Establish his throne forever"—No king can stay on his throne forever except Jesus. Only Jesus is the First and the Last, the Alpha and the Omega.

"I will be his father, and he will be my son"—Many times in the New Testament Jesus said God was His Father. This time God said it about Jesus His Son (see also Matthew 3:17, John 3:16).

"I will establish him over my dynasty and my kingdom for all time, and his throne will be secure forever"—Jesus said in Revelation: "I am the Alpha and the Omega, the First and the Last, the Beginning and the End." (Revelation 22:13) Jesus further said: "I, Jesus, have sent my angel to give you this message for the churches. I am both the source of David and the heir to his throne. I am the bright morning star." (Revelation 22:16)

The apostle John described Jesus as the only Son of God, and He is God: "No one has ever seen God. But his only Son, who is himself God, is near to the Father's heart; he has told us about him." (John 1:18)

The Pharisees judged Jesus with their human wisdom. They did not believe what Jesus told them: "Where is your father?" they asked.

Jesus answered, "Since you don't know who I am, you don't know who my Father is. If you knew me, then you would know my Father, too." (John 8:19)

Jesus also identified Himself to the Pharisees this way: "Jesus told them, 'If God were your Father, you would love me, because I have come to you from God. I am not here on my own, but he sent me." (John 6:42)

He Is God, Jehovah, and the Spirit of God

Since Jesus is God, He was present at the creation as the Spirit of God:

> In the beginning God created the heavens and the earth. The earth was empty, a formless mass cloaked in darkness. And the Spirit of God was hovering over its surface. (Genesis 1:1–2)

Only God could identify Himself with the awe-inspiring statement "I am who I am!" "I am" and "I am He" both mean "I am God" or "I am Jehovah".

About 1445 before Christ, after Moses led the Israelites out of Egypt, God told him how to tell the people of Israel who was giving him instructions:

> I am the one who always is. Just tell them, 'I AM has sent me to you.' God also said, Tell them, 'The Lord, the God of your ancestors—the God of Abraham, the God of Isaac, and the God of Jacob—has sent me to you. This will be my name forever; it has always been my name, and it will be used throughout all generations.' (Exodus 3:14–15)

From that time, only God would use the phrase, "I AM!" to identify Himself. Some 1,477 years later, Jesus invoked the mighty name when He spoke to the Jews and the Pharisees:

> Therefore, I said to you that you will die in your sins; for if you do not believe that I am He, you will die in your sins. (John 8:24 NKJV, also see Isaiah 41:4, John 10:30, Revelation 1:18 NKJV)

To make His deity absolutely clear, Jesus repeatedly used that phrase when speaking to the Jews:

> When you lift up the Son of Man, then you will know that I am He. (John 8:28 NKJV)

> "Your father Abraham rejoiced to see My day, and he saw it and was glad." Then the Jews said to Him, "You are not yet fifty years old, and have You seen Abraham?" Jesus said to them, "Most assuredly, I say to you, before Abraham was, I AM." (John 8:56–58 NKJV, also see Isaiah 52:6, Jeremiah 31:34, John 6:38)

Only God is the First and the Last, the Alpha and the Omega. The Old Testament contains so many statements from God Himself confirming this. Isaiah prophesied that there is only one God and many times it is stated that He is the First and the Last (see

Isaiah 41–46). This statement that He is the Alpha and the Omega, the First and the Last, the Beginning and the End was confirmed by the Resurrected Jesus not once, but many times (see Revelation 1:8, 17–18; 2:8; 21:6; 22:13).

The Resurrection and the Life

Jesus invoked that awesome name again as He talked with Martha, the sister of Lazarus, before he raised Lazarus from the dead:

> I am the resurrection and the life. Those who believe in me, even though they die like everyone else, will live again. They are given eternal life for believing in me and will never perish. (John 11:25–26)

Only God can say that He Himself is "the Resurrection and the Life." Jesus foretold that He would resurrect His own body in three days (see John 2:19–22). Only God has the authority to say so and to do so. He did fulfill His own statement. That is the reason why we need to praise Him and give Him all the glory. If He did not raise Himself from the dead, then there is no reason for anyone to believe in Him.

The Creator

About 931 years before Christ, God's Spirit filled King Solomon and the entire eighth chapter of Proverbs describes Jesus. Jesus is the Word, and He is also the wisdom in the Word. It was the Spirit of Jesus who spoke through King Solomon. The most obvious part of the chapter is highlighted in the following:

> The Lord possessed me at the beginning of His way, before His works of old. I have been established from everlasting, from the beginning, before there was ever an earth. When there were no

> depths I was brought forth, when there were no fountains abounding with water. Before the mountains were settled, before the hills, I was brought forth; while as yet He had not made the earth or the fields, or the primeval dust of the world. When He prepared the heavens, I was there, when He drew a circle on the face of the deep, when He established the clouds above, when He strengthened the fountains of the deep, when He assigned to the sea its limit, so that the waters would not transgress His command, when He marked out the foundations of the earth, then I was beside him, as a master craftsman; And I was daily His delight, rejoicing always before Him, rejoicing in His inhabited world, And my delight was with the sons of men.
>
> Now therefore, listen to me, my children, for blessed are those who keep my ways. Hear instruction and be wise, and do not disdain it. Blessed is the man who listens to me, watching daily at my gates, waiting at the posts of my doors. For whoever finds me finds life, and obtains favor from the Lord; but he who sins against me wrongs his own soul; all those who hate me love death. (Proverbs 8:22–36 NKJV, also refer to Jeremiah 5:21; Matthew 3:17; Luke 11:28; John 1:1–3; 6:35, 47–48, 63; 8:56–58; 11:25–26; and 14:6)

"As a master craftsman"—Everything that was created was created by the Word of God. Jesus is the Word of God. (refer to Genesis 1; John 1:1–3; and Revelation 19:13)

"Whoever finds me finds life"—The apostle John confirmed this 1020 years later: "So whoever has God's Son has life; whoever does not have his Son does not have life." (1 John 5:12)

Mighty God, Everlasting Father

More than 700 years before Jesus was born as a man, Isaiah prophesied about Jesus:

> For a child is born to us, a son is given to us. And the government will rest on his shoulders. These will be his royal titles: Wonderful, Counselor, Mighty God, Everlasting Father, Prince of Peace. (Isaiah 9:6)

Jesus is God the Father and also the Son of God. Jesus was also the Child of man and the Son of man. The most important fact is that He was born as a man and God gave Him to man. Only as a man could He die. Because He died for the sins of man (He had no sin Himself) and was resurrected on the third day, the way to God (the New Covenant) was created for man to follow. Only by following Jesus will man receive eternal life.

That is why John emphasized the importance about accepting the Son of God—Jesus:

> Anyone who denies the Son doesn't have the Father either. But anyone who confesses the Son has the Father also. (1 John 2:23)

The Spirit of God spoke through the prophet Isaiah:

> Who has done such mighty deeds, directing the affairs of the human race as each new generation marches by? It is I, the Lord, the first and the last. I alone am He. (Isaiah 41:4; also refer to Isaiah 44:6, 48:12; Revelation 1:8, 1:17–18; 21:6; and 22:13)

> This is what the Lord, Israel's king and redeemer, the Lord almighty, says: "I am the first and the last, there is no other God. Who else can tell you what is going to happen in the days ahead? Let them tell you if they can and thus prove their power. Let them do as I have done since ancient times. Do not tremble; do not be afraid. Have I not proclaimed from ages past what my purposes are for you? You are my witnesses—is there any other God? No! There is no other Rock—not one!" (Isaiah 44:6–8; also refer to Revelation 1:8, 17–18; 21:6; and 22:13)

Only God can tell us what is going to happen in the days ahead. There are many examples to show that what Jesus predicted came to pass. One of the typical examples concerns Peter's denial of Jesus three times the night before Jesus' crucifixion.

Jesus is both God and the Rock. The apostle Paul wrote:

> As followers of Moses, they were all baptized in the cloud and the sea. And all of them ate the same miraculous food, and all of them drank the same miraculous water. For they all drank from the miraculous rock that traveled with them, and that rock was Christ. (1 Corinthians 10:2–4)

There Is No Other God

Jesus is the unique source of creation, salvation and righteousness. Again, Isaiah spoke from the Spirit of Jesus:

> I am the Lord; there is no other God. I have prepared you, even though you do not know me, so all the world from east to west will know there is no other God. I am the Lord and there is no other. I am the one who creates the light and makes the darkness. I am the one sends good times and bad times. I, the Lord, am the one who does these things. Open up, O heavens, and pour out your righteousness. Let the earth open wide so salvation and righteousness can sprout up together. I, the Lord, created them. (Isaiah 45:5–8; see also John 1:3–5)

Jesus is the Word of God, the God and the Creator:

> In the beginning the Word already existed. He was with God, and he was God. He was in the beginning with God. He created everything there is. Nothing exists that he didn't make. (John 1:1–3)

The Word of God is very powerful. God created everything by His Word (see Genesis 1, the very beginning of the Holy Bible).

The Holy Bible confirms again at the end that Jesus is the Word of God (see Revelation 19:13).

In Isaiah 43–46, God reminded all man that He is the only God. He mentioned 16 times that He is the only God and besides Him there is no other god. Only He is the Alpha and the Omega, the First and the Last. This is the most important message God gives to man in the entire Holy Bible. It is also the first and the most important commandment. Besides the book of Isaiah, the same statement has also been given by God many times in the Old Testament: Exodus 20:3 (the First Commandment); Deuteronomy 5:7; 32:39; 1 Kings 8:60; 2 Kings 17:35–39; Jeremiah 25:6, 35:15; Hosea 13:4; and Joel 2:27.

"I Will Be Found by You"

God desires that we know Him through Jesus. About 950 before Christ, God's Spirit spoke through King Solomon:

"I love those who love me, and those who seek me diligently will find me" (Proverbs 8:17 NKJV), and ". . . whoever finds me finds life and wins approval from the Lord." (v. 35)

About 600 before Christ, the prophet Jeremiah sent a letter to the priests, the prophets, the elders and all the people of Israel whom Nebuchadnezzar had carried away captive from Jerusalem to Babylon. In the letter, Jeremiah mentioned what God said:

> "In those days when you pray, I will listen. If you look for me in earnest, you will find me when you seek me. I will be found by you," says the Lord. "I will end your captivity and restore your fortunes. I will gather you out of the nations where I sent you and bring you home again to your own land." (Jeremiah 29:12–13)

Many years later, in about 31 A.D., Jesus told His disciples and followers: "Ask, and it will be given to you; seek, and you will find; knock, and it will be opened to you. For everyone who asks receives, and he who seeks finds, and to him who knocks it will be opened." (Matthew 7:7–8 NKJV; also see Luke 11:9–10)

"Do Not Test the Lord Your God"

Jesus once again revealed Himself as God by His statements to Satan. After forty days and forty nights without food, Jesus was led by the Holy Spirit to the wilderness to be tempted by Satan. Although Jesus carried an earthly body as a man, He identified Himself as God twice when He denounced Satan:

> Jesus responded, "The Scriptures also say, 'Do not test the Lord your God.'" (Matthew 4:7)

> "Get out of here, Satan," Jesus told him. "For the Scriptures say, You must worship the Lord your God; serve only him." (Matthew 4:10)

The Authority to Forgive Sins

As God, Jesus had the power to forgive sins. No one can forgive sin but God. When Jesus healed a paralyzed man, He said: "Son, your sins are forgiven." (Luke 5:20) The Pharisees and teachers of religious law heard about this and said to each other: "This is blasphemy! Who but God can forgive sins?" (v. 21) Jesus knew what they were thinking and told them: "I will prove that I, the Son of Man, have the authority on earth to forgive sins." (v. 24) Only God can forgive sins. There is only one God. Jesus is God, and He is the same God, the Father!

Who Is Himself God

The apostle John said this about Jesus as God:

> No one has ever seen God. But his only Son, who is himself God, is near to the Father's heart; he has told us about him. (John 1:18)

"His only Son" refers to Jesus, and "about him" means about God the Father. The Father and the Son are one party spiritually at all times.

To further confirm that Jesus is God, about 24 years following the resurrection of Jesus, a letter the apostle Paul wrote to the Christians in Rome reads:

> They are the people of Israel, chosen to be God's special children. God revealed his glory to them. He made covenants with them and gave his law to them. They have the privilege of worshiping him and receiving his wonderful promises. Their ancestors were great people of God, and Christ himself was a Jew as far as his human nature is concerned. And He is God, who rules over everything and is worthy of eternal praise! Amen. (Romans 9:4–5)

There is no mistaking this truth. Jesus said, "The Father and I are one" (John 10:30). "Are" is the present tense. Jesus didn't say "were one" or "will be one." It will stay this way from the beginning to the end. Before Jesus was born as a man; during the time when Jesus was a man; after Jesus died and resurrected; and in the future—forever Jesus is God.

The relationship between God the Father and Jesus can be visualized as mercury in a bottle. When Jesus became the Son of God and was born as a man, it was like a small portion of mercury poured out of the bottle. When Jesus was resurrected, it is like that portion of mercury being put back to its original place. Both the mercury inside the bottle and the small portion poured out of the bottle are the same in every respect. There is only one God.

He Is the Holy Spirit

Jesus said to a Samaritan woman near Jacob's well: "For God is Spirit, so those who worship him must worship in spirit and in truth." (John 4:24)

Jesus is God. Jesus is also the Holy Spirit. About 50 years after Jesus' resurrection, John said: "And we know he [Jesus] lives in us because the Holy Spirit lives in us." (1 John 3:24)

The following four segments of the Holy Bible clearly confirm that Jesus is also the Holy Spirit:

> When the Jewish leaders asked Jesus to show them a miraculous sign, Jesus replied: "All right," Jesus replied. "Destroy this temple, and in three days I will raise it up." "What!" they exclaimed. "It took forty-six years to build this Temple, and you can do it in three days?" But by "this temple," Jesus meant his body. After he was raised from the dead, the disciples remembered that he had said this. (John 2:19–22)
>
> Jesus told the Jews: "No one can take my life from me. I lay down my life voluntarily. For I have the right to lay it down when I want to and also the power to take it again." (John 10:18)
>
> Jesus told Martha, the sister of Lazarus whom Jesus raised from the dead: "I am the resurrection and the life. Those who believe in me, even though they die like everyone else, will live again." (John 11:25)
>
> In the letter Paul wrote to the Romans, he emphasized: This Spirit of God, who raised Jesus from the dead, lives in you. And

> just as he raised Christ from the dead, he will give life to your mortal body by this same Spirit living within you. (Romans 8:11)

Jesus continued His teaching of His disciples:

> And I will ask the Father, and he will give you another Counselor, who will never leave you. He is the Holy Spirit, who leads into all truth. The world at large cannot receive him, because it isn't looking for him and doesn't recognize him. But you do, because he lives with you now and later will be in you. (John 14:16–17)

"Another Counselor" means the Holy Spirit and also Jesus Himself (see Isaiah 9:6). When He said "He lives with you now" Jesus meant that He was living with His disciples in the same premises at that time, but after His resurrection, the Holy Spirit (the representative of Jesus) would live inside His disciples' hearts.

To make this relationship clearer, Jesus further told His disciples:

> It is the Spirit who gives eternal life, Human effort accomplishes nothing. And the very words I have spoken to you are spirit and life. (John 6:63)

> But when the Father sends the Counselor as my representative—and by the Counselor I mean the Holy Spirit—he will teach you everything and will remind you of everything I myself have told you. (John 14:26)

> But I will send you the Counselor—the Spirit of truth. He will come to you from the Father and will tell you all about me. (John 15:26)

> But it is actually best for you that I go away, because if I don't, the Counselor won't come. If I do go away, he will come because I will send him to you. (John 16:7)

> He will bring me glory by revealing to you whatever he receives from me. (John 16:14)

Who sends the Holy Spirit to us, the Father or His Son Jesus? Is there any contradiction here? There is no contradiction, as both the Father and the Son are the same God. God exists as the Trinity. The apostle Paul also explained that Jesus is the Holy Spirit: "And you Gentiles have become his children, God has sent the Spirit of his Son into your hearts, and now you can call God your dear Father." (Galatians 4:6)

The Visible Image of the Invisible God

In his letter to the church in Colosse, a small city about 100 miles east of Ephesus in today's Turkey, the apostle Paul gave a quite detailed description of Jesus:

> Christ is the visible image of the invisible God. He existed before God made anything at all and is supreme over all creation. Christ is the one through whom God created everything in heaven and earth. He made the things we can see and the things we can't see—kings, kingdoms, rulers, and authorities. Everything has been created through him and for him. He existed before everything else began, and he holds all creation together.

> Christ is the head of the church, which is his body. He is the first of all who will rise from the dead, so he is first in everything. For God in all his fullness was pleased to live in Christ, and by him God reconciled everything to himself. He made peace with everything in heaven and on earth by means of his blood on the cross. This includes you who were once so far

away from God. You were his enemies, separated from him by your evil thoughts and actions, yet now he has brought you back as his friends. He has done this through his death on the cross in his own human body. As a result, he has brought you into the very presence of God, and you are holy and blameless as you stand before him without a single fault. (Colossians 1:15–22, also see John 14:6–11)

Seven Images for Seven Churches

In about A.D. 95, the apostle John was probably the only apostle of Jesus who was still alive. He wrote the Book of Revelation from the visions he received from the Lord. Revelation describes the Resurrected Jesus in seven different images, one each for the seven churches in seven specific cities throughout the Roman Province of Asia:

1. "He who holds the seven stars in His right hand, who walks in the midst of the seven golden lampstands." (Revelation 2:1 NKJV)
2. "The First and the Last, who was dead, and came to life." (Revelation 2:8 NKJV)
3. "He who has the sharp two-edged sword." (Revelation 2:12 NKJV)
4. "Who has eyes like a flame of fire, and His feet like fine brass." (Revelation 2:18 NKJV)
5. "He who has the seven Spirits of God and the seven stars." (Revelation 3:1 NKJV)
6. "He who is holy, He who is true, He who has the key of David, He who opens and no one shuts, and shuts and no one opens." (Revelation 3:7 NKJV, also see Isaiah 22:22)
7. "The Amen, the Faithful and True Witness, the Beginning of the Creation of God." (Revelation 3:14 NKJV)

In Revelation, it is plain that Jesus is the only God from the very beginning and to the end: "I am the Alpha and the Omega—the beginning and the end," says the Lord God. "I am the one who is, who always was, and who is still to come, the mighty one." (Revelation 1:8; see also Revelation 1:17–18; 2:8; 21:6; and 22:13)

Only God can say that He is the Alpha and the Omega, the Beginning and the End. In the Old Testament, God said many times that He is the First and the Last:

> This is what the Lord, Israel's King and Redeemer, the Lord Almighty, says: "I am the First and the Last; there is no other God." (Isaiah 44:6).

> Listen to me, O family of Jacob, Israel my chosen one! I alone am God, the First and the Last. (Isaiah 48:12)

Since there is only One God, obviously, "the Lord, Israel's King and Redeemer, the Lord Almighty" are all titles referring to Jesus as well.

"I Am He Who Lives"

The apostle John recorded his encounter with the resurrected Jesus through a vision:

> And when I saw Him, I fell at His feet as dead. But he laid His right hand on me saying to me, "Do not be afraid; I am the first and the last. I am HE who lives, and was dead, and behold, I am alive forevermore. Amen. And I have the keys of Hades and of Death." (Revelation 1:17–18 NKJV)

The prophet Isaiah made the following prophesies about 800 years before the above incident:

> Who has done such mighty deeds, directing the affairs of the human race as each new generation marches by? It is I, the Lord, the First and the Last. I alone am He. (Isaiah 41:4)

> "But you are my witnesses, O Israel!" says the Lord. "And you are my servant. You have been chosen to know me, believe in me, and understand that I alone am God. There is no other God; there never has been and never will be. I am the Lord, and there is no other Savior." (Isaiah 43:10–11)

God does not die. Only as a human being could Jesus die. Jesus was the first man resurrected by God (through the Holy Spirit) to eternal life —the way for all man to follow.

The Alpha and the Omega

Even at the very last moments of the world, Jesus still keeps the door of salvation open and free of charge to those who are willing to accept Him.

> And the one sitting on the throne said "Look, I am making all things new!" And then he said to me, "Write this down, for what I tell you is trustworthy and true." And he also said, "It is finished! I am the Alpha and the Omega—the Beginning and the End. To all who are thirsty I will give the springs of the water of life without charge." (Revelation 21:5–6, also refer to Matthew 4:17)

From the beginning of Jesus' preaching to the end of the world, Jesus emphasized the importance of repentance (that's what He means by "thirsty" above). We need to believe in Jesus and to repent so that God will give us the free gift of the Holy Spirit (i.e., Springs of the Water of Life).

Only God is the Alpha and the Omega. Only Jesus is HE, the First and the Last, the Beginning and the End. The Resurrected

Jesus further told the apostle John: "See, I am coming soon, and my reward is with me, to repay all according to their deeds. I am the Alpha and the Omega, the First and the Last, the Beginning and the End" (Revelation 22:12–13, also see Isaiah 40:10, 62:11).

God Chooses to Reveal Himself to Us

Jesus told His disciples: "No one really knows the Son except the Father, and no one really knows the Father except the Son and those to whom the Son chooses to reveal Him" (Luke 10:22). We are the fortunate ones as God chooses to reveal Himself to us. All the people who read this book are those to whom Jesus chooses to reveal the Father and Himself.

Every thing that was created was created through Jesus and for Him; both with life and without life, both what we can see and we cannot see, both things we can feel and things we cannot feel. We are now situated in a scientifically advanced era. Human beings can make many sophisticated things. However, no life can be created without Jesus. We cannot find any two things God made that look exactly alike, act the same, and live the same, whether animals, plants, fish, birds, mountains, seas, stars, the clouds, or even grass. Is that wonderful?

There is only one man in the world Who gave a name to Himself before He was born (see Matthew 1:21; Luke 1:31–33). There is also only one man in the world who resurrected Himself after He died (see John 2:19; 10:18). He is no other than Jesus. Everything is possible in Jesus, because He is also God.

Without exception, every man was created by God (or by Jesus). To those who believe in Jesus and accept Him as the Savior or Messiah, He gives the right to become children of God (see John 1:12). The relationship between God and every man is unique and direct. The only barrier between them is the sin man commits.

The curtain in the Temple was torn into two by God Himself when Jesus gave up His life as a man to bear the sins for all man about 2,000 years ago. Starting from that moment, each person can pray freely to God, asking for the forgiveness of sin, whenever he or she wishes. And when we ask in faith, God forgives our sin, and we can then be made whole.

God is holy. Unless we are made holy by accepting Jesus into our hearts, we cannot see God. We owe Jesus our lives as He sacrificed His life for us. Now we can be made holy because Jesus acted as the one-time priest and used His own blood to wash our sins away.

Jesus not only died, He was resurrected on the third day. Thus, He provides us with the way to eternal life. Jesus promised that we would have eternal life as soon as we accepted Him as our Savior or Messiah. All we need to do is follow Him—His words, the New Covenant.

"Thank You Father for revealing to us the Savior—Jesus Christ"

chapter three

Why Was Jesus Born as a Man?

The First Punishment

THE FIRST TIME MAN SINNED AND MADE GOD ANGRY IS RECORDED in Genesis 2 and 3. Adam and Eve ate the fruit God told them not to eat. As a result, they were punished by being banished from the Garden of Eden and by eventual death. (see Genesis 2:15–17 and 3:19)

> Then the Lord God said, "The people have become as we are, knowing everything, both good and evil. What if they eat the fruit of the tree of life? Then they will live forever!" So the Lord God banished Adam and his wife from the Garden of Eden, and He sent Adam out to cultivate the ground from which he had been made.
>
> After banishing them from the garden, the Lord God stationed mighty angelic beings to the east of Eden. And a flaming sword

flashed back and forth, guarding the way to the tree of life. (Genesis 3:22–24) **This was the first punishment.**

The Second Punishment

The second time God punished man as they sinned and made Him angry was during the generation of Noah:

> Now the Lord observed the extent of the people's wickedness, and he saw that all their thoughts were consistently and totally evil. So the Lord was sorry he had ever made them. It broke his heart. And the Lord said, 'I will completely wipe out this human race that I have created. Yes, and I will destroy all the animals and birds, too. I am sorry I ever made them.' But Noah found favor with the Lord. (Genesis 6:5–8)

God subsequently sent a great flood to destroy everything on earth. The only survivors were Noah's family of eight, the animals, insects, and birds that stayed on that great ship that Noah made according to God's instructions. This was the second punishment.

The Third Punishment

The third time God became angry and punished man was when men wished to demonstrate their own greatness by building the Tower of Babel. God said:

> If they can accomplish this when they have just begun to take advantage of their common language and political unity, just think of what they will do later. Nothing will be impossible for them! Come, let's go down and give them different languages. Then they won't be able to understand each other.

> In that way, the Lord scattered them all over the earth; and that ended the building of the city. That is why the city was called

> Babel, because it was there that the Lord confused the people by giving them many languages, thus scattering them across the earth. (Gen. 11:6–9)

The Fourth Punishment

The fourth time man's sin made God extremely angry was when the people of Sodom and Gomorrah reached extremes of evil and showed no interest in doing right. After removing the one righteous family, God destroyed these two cities (see Genesis 18 and 19).

The Way to Avoid the Final Punishment

After the destruction of Sodom and Gomorrah, people continued to sin. Instead of destroying the world and all the people, God made a decision to save the people by sending His own Son to the world to take upon Himself the sins of the world. One of the early references to Jesus in the Holy Bible can be found in Genesis 49:1 and 49:8–12.

Although Jesus had no sin, it was necessary that He die as a man for the sins committed by all men. God made this decision based on His unlimited love. Every man will be given a chance and a choice. Those who believe in His Son will become children of God and have eternal life. Non-believers will be judged and cast to the lake of fire.

When Jesus was a man, He did everything God the Father instructed Him to do. He did not do anything based on His own will. He was crucified by His own people, the Jews. He was resurrected on the third day, when He defeated Satan and death. After His resurrection, He joined God the Father again and was received complete authority in heaven and on earth (see Matthew 28:18).

But many of His people did not believe that Jesus had come from God. To the unbelieving Jewish leaders, Jesus said:

> You are from beneath; I am from above. You are of this world; I am not of this world. Therefore I said to you that you will die in your sins; for if you do not believe that I am He, you will die in your sins. (John 8:23–24)

> Jesus told them, "If God were your Father, you would love me, because I have come to you from God. I am not here on my own, but he sent me." (John 8:42)

> Jesus shouted to the crowds, "If you trust me, you are really trusting God who sent me. For when you see me, you are seeing the one who sent me. I have come as a light to shine in this dark world, so that all who put their trust in me will no longer remain in the darkness. If anyone hears me and doesn't obey me, I am not his judge—for I have come to save the world and not to judge it. But all who reject me and my message will be judged at the day of judgment by the truth I have spoken." (John 12:44–48)

Several years ago, I used to imagine that it would take a very long time, maybe years, for the judgment to conclude, since Jesus will be the only judge and there are so many people, both those who died and those who are still alive. The picture in my mind is quite different now. Since we know that Jesus is the Word of God (see John 1:1), the judgment will be made on a spirit-to-spirit basis (not person-to-person), directly and simultaneously. The speed of judgment can be much faster than the speed of the fastest computer.

Jesus Defeated Satan as a Man

> Then Jesus was led out into the wilderness by the Holy Spirit to be tempted there by the Devil. For forty days and forty nights he ate nothing and became very hungry. Then the Devil came and said to him, "If you are the Son of God, change these stones into

> loaves of bread." But Jesus told him, "No! The scriptures say, people need more than bread for their life; they must feed on every word of God." Then the Devil took him to Jerusalem, to the highest point of the Temple, and said, "If you are the Son of God, jump off! For the Scriptures say, He orders his angels to protect you. And they will hold you with their hands to keep you from striking your foot on a stone."
>
> Jesus responded, "The Scriptures also say, Do not test the Lord your God."
>
> Next the Devil took him to the peak of a very high mountain and showed him the nations of the world and all their glory. "I will give it all to you," he said, "if you will only kneel down and worship me."
>
> "Get out of here, Satan," Jesus told him. "For the Scriptures say, You must worship the Lord your God; serve only him."
>
> Then the Devil went away, and angels came and cared for Jesus. (Matthew 4:1–11; also see Luke 4:1–13)

No one should take Satan's temptations lightly, but we should all strive to resist them by the Word of God. In the above case, Satan tried to tempt Jesus (as a man) from three different aspects:

1. Satan tried to tempt Jesus through His physical need. Jesus was very hungry because He had not eaten any food for forty days.
2. Satan challenged the pride of Jesus and tried to provoke Jesus to do something according to his ambition.
3. Satan tried to offer lust as a bait, aiming to take Jesus as his slave, as he had done to Eve.

Adam's wife (later named Eve) failed to resist the temptation from Satan. She committed sin by eating the fruit from the tree of knowledge of good and evil, which God had told Adam not to eat. She also asked her husband to eat it. They both disobeyed God and followed the lies and temptations of Satan (see Genesis 3). From that time on, human beings became slaves of Satan.

One of the most important acts Jesus performed was that, as a man, He defeated Satan. Clearly, it was an order and an arrangement made by God the Father as Jesus was led out into the wilderness by the Holy spirit (not by Satan) to be tempted there by the devil. Following the victory of Jesus, man can be set free from Satan's slavery by accepting Jesus as their Savior or Messiah.

Jesus Could Die Only as a Human Being

In a letter the apostle Paul wrote to the Christian Jews, he explained the reason Jesus was born as a man:

> We all know that Jesus came to help the descendants of Abraham, not to help the angels. Therefore, it was necessary for Jesus to be in every respect like us, his brothers and sisters, so that he could be our merciful and faithful High Priest before God. He then could offer a sacrifice that would take away the sins of the people. Since he himself has gone through suffering and temptation, he is able to help us when we are being tempted. (Hebrews 2:16–18)

> Because God's children are human beings—made of flesh and blood—Jesus also became flesh and blood by being born in human form. For only as a human being could he die, and only by dying could he break the power of the Devil, who had the power of death. Only in this way could he deliver those who have lived all their lives as slaves to the fear of dying. (Hebrews 2:14–15)

Man must die because of his sin (see Genesis 2:17; 3:19). Jesus died as a man, yet He was resurrected on the third day, breaking the power of sin and death so that all who believe in Him can follow Him. The main purpose Jesus died as a man was to defeat Satan and death.

Several decades after the death and resurrection of Jesus, the apostle John shared his understandings with us regarding the main reason that Jesus came to the world as a man:

> But when people keep on sinning, it shows they belong to the Devil, who has been sinning since the beginning. But the Son of God came to destroy these works of the Devil. Those who have been born into God's family do not sin, because God's life is in them. So they can't keep on sinning, because they have been born of God. (1 John 3:8–9)

He Rose from the Dead

Paul wrote to the Christians in Rome emphasizing the importance of being born again in Jesus' death and resurrection:

> Since we have been united with him in his death, we will also be raised as he was. Our old sinful selves were crucified with Christ so that sin might lose its power in our lives. We are no longer slaves to sin. For when we died with Christ we were set free from the power of sin. And since we died with Christ, we know we will also share his new life. We are sure of this because Christ rose from the dead, and he will never die again. Death no longer has any power over him. He died once to defeat sin, and now he lives for the glory of God. (Romans 6:5–10)

"We will also be raised as he was" refers to the fact that all Christians who died will be resurrected when Jesus comes again at the end of the world.

"When we died with Christ" refers to the time when those who accepted Jesus as their Savior (or Messiah) gave up their old sinful life and starting a new Christian life.

"Share his new life" refers to the eternal life of a Christian promised by God after being born again.

Paul also wrote to the church in Corinth to point out how Christ's resurrection will bring about the resurrection of Christians at His return:

> But the fact is that Christ has been raised from the dead. He has become the first of a great harvest of those who will be raised to life again. So you see, just as death came into the world through a man, Adam, now the resurrection from the dead has begun through another man, Christ. Everyone dies because all of us are related to Adam, the first man. But all who are related to Christ, the other man, will be given new life. But there is an order to this resurrection: Christ was raised first; then when Christ comes back, all his people will be raised. (1 Corinthians 15:50–54)

To Create the New Covenant

When Jesus gave up His life as a man, God gave us the New Covenant. Man no longer need to rely on the Old Covenant to save them. This was signified when God tore in two the temple veil that separated the Holy of Holies from the outer area of the temple. In the Old Covenant, God had ordered Moses to make a curtain to enclose the Ark of the Covenant inside the Temple as the Most Holy Place (refer to Exodus 40). Only the priest was allowed to enter to the Most Holy Place.

> By this time it was noon, and darkness fell across the whole land until three o'clock. The light from the sun was gone. And suddenly, the thick veil hanging in the Temple was torn apart. Then

> Jesus shouted, "Father, I entrust my spirit into your hands!" And with those words he breathed his last." (Luke 23:44–46; also refer to Matthew 27:51 and Mark 15:38)

Paul, a religious leader of Judaism, persecuted Christians before he met the Resurrected Jesus. After Paul repented of his sins and accepted Jesus as his Messiah, his name was changed by Jesus to Paul from Saul. Jesus further appointed Paul as the chosen instrument to deliver His message to the Gentiles in addition to the people of Israel (refer to Acts 9:15). So it was the apostle Paul who first spread the Gospel to the Gentiles.

Afterwards, he also wrote a letter to the Christian Jews (those Jews who converted from Judaism). In those days, most of the Jews were very stubborn and refused to accept Jesus as their Messiah. In this letter, the Book of Hebrews, Paul mentioned many verses of the Old Testament, and referred to many Jewish traditional customs and beliefs so Jews can understand his letter easily. Paul explained the most important reason Jesus came to this world as a man—for our salvation!

> So Christ has now become the High Priest over all the good things that have come. He has entered that great, perfect sanctuary in heaven, not made by human hands and not part of this created world. Once for all time he took blood into that Most Holy Place, but not the blood of goats and calves. He took his own blood and with it he secured our salvation forever. (Hebrews 9:11–12)

> And so, dear brothers and sisters, we can boldly enter heaven's most holy place because of the blood of Jesus. This is the new, life-giving way that Christ has opened up for us through the sacred curtain by means of his death for us. (Hebrews 10:19–20; also refer to Matthew 27:51)

When Jesus died as our High Priest, He used His own blood to cover the sins of mankind once and for all. The priest, the veil, the sacrifices and the Ark of the Covenant were, therefore, no longer necessary. On the other hand, God used Jeremiah to prophesy that the Jewish people broke the Old Covenant. In order to save His people, God would give them a New Covenant. Thank God for sending Jesus to save us! The words of Jesus sealed with His own blood is the New Covenant (see Jeremiah 31:31–34; Matthew 26:26–28; and Luke 22:20). Because of Jesus, we can now pray and worship God directly and at any place.

Bringing His People Home—to Eternal Life

Jesus was born as a man not to condemn the world, but to save it:

> For God so loved the world that he gave his only Son, so that everyone who believes in him will not perish but have eternal life. God did not send his Son into the world to condemn it, but to save it. There is no judgment awaiting those who trust him. But those who do not trust him have already been judged for not believing in the only Son of God. (John 3:16–18, also refer to Romans 8:1)

Jesus continued His preaching on the New Covenant to the Jews at Capernaum following the day He fed a crowd of more than 5,000 with five loaves and two fish:

> For I have come down from heaven to do the will of God who sent me, not to do what I want. And this is the will of God, that I should not lose even one of all those he has given me, but that I should raise them to eternal life at the last day. For it is my Father's will that all who see his son and believe in him

> should have eternal life—that I should raise them at the last day. (John 6:38–40)

This is the secret that Ezekiel prophesied 600 years before: "Then my people will know that I am the Lord their God—responsible for sending them away to exile and responsible for bringing them home. I will leave none of my people behind." (Ezekiel 39:28, see also Jeremiah 23:3–4)

Although the original mission for Jesus was to help the people of Israel— God's lost sheep (see Matthew 15:24 and 10:5–6), His own people (the Jews) did not accept Him (see John 1:11). There is no doubt that God's words will be fulfilled. When God's time arrives, all the Jews will be saved by accepting the New Covenant into their hearts (see Romans 11:25–27, Jeremiah 31:33).

That was, is, and will always be the mission of Jesus—to bring people into the Father's house. Jesus told His disciples:

> There are many rooms in my Father's home, and I am going to prepare a place for you. If this were not so, I would tell you plainly. When everything is ready, I will come and get you, so that you will always be with me where I am. And you know where I am going and how to get there. (John 14:2–4)

> I am the Way, the Truth and the Life. No one can come to the Father except through me. (John 14:6)

Jesus did not say: "go to the Father." Instead, He said: "come to the Father." This is because Jesus is the Father as well. The most important duty God the Father gave to Jesus (as a man) is to provide the way for His selected people (Christian—both Jews and Gentiles) to the New Jerusalem (see Revelation 21). However, God let man make his own choice.

To Save God's Lost Sheep—the Jews

In those days when Jesus walked the earth, tax collectors were considered sinners due to their abuse of their authority and greed. Jesus, however, asked one of them to become His disciple:

> As Jesus was going down the road, he saw Matthew sitting at his tax-collection booth. 'Come, be my disciple,' Jesus said to him. So Matthew got up and followed him.
>
> That night Matthew invited Jesus and his disciples to be his dinner guests, along with his fellow tax collectors and many other notorious sinners. The Pharisees were indignant. "Why does your teacher eat with such scum?" they asked his disciples.
>
> When he heard this, Jesus replied, "Healthy people don't need a doctor—sick people do." Then he added, "Now go and learn the meaning of this Scripture: I want you to be merciful; I don't want your sacrifices. For I have come to call sinners, not those who think they are already good enough." (Matthew 9:9–13)

Jesus was pleased with another tax collector, Zacchaeus, one of the richest and most influential Jews in the Roman tax-collecting business. As Zacchaeus repented of his sins, Jesus told the crowd of Jews including His disciples:

> Salvation has come to this home today, for this man has shown himself to be a son of Abraham. And I, the Son of Man, have come to seek and save those like him who are lost. (Luke 19:9–10)

Every man has sin (both the sins inherited from Adam and from his own actions), therefore every man must die. Jesus offered Himself as one-time priest. By His own blood, the sins of man can be washed clean. The only way man may receive eternal life is to accept Jesus as his/her Savior/Messiah and obey the words of God. The original mission God gave to His Son Jesus was to look after God's lost sheep—the people of Israel. This fulfilled many prophecies of the Old Testament (one of the most obvious prophecies is given in Ezekiel 37:24–28). See the two cases below:

> Jesus sent the twelve disciples out with these instructions: "Don't go to the Gentiles or the Samaritans, but only to the people of Israel—God's lost sheep. Go and announce to them that the Kingdom of Heaven is near. Heal the sick, raise the dead, cure those with leprosy, and cast out demons. Give as freely as you have received!" (Matthew 10:5–8)

> Jesus then left Galilee and went north to the region of Tyre and Sidon. A Gentile woman who lived there came to him, pleading, "Have mercy on me, O Lord, Son of David! For my daughter has a demon in her, and it is severely tormenting her." But Jesus gave her no reply—not even a word. Then his disciples urged him to send her away. "Tell her to leave," they said. "She is bothering us with all her begging." Then he said to the woman, "I was sent only to help the people of Israel—God's lost sheep—not the Gentiles." (Matthew 15:21–24)

Only after Jesus was rejected, died and resurrected, did He instruct His apostles Peter and Paul to preach the Gospel to the Gentiles as well. This happened when most of the Jews had their ears shut and eyes closed to the New Covenant, not accepting Jesus as Messiah. Therefore the Good News went to the Gentiles:

> Then Paul and Barnabas spoke out boldly and declared, "It was necessary that this Good News from God be given first to you Jews. But since you have rejected it and judged yourselves unworthy of eternal life —well, we will offer it to Gentiles. For this

> is as the Lord commanded us when he said, 'I have made you a light to the Gentiles, to bring salvation to the farthest corners of the earth.'" (Acts 13:46–47; also see Acts 9 and 10)

Serving Others

Jesus called His disciples together and emphasized the importance of serving others:

> You know that in this world kings are tyrants, and officials lord it over the people beneath them. But among you it should be quite different. Whoever wants to be a leader among you must be your servant, and whoever wants to be first must become your slave. For even I the son of man, came here not be served but to serve others, and to give my life as a ransom for many. (Matthew 20:25–28; also see Mark 10:42–45)

The Good Shepherd

Jesus established Himself as the Shepherd and all His followers (believers) as His Sheep:

> The thief's purpose is to steal and kill and destroy. My purpose is to give life in all its fullness. I am the good shepherd. The good shepherd lays down his life for the sheep. A hired hand will run when he sees a wolf coming. He will leave the sheep because they aren't his and he isn't their shepherd. And so the wolf attacks them and scatters the flock. The hired hand runs away because he is merely hired and has no real concern for the sheep.
>
> I am the good shepherd; I know my own sheep, and they know me, just as my Father knows me and I know the Father. And I lay down my life for the sheep. I have other sheep, too, that are not in this sheepfold. I must bring them also, and they will listen to my voice; and there will be one flock with one shepherd.

> The Father loves me because I lay down my life that I may have it back again. No one can take my life from me. I lay down my life voluntarily. For I have the right to lay it down when I want to and also the power to take it again. For my Father has given me this command. (John 10:10–18)

"The thief" refers to Satan, the devil, a demon, or evil spirit.

"Other sheep" refers to the Gentiles. Jesus prophesied that salvation will also go to them when they accept Jesus as their Savior.

Jesus is God. He could not die as God. He could die only as a man so He could fulfill the responsibilities given to Him by the God the Father—to bear the sins of all men. When Jesus came to this world as a man and died as a man, He defeated the death and Satan. Only in this way, His followers may also be resurrected and to receive eternal life.

There is only one man who was resurrected by the power of His own Spirit—Jesus.

He Gives Glory to God, the Father

The following statement is found in a letter the apostle Paul sent to the church in Philippi, Macedonia, about 30 years after the resurrection of Jesus:

> Though He was God, he did not demand and cling to his rights as God. He made himself nothing; he took the humble position of a slave and appeared in human form. And in human form he obediently humbled himself even further by dying a criminal's death on a cross. Because of this, God raised him up to the heights of heaven and gave him a name that is above every other name, so that at the name of Jesus every knee will bow, in heaven and on earth and under the earth, and every tongue will confess that Jesus Christ is Lord, to the glory of God the Father. (Philippians 2:6–11, also see Isaiah 45:23, Romans 14:11)

Free Gifts from Jesus to All Mankind

The following lists some of the Free Gifts Jesus gives to us:

- Created the Way for man to God the Father (man may have eternal life via the New Covenant, the Word of God).
- Defeated Satan as a man (only by Him can man be freed from being Satan's slave).
- Died for the sins of all mankind (sins of man can then be washed clean only by His blood).
- Healed the sick and raised the dead (miracles on earth, He also gives this power to His believers).
- Provided man with the visible image of the invisible God (He was born as a man so that man may go closer to God).
- Sent the Holy Spirit to man (strengthens man's faith and reminds man about the truth—the words of God).
- Glorified the Father as a man (set an example for man to follow).

"Father, thank you for the New Covenant,
sealed with the blood of Jesus Christ to save us."

chapter four

Ears Can Hear, Eyes Can See

God Blinded the Jews and Hardened Their Hearts

God instructed Isaiah to tell the people of Israel:

> You will hear my words, but you will not understand. You will see what I do, but you will not perceive its meaning. Harden the hearts of these people. Close their ears, and shut their eyes. That way, they will not see with their eyes, hear with their ears, understand with their hearts, and turn to me for healing. (Isaiah 6:9–10, also refer to Jeremiah 5:21; John 12:40)

[Isaiah asked:] "Lord, how long must I do this?" [God replied:] "Until their cities are destroyed, with no one left in them. Until their houses are deserted and the whole country is an utter wasteland. Do not stop until the Lord has sent everyone away to distant lands and the entire land of Israel lies deserted. Even if only a tenth—a remnant—survive, it will be invaded again and

> burned. Israel will remain a stump, like a tree that is cut down, but the stump will be a holy seed that will grow again." (Isaiah 6:11–13; also refer to Matthew 13:14–17; 23:37–39; Mark 4:10–12; Isaiah 53:1; Acts 28:26–27; and 1 Corinthians 14:21)

Three important events happened following the above prophecy:

First, from the time Jesus was born as a man until the generation immediately before the second Coming of Jesus, the Jews will continue to have their ears and eyes shut. All the Jews will accept Jesus as their Messiah in the same generation of the Second Coming of Jesus.

Second, during the period in which the Jews refuse to accept Jesus as their Messiah, Gentiles are given an opportunity to receive eternal life by accepting Jesus as their Savior.

Finally, today, God removes all the obstacles in the ears and the eyes of the Jews. Today, they are able to hear and to see clearly who their Messiah is. Only their Messiah can bring them back to their own land (the New Jerusalem) as promised by God. The Holy seed will grow, and grow quickly. (see Isaiah 29:18)

God Opens the Eyes and Ears of the Jews Today

Isaiah also prophesied:

> I will bring the blind by a way they did not know; I will lead them in paths they have not known. I will make darkness light before them, and crooked places straight. These things I will do for them, and not forsake them. (Isaiah 42:16)

God chooses today to open the ears and eyes of His people:

> "Look, a righteous King is coming! And honest princes will rule under him. He will shelter Israel from the storm and the wind. He will refresh her as a river in the desert and as the cool shadow of

> a large rock in a hot and weary land. Then everyone who can see will be looking for God, and those who can hear will listen to his voice." (Isaiah 32:1–3, also refer to Isaiah 9:6 and Matthew 23:39)

> Hear, you deaf; And look, you blind, that you may see. (Isaiah 42:18)

Today is the day of God's healing of His people—the Jews! He will heal their hearts and minds so that they may hear and see. All the Jews (the people of Israel) will be able to find the way to their own land —the land God promised Abraham and Jacob, for them and their descendants. God also shows them how to get there, as this chapter makes plain.

Why the Jews Refused Jesus

According to the descriptions in the Holy Bible, Jews are religious, superstitious and stubborn people, yet they always desire to worship. Whenever they strayed away from God, they worshipped idols. God loves His chosen people the Jews because of the faith of their ancestors Abraham, Isaac and Jacob. He wants them to worship Him alone, instead of the idols, since He is a jealous God. (refer to Exodus 20:5) For this reason, God repeatedly warned them through the prophets that besides Him there was no other God. But they remained obstinate and refused to listen to the prophecies. Instead, they persecuted the prophets and stoned them to death.

God punished His chosen people every now and then, as recorded in the Old Testament, including their dispersion into other countries all over the world. While Jews did not wish to be punished again for choosing the wrong god or idols, they refused to accept Jesus as well.

The main reason Jews did not accept Jesus was they believed Jesus was merely a man or another prophet. When Jesus told them He was the Son of God, He was accused by the Jews of blasphemy.

About 750 before Christ, God instructed Hosea to make the following prophecy:

> I am the Lord your God, who rescued you from your slavery in Egypt. You have no God but me, for there is no other savior. (Hosea 13:4)

"Do Not Worship Any Other Gods Besides Me"

God told the Jews that worshiping idols would be the most important offense. Since the time Moses led the Jews out of Egypt through the time of Hosea, the Jews experienced numerous punishments for worshiping the wrong gods and idols. God made the priority clear in the first two commandments He gave Moses:

> I am the Lord your God, who rescued you from slavery in Egypt. Do not worship any other gods besides me. Do not make idols of any kind, whether in the shape of birds or animals or fish. You must never worship or bow down to them, for I, the Lord your God, am a jealous God who will not share your affection with any other god! I do not leave unpunished the sins of those who hate me, but I punish the children for the sins of their parents to the third and fourth generations. But I lavish my love on those who love me and obey my commands, even for a thousand generations. (Exodus 20:2–6)

About 720 years before Christ, God instructed Isaiah to again remind the Jews of His command:

> "But you are my witnesses, O Israel!" says the Lord. "And you are my servant. You have been chosen to know me, believe in me, and understand that I alone am God. There is no other God; there never has been and never will be. I am the Lord, and there is no other Savior." (Isaiah 43:10–11)

> For Jacob My servant's sake, and Israel My elect, I have even called you by your name; I have named you, though you have not known Me. I am the Lord, and there is no other; there is no God besides me. I will gird you, though you have not known Me, that they may know from the rising of the sun to its setting that there is none besides Me. I am the Lord, and there is no other; I form the light and create darkness, I make peace and create calamity; I, the Lord, do all these things. (Isaiah 45:4–7)

God was then and is now absolutely serious when He states, "I alone am God." This fact was mentioned by Isaiah 16 times in Isaiah 43 to 46.

"Greater Than Our Father Abraham?"

When Jesus was teaching, the Jewish leaders and Pharisees denounced Him:

> Jesus said . . . "I assure you, anyone who obeys my teaching will never die!"
>
> The people said, "Now we know you are possessed by a demon. Even Abraham and the prophets died, but you say that those who obey your teaching will never die! Are you greater than our father Abraham, who died? Are you greater than the prophets, who died? Who do you think you are?"
>
> Jesus answered, "If I am merely boasting about myself, it doesn't count. But it is my Father who says these glorious things about me. You say, 'He is our God,' but you do not even know Him. I know Him. If I said otherwise, I would be as great a liar as you! But it is true—I know Him and obey Him. Your ancestor Abraham rejoiced as he looked forward to my coming. He saw it and was glad."

> The people said, "You aren't even fifty years old. How can you say you have seen Abraham?"
>
> Jesus answered, "The truth is, I existed before Abraham was even born!" At that point they picked up stones to kill him. But Jesus hid himself from them and left the Temple. (John 8:51–59, see also Proverbs 8:22–36 and John 17:5)

The Pharisees could not deal with the truth that before Jesus was born as a man, He was God. They told Jesus: "For a good work we do not stone you, but for blasphemy, and because you, being a man, make yourself God" (John 10:33). He knew Abraham because He created Abraham. When Jesus was born as a man, He was the Son of God—and still God. There is only one God. Meantime, He was also a Son of man. God is a spirit. He exists in the same from the Beginning to the End. God the Father—Jehovah, the Holy Spirit, and Jesus (even during the period when He was a man) were, in fact, One God at all times!

Breaking the Sabbath Rules

One Sabbath day, Jesus healed a man who had been sick for 38 years, near the Pool of Bethesda in the city of Jerusalem. Instead of praising God for the miracles, the Pharisees were offended, because they saw it was working on the Sabbath. In fact, the Sabbath was set up by Jesus Himself after He created everything (see Proverbs 8:22–36; John 1:3).

> Then the man went to find the Jewish leaders and told them it was Jesus who had healed him. So the Jewish leaders began harassing Jesus for breaking the Sabbath rules. But Jesus replied, "My Father never stops working, so why should I?"

> So the Jewish leaders tried all the more to kill him. In addition to disobeying the Sabbath rules, he had spoken of God as his Father, thereby making himself equal with God. (John 5:15–18)

Although the original mission of Jesus from God the Father was to "look for God's lost sheep"—i.e., the Jews—most of them have not accepted Jesus as their Messiah.

Most Jews believed Jesus was merely a prophet or an ordinary man. (refer to Luke 24:19) Even Jesus' own brothers did not believe He was God or Son of God. (refer to John 7:2–5) However, when Jesus died and was resurrected, at least two of his brothers believed in Him, and wrote the books of James and Jude. Neither did His disciples believe He was resurrected until they saw and gathered together with Him (see Luke 24:36–42).

The following Bible verses may explain that Jesus was God before He was born as a man. He existed with God before the world was being created. The quoted verses of the Holy Bible can be found inside this book by referring to the index for their respective page numbers:

Genesis 1:2
Proverb 8:22–36
Isaiah 7:14; 9:6–7; 11:1–11; 44:6–8; 48:12; 49:1–12; 53:2
Ezekiel 34:11, 23
Daniel 7:13–14
Micah 5:2–5
John 1:1–3; 1:18; 8:24, 28, 56–58; 10:30; 14:7–10; 17:5, 24
Revelation 1:8; 1:17–18; 2:8, 21:6–7; 22:13, 16

"I Have Come Down from Heaven"

To ensure that there was no mistaking who He was, Jesus taught the Jewish people in Capernaum, a town near His home in Galilee:

> Those the father has given me will come to me, and I will never reject them. For I have come down from heaven to do the will of God who sent me, not to do what I want. And this is the will of God, that I should not lose even one of all those he has given me, but that I should raise them to eternal life at the last day. For it is my father's will that all who see his son and believe in him should have eternal life—that I should raise them at the last day. (John 6:37–40, see also Jeremiah 23:3–4; Ezekiel 39:28)

In addition to the fact that Jesus told the audience that He would never reject those given to Him by God the Father, He made two important points:

1. He told the Jewish audience loud and clear that He came down from heaven (not that He was merely a man), and
2. He repeatedly said He would raise those who believed in Him to eternal life at the last day. This is a strong and positive statement, no ambiguity!
3. This statement fulfills God the Father's promise to the Jews: "I will leave none of my people behind." (see Ezekiel 39:27–28; Jeremiah 23:3–4)

Jesus told the Jews repeatedly that He was sent by God the Father and acted completely on the instructions of the Father. He also confirmed again about raising His believers from the dead at the last day:

> For people can't come to me unless the Father who sent me draws them to me, and at the last day I will raise them from the dead. (John 6:44)

> That is what I meant when I said that people can't come to me unless the Father brings them to me. (John 6:65; also refer to Ezekiel 34:23–24)

> So Jesus said, "When you have lifted up the Son of Man on the cross, then you will realize that I am he and that I do nothing on my own, but I speak what the Father taught me." (John 8:28)

> I don't speak on my own authority. The Father who sent me gave me his own instructions as to what I should say. And I know his instructions lead to eternal life; so I say whatever the Father tells me to say! (John 12:49–50)

> Jesus shouted to the crowds, "If you trust me, you are really trusting God who sent me. Or when you see me, you are seeing the one who sent me." (John 12:44–45)

> Jesus told His disciples shortly before His arrest by the Jews: "If you had known who I am, then you would have known who my Father is. From now on you know him and have seen him!" (John 14:7)

> Don't you believe that I am in the Father and the Father is in me? The words I say are not my own, but my Father who lives in me does his work through me. Just believe that I am in the Father and the Father is in me. Or at least believe because of what you have seen me do. The truth is, anyone who believes in me will do the same works I have done, and even greater works, because I am going to be with the Father. (John 14:10–12)

During the night of Jesus' arrest, perhaps only one young disciple of Jesus remained awake. He heard and recorded Jesus' prayer in John 17:

> I brought glory to you here on earth by doing everything you told me to do. (John 17:4)
>
> As you sent me into the world, I am sending them into the world. And I give myself entirely to you so they also might be entirely yours. (John 17:18–19)

The above ten scriptures from the book of John tell us clearly that Jesus did not do anything on His own when He was a man. He acted completely under the instructions of God the Father. God the Father said through many prophets that He would establish a shepherd from the family of David to look after His sheep. The shepherd is none other than Jesus. (refer to Revelation 22:16)

The True Bread of God

Most of the people of Israel have not accepted Jesus as the Son of God. (refer to John 1:10–11) On the day following the miracle in which Jesus used five barley loaves and two small fish to feed more than 5,000 people, Jesus continued His preaching to the Jewish people:

> Jesus replied, "The truth is, you want to be with me because I fed you, not because you saw the miraculous sign. But you shouldn't be so concerned about perishable things like food. Spend your energy seeking the eternal life that I, the Son of Man, can give you. For God the Father has sent me for that very purpose."
>
> They replied, "What does God want us to do?"
>
> Jesus told them, 'This is what God wants you to do: Believe in the one he has sent.'
>
> They replied, 'You must show us a miraculous sign if you want us to believe in you. What will you do for us? After all, our ancestors

> ate manna while they journeyed through the wilderness! As the Scriptures say, 'Moses gave them bread from heaven to eat.'
>
> Jesus said, "I assure you, Moses didn't give them bread from heaven. My Father did. And now he offers you the true bread from heaven. The true bread of God is the one who comes down from heaven and gives life to the world."
>
> "Sir," they said, "give us that bread every day of our lives"
>
> Jesus replied, "I am the bread of life. No one who comes to me will ever be hungry again. Those who believe in me will never thirst. But you haven't believed in me even though you have seen me." (John 6:26–36)

The "bread of life" is in fact the "Word of God" as can be found in the Holy Bible. One of the titles of Jesus is "the Word of God." (see Revelation 19:13 and John 1:1)

Who Will Bring Back the Jews to Their Land?

About 760 years before Christ, the prophet Amos documented:

> "The time will come," says the Lord, "when the grain and grapes will grow faster than they can be harvested. Then the terraced vineyards on the hills of Israel will drip with sweet wine! I will bring my exiled people of Israel back from distant lands, and they will rebuild their ruined cities and live in them again. They will plant vineyards and gardens; they will eat their crops and drink their wine. I will firmly plant them there in the land I have given them," says the Lord your God. "Then they will never be uprooted again." (Amos 9:13–15)

Amos prophesied that God Himself will bring His people back to the land God will give them.

Only in New Jerusalem will Jews "never be uprooted again." The world we live now is not a permanent place. God uses a plant to represent the Jews. When a plant is uprooted, it will die. No one can escape death in this world. Eternal life can only be found in the New Jerusalem. Only there life will be everlasting.

About 740 before Christ, Hosea prophesied Israel would return to the Lord their God and their King:

> This illustrates that Israel will be a long time without a king or prince and without sacrifices, temple, priests, or even idols! But afterward the people will return to the Lord their God and to David's descendant, their king. They will come trembling in awe to the Lord, and they will receive his good gifts in the last days. (Hosea 3:4–5)

The first sentence in this prophecy has already been fulfilled, as most of the Jews have not accepted Jesus as their Messiah over the past 2,000 years. We can see that the Holy Spirit has already started His work. All the Jews will soon return to their God and their king. Special attention is needed regarding the phrase: "in the last days" (see Matthew 23:39). "His good gifts" refers to the eternal life that God will give to the believers of Jesus.

About 720 before Christ, the prophet Micah prophesied:

> But you, Bethlehem Ephrathah, are only a small village in Judah. Yet a ruler of Israel will come from you, one whose origins are from the distant past. The people of Israel will be abandoned to their enemies until the time when the woman in labor gives birth to her son. Then at last his fellow countrymen will return from exile to their own land. And he will stand to lead his flock with the Lord's strength, in the majesty of the name of the Lord his God. Then his people will live there undisturbed, for he will be highly honored all around the world. And he

will be the source of our peace. (Micah 5:2–5; also refer to Luke 2:4–7, John 14:2–4 and Isaiah 52:8–10)

"Whose origins are from the distant past" refers to Jesus. He was God before He was born as a man. (see Exodus 3:14–15; John 8:24, 28, 56–58; Revelation 1:8, 17–18; 21:6; 22:12)

"Then at last" means something positive will happen after something negative. In this case, it is referring to the Jewish people who will accept Jesus after they had denied Him. It will happen only in the last days.

The shepherd prophesied by Micah is no other than Jesus. The most important responsibility delegated to Jesus by God the Father is to give eternal life to those who believe in Jesus at the last day. (refer to John 6:37–40, 44–51, 54, 65). The place for eternal life is not Jerusalem, Israel or Canaan, but in the New Jerusalem. (refer to Revelation 21) Canaan was God's promised land to the Jews under the Old Covenant. It was the first time God saved the Jews. The second time God will save the Jews (only a remnant of them will return, see Isaiah 10:21–22) by leading them to the New Jerusalem, through Jesus, via the New Covenant.

The Last Flight

An illustration of "the last flight" can describe the situation on the last day:

There is a scheduled last flight from the world to the New Jerusalem. The plane has a total of 100 passenger seats, out of which 88 seats have already been occupied. The remaining twelve seats were reserved for the 12 children of the owner of the airline, who also owns the New Jerusalem.

About one hour ago, the owner told the Captain of the plane that his children might not be on time, as most of them are very stubborn. He also told the Captain that the tickets and boarding passes had already been issued and given to his children. He instructed the Captain that the plane must not depart without all his children on board. The Captain replied: "Boss, your instructions have been acknowledged and the message passed to all relevant personnel of the airline."

On the other hand, there are many people on the waiting list for this flight. Although the airline service representatives repeatedly told these people that they should have made their reservations before their departure date a long time ago, they still stand in line and hope for a last-minute miracle.

- The "last flight" stands for the end of the world;
- 88 passengers represent the Gentiles;
- 12 seats were reserved for the people of Israel;
- God is the owner of the airline and New Jerusalem;
- "Very stubborn" refers to the stubbornness of Jews who have not yet accepted Jesus as their Messiah;
- The Captain and airline ground service representatives are the angels;
- The tickets are the words of Jesus;
- The boarding passes are the faith and behavior of believers;
- People on the waiting list are the Gentiles who still have not accepted Jesus as their Savior and those Christians who have not obeyed the Father (words of Jesus) at a time when the Jews started to accept Jesus as their Messiah.

The Land Where He Lives Will Be a Glorious Place

About 700 years before Christ, Isaiah prophesied the following:

> In that day the heir to David's throne will be a banner of salvation to all the world. The nations will rally to him, for the land

> where he lives will be a glorious place. In that day the Lord will bring back a remnant of his people for the second time, returning them to the land of Israel from Assyria, Lower Egypt, Upper Egypt, Ethiopia, Elam, Babylonia, Hamath, and all the distant coastlands.
>
> He will raise a flag among the nations for Israel to rally around. He will gather the scattered people of Judah from the ends of the earth. (Isaiah 11:10–12)

"The heir to David's throne will be a banner of salvation to all the world" refers to none other than Jesus (see Revelation 22:16).

"The Lord will bring back a remnant of his people for the second time" means that this time, God asks His Son Jesus to save all the Jews via the New Covenant. According to God's own words, it is only a matter of time (it had already been earmarked in God's calendar) that all Jews still alive will accept Jesus as their Messiah. This is the condition Jesus gave to the Jews. (refer to Chapter One and Matthew 23:37–39)

Jesus also said: "Heaven and earth will disappear, but my words will remain forever" (Matthew 24:35). Only by accepting Jesus as their Messiah may they enter into the New Jerusalem, the land promised by God. It will happen right at the same generation (a period between 20 and 40 years since the beginning of this sign).

The phrases, "a glorious place" and "the land of Israel," both refer to God's Resting Place—the New Jerusalem—where God will live with His people. (refer to Genesis 28:13; Hebrews 4:9; Revelation 21:1–3)

To Bring His People of Israel Back to Him

About 700 years before Jesus was born as a man, His spirit spoke through Isaiah (the numerals in parenthesis are being explained following the text):

Listen to me, all of you in far-off lands! The Lord called me before my birth; from within the womb he called me by name (1). He made my words of judgment as sharp as a sword (2). He has hidden me in the shadow of his hand. I am like a sharp arrow in his quiver.

He said to me, "You are my servant, Israel, and you will bring me glory."

I replied, "But my work all seems so useless! I have spent my strength for nothing and to no purpose at all (3). Yet I leave it all in the Lord's hand; I will trust God for my reward."

And now the Lord speaks—he who formed me in my mother's womb to be his servant, who commissioned me to bring his people of Israel back to him (4). The Lord has honored me (5), and my God has given me strength. He says, "You will do more than restore the people of Israel to me. I will make you a light to the Gentiles, and you will bring my salvation to the ends of the earth" (6).

The Lord, the Redeemer and Holy One of Israel, says to the one who is despised and rejected by a nation (7), to the one who is the servant of rulers: "Kings will stand at attention when you pass by. Princes will bow low because the Lord has chosen you. He, the faithful Lord, the Holy One of Israel, chooses you."

This is what the Lord says: "At just the right time, I will respond to you. On the day of salvation (8), I will help you. I will give you as a token and pledge to Israel (9). This will prove that I will reestablish the land of Israel and reassign it to its own people again (10). Through you I am saying to the prisoners of darkness (11), 'Come out! I am giving you your freedom!' They will be my sheep, grazing in green pastures and on hills that were previously bare. They will neither hunger nor thirst. The searing sun and scorching desert winds will not reach them anymore (12). For the Lord in his mercy will lead them beside cool waters. And I will make my mountains into level paths for them. The highways will be raised above the valleys. See, my people will return from far away, from lands to the north and west, and from as far south as Egypt (10)." (Isaiah 49:1–12)

All these prophecies have been fulfilled except the judgment that is still pending and forthcoming (to be fulfilled when Jesus returns). The explanations are:

1. God's angel told Joseph in a dream that the child within Mary has been conceived by the Holy Spirit. The angel also told Joseph that Mary would have a son; and Joseph should name Him Jesus. (refer to Matthew 1:20–21)
2. Jesus said: "the word that I have spoken will judge him in the last day" (John 12:48)
3. The original mission of Jesus sent by God the Father was to look after the lost sheep of the house of Israel. (refer to Matthew 15:24) He died for their sins (see Isaiah 53). However, the people of Israel did not believe in Him.
4. Under many paragraphs in this chapter describe God's appointment of Jesus as the Shepherd and also the King to His selected people and He is responsible to bring them back to God.
5. Jesus will be honored by God the Father to sit at His right hand side and humble His enemies making them a footstool under His feet. (refer to Psalm 110:1) Jesus was also awarded with the complete authority in heaven and on earth. (refer to Matthew 28:18)
6. The Resurrected Jesus appointed Paul to preach to the Gentiles. (refer to Acts 9:15 and 13:46–49) He also instructed Apostle Peter to spread the Gospel to the Gentiles. (refer to

Acts 10:9–16) It also fulfilled the prophecy made by Simeon. (refer to Luke 2:32)

7. In addition to His own countrymen, Jesus was even despised by His own brothers. (refer to John 7:1–5) Jesus also said that He does not belong to this world. (refer to John 17:14–15, 18:36) He was persecuted and crucified by His own people.
8. The day of salvation is today when the door is still open to all.
9. The word of Jesus is the New Covenant, which God the Father promised His people to save them. (refer to Jeremiah 31:31)
10. This land is not the geographic location of today's Israel as it was the land God the Father promised the Jews under the Old Covenant. The "Promised Land" and "Jews' own land" under the New Covenant is the New Jerusalem. (refer to Isaiah 65:17–19, 66:18–22, Jeremiah 31:15–17, Hebrews 4:1–11, 12:22; 2 Peter 3:13; Revelation 21)
11. Jesus preached to the dead in Paradise, those who died from the generation of Noah to the moment Jesus was being crucified. (refer to 1 Peter 3:19–20)
12. It is only in the New Jerusalem there is peace and no more suffering. By that time, Satan has already been cast into the lake of fire and he will stay there permanently. (refer to Revelation 20:10, 14–15)

Not a Single One of Them Will Be Lost or Missing

About 600 before Christ, the prophet Jeremiah made the following prophecies:

> "I will send disaster upon the leaders of my people—the shepherds of my sheep—for they have destroyed and scattered the very ones they were expected to care for," says the Lord.

> This is what the Lord, the God of Israel, says to these shepherds: "Instead of leading my flock to safety, you have deserted them and driven them to destruction. Now I will pour out judgement on you for the evil you have done to them. But I will gather together the remnant of my flock from wherever I have driven them. I will bring them back into their own fold, and they will be fruitful and increase in number. Then I will appoint responsible shepherds to care for them, and they will never be afraid again. Not a single one of them will be lost or missing," says the Lord.
>
> "For the time is coming," says the Lord, "when I will place a righteous branch on King David's throne. He will be a King who rules with wisdom. He will do what is just and right throughout the land. And this is his name: "THE LORD IS OUR RIGHTEOUSNESS." In that day Judah will be saved, and Israel will live in safety."
>
> "In that day," says the Lord, "when people are taking an oath, they will no longer say, 'As surely as the Lord lives, who rescued the people of Israel from the land of Egypt.' Instead, they will say, 'As surely as the Lord lives, who brought the people of Israel back to their own land from the land of the north and from all the countries to which he had exiled them.' Then they will live in their own land." (Jeremiah 23:1–8; also refer to John 6:39, Ezekiel 39:28)

"Their own fold" and "their own land" both referring to the New Jerusalem. (see Isaiah 65:17–19, 66:18–22; Jeremiah 31:17 and Revelation 21)

"A righteous branch on King David's throne", "He will be a king who rules with wisdom" and "the Lord is our righteousness" all stand for Jesus. This prophecy was made more than 300 years after King David. Therefore, it is not referring to King David or his son King Solomon. In Revelation 22:16, a confirmation is given by the Resurrected Jesus Himself. In Proverbs 8:12, the Spirit of Jesus spoke through King Solomon that He is wisdom. (Also refer to Isaiah 16:5 and Jeremiah 33:14–16)

Bring Them to God's Home

> For the time is coming when I will restore the fortunes of my people of Israel and Judah. I will bring them home to this land that I gave to their ancestors, and they will possess it and live here again. I, the Lord, have spoken! (Jeremiah 30:3)

"This land" refers to the New Jerusalem where God and His people will live together in one "home". God said "here" to describe His Resting Place when He talked to Jacob above the ladder. (refer to Genesis 28:10–15) The ladder is Jesus (see John 1:51) or the Way to God (see John 14:6). There is a special rest still waiting for the people of God—the New Jerusalem. (refer to Hebrews 4:1–9; Revelation 3:12, 21:1–3)

Jesus told His disciples: "There are many rooms in my Father's home, and I am going to prepare a place for you. If this were not so, I would tell you plainly. When everything is ready, I will come and get you, so that you will always be with me where I am. And you know where I am going and how to get there" (John 14:2–4; see also Hebrews 4:9). It is clear that Jesus will not lead His disciples to the spot on the earth we call Israel. He is referring to God's Resting Place, the New Jerusalem. (also refer to John 17:24 and Revelation 21)

Only Jesus can bring the people of Israel home to their own land, because He is the Way, the Truth and Life (John 14:6), the Word of God (Revelation 19:13), the New Covenant (Jeremiah 31:31; Luke 22:19–20), the Shepherd and the King of Israel (Ezekiel

34:11, 23–24), the One-Time Priest who uses His own blood to clean the sins of all mankind (Hebrews 7:20–22, 27); the Everlasting Father (Isaiah 9:6), the Messiah (John 4:26); and the Almighty God (Exodus 3:14; Isaiah 9:6; 44:6; 48:12; John 1:1; 8:58; Revelation 1:8, 17–18; 2:8; 21:6; 22:12–13). Hallelujah!

Serve God and the King

> For in that day, says the Lord Almighty, I will break the yoke from their necks and snap their chains. Foreigners will no longer be their masters. For my people will serve the Lord their God and David their king, whom I will raise up for them. So do not be afraid, Jacob, my servant; do not be dismayed, Israel, says the Lord. For I will bring you home again from distant lands, and your children will return from their exile. Israel will return and will have peace and quiet in their own land, and no one will make them afraid. For I am with you and will save you, says the Lord. I will completely destroy the nations where I have scattered you, but I will not destroy you. But I must discipline you; I cannot let you go unpunished. (Jeremiah 30:8–11)

God asked Jeremiah to tell the Jews that they will serve "the Lord their God and David their king." Obviously "David their king" is not King David, son of Jesse and father of King Solomon, because King David died about 300 years before Jeremiah became a prophet. It is referring to Jesus.

"Raise up" means God raised up Jesus from the dead. If Jesus was not being raised up (resurrected) by God the Father through the Holy Spirit, then we also would not have hope for eternal life.

"I will completely destroy the nations where I have scattered you" means that the old heaven and the old earth (this world) will be destroyed and will disappear (see Revelation 21:1). The Second Coming of Jesus (or the Return of Jesus) will take place in the same generation when all the Jew have accepted Jesus as their Messiah. (see Matthew 23:39; 24:32–35; Revelation 21:1; and Isaiah 10:21–22)

"Who Would Dare to Come Unless Invited?"

> But the Lord says this: When I bring you home again from your captivity and restore your fortunes, Jerusalem will be rebuilt on her ruins. The palace will be reconstructed as it was before. There will be joy and songs of thanksgiving, and I will multiply my people and make of them a great and honored nation. Their children will prosper as they did long ago. I will establish them as a nation before me, and I will punish anyone who hurts them. They will have their own ruler again, and he will not be a foreigner.
>
> I will invite him to approach me, say the Lord, for who would dare to come unless invited? You will be my people, and I will be your God. (Jeremiah 30:18–22)

"Jerusalem will be rebuilt on her ruins" refers promises that all the Jews will accept Jesus as their Messiah.

"The Palace" refers to the rest place of the "ruler." Instead of a physical building, God chooses to rest among His people, in their hearts. (see 1 Corinthians 3:16–17 and 6:19)

Who will be their ruler and not a foreigner? Who is worth the invitation of God? Who dares to face God directly? The answer to all these questions: Jesus.

"David Will Forever Have a Descendant Sitting on the Throne of Israel"

> "The day will come," says the Lord, "when I will do for Israel and Judah all the good I have promised them. At that time I will

> bring to the throne of David a righteous descendant, and he will do what is just and right throughout the land. In that day Judah will be saved, and Jerusalem will live in safety. And their motto will be 'the Lord is our righteousness!' For this is what the Lord says: David will forever have a descendant sitting on the throne of Israel." (Jeremiah 33:14–17)

"I will bring to the throne of David a righteous descendant" refers to the prophecy God promised the Jews to send Jesus to them. Only Jesus is qualified to sit on King David's throne forever: And it is one of King David's descendants, Jesus, who is God's promised Savior of Israel! (Acts 13:23)

> I, JESUS, have sent my angel to give you this message for the churches. I am both the source of David and the heir to his throne. I am the bright morning star. (Revelation 22:16).

"I Myself Will Search and Find My Sheep"

Ezekiel made the following prophecies:

> For this is what the Sovereign Lord says: "I myself will search and find my sheep. I will be like a shepherd looking for his scattered flock. I will find my sheep and rescue them from all the places to which they were scattered on that dark and cloudy day. I will bring them back home to their own land of Israel from among the peoples and nations. I will feed them on the mountains of Israel and by the rivers in all the places where people live. Yes, I will give them good pastureland on the high hills of Israel. There they will lie down in pleasant places and feed in lush mountain pastures. I myself will tend my sheep and cause them to lie down in peace, says the Sovereign Lord. I will search for my lost ones who strayed away, and I will bring them safely home again. I will bind up the injured and strengthen the weak. But I will destroy those who are fat and powerful. I will feed them, yes—feed them justice!" (Ezekiel 34:11–16)

> And I will set one shepherd over them, even my servant David. He will feed them and be a shepherd to them. And I, the Lord, will be their God, and my servant David will be a prince among my people. (Ezekiel 34:23–24)

"The mountains of Israel" and "the high hills of Israel" refer to the New Jerusalem. As soon as a person believes in Jesus as his/her Savior or Messiah, that person's name has already been recorded in the Book of Life (a visa to the New Jerusalem).

"Fat and powerful" refers to those who refuse to accept Jesus as their Savior or Messiah.

"One shepherd" and "my servant David" both refer to Jesus. "I myself" refers to God the Father Himself and also to Jesus since God the Father and Jesus are one. (refer to Isaiah 9:6 and John 10:30)

God will lead the Jews to become believers of Jesus. As soon as Jews believe in Jesus as their Messiah, they will be given valid passports and visas (God's promise of salvation with eternal life) so they may return home to their own land—the New Jerusalem.

"They Shall All Have One Shepherd"

> David My servant shall be king over them, and they shall all have one shepherd; they shall also walk in My judgments and observe My statutes, and do them. Then they shall dwell in the land that I have given to Jacob My servant, where your fathers dwelt; and they shall dwell there, they, their children, and their children's children, forever; and My servant David shall be their prince forever. Moreover I will make a covenant of peace with them and it shall be an everlasting covenant with them; I will establish them and multiply them, and I will set my sanctuary in their midst forevermore. My tabernacle also shall be with them;

> indeed I will be their God and they shall be My people. The nations also will know that I, the Lord, sanctify Israel, when my sanctuary is in their midst forevermore. (Ezekiel 37:24–28 NKJV)

Jeremiah and Ezekiel were not the only prophets who prophesied that an heir of David would provide salvation to the people of Israel. Before their time, Isaiah made a prophecy in Isaiah 11:10: "In that day the heir to David's throne will be a banner of salvation to all the world."

In Matthew 15:22 a Gentile woman called Jesus "O Lord, Son of David."

"The land I have given to Jacob"—God did not mean to give Jacob and his descendants a small parcel of land merely big enough for Jacob to sleep. (refer to Genesis 28:10–15.) In Jacob's dream God was standing above a ladder, and angels were going up and down that ladder. The ladder is the way for man to God. (refer to John 1:51; 14:6) Since there is still a special Resting Place waiting for the people of God. (refer to Hebrews 4:9) The place promised by God to Jacob is in fact His own place of rest, the New Jerusalem where God will live among His people. (refer to Exodus 29:45; Luke 17:21; and Revelation 21:3) That is why God mentioned twice that "my sanctuary is in their midst forevermore." God will live in the hearts of His people. (refer to 1 Corinthians 3:16–17, 6:19)

Bless the One Who Comes in the Name of the Lord

About 480 before Christ, Zechariah Prophesied:

> "Rejoice greatly, O people of Zion! Shout in triumph, O people of Jerusalem! Look, Your king is coming to you. He is righteous and victorious, yet he is humble, riding on a donkey—even on a donkey's colt. I will remove the battle chariots from Israel and the war-horses from Jerusalem, and I will destroy all the weapons used in battle. Your King will bring peace to the nations. His

> realm will stretch from sea to sea and from the Euphrates River to the ends of the earth.
>
> Because of the covenant I made with you, sealed with blood, I will free your prisoners from death in a waterless dungeon. Come back to the place of safety, all you prisoners, for there is yet hope! I promise this very day that I will repay you two mercies for each of your woes!" (Zechariah 9:9–12; also refer to Jeremiah 31:31–34)

"Your king" refers to Jesus. (see Luke 19:29–40)

"The covenant I made with you, sealed with blood" refers to the New Covenant and the words of Jesus. The Blood refers to the blood of Jesus shed for all man on the day of crucifixion. (refer to Luke 22:19–20)

"All you prisoners" refers to the Jews who still haven't believed in Jesus. Only by accepting Jesus may man go free from being a Satan's slave.

"Place of safety" refers to the Jews accepting Jesus as their Messiah.

"Two mercies"; God promised the Jews that the believers in Jesus will have a pleasant life in this world and the eternal life in the new heavens and a new earth—the New Jerusalem.

To fulfill the prophecy of Zechariah, Matthew, the former tax collector and one of Jesus' apostles, wrote the following:

> As Jesus and the disciples approached Jerusalem, they came to the town of Bethphage on the Mount of Olives. Jesus sent two of them on ahead. "Go into the village over there," he said, "and you will see a donkey tied there, with its colt beside it. Untie them and bring them here. If anyone asks what you are doing, just say, 'The Lord needs them,' and he will immediately send them." This was done to fulfill the prophecy,

"Tell the people of Israel,
'Look, your King is coming to you.
He is humble, riding on a donkey—
even on a donkey's colt.'"

The two disciples did as Jesus said. They brought the animals to him and threw their garments over the colt, and he sat on it.

Most of the crowd spread their coats on the road ahead of Jesus, and others cut branches from the trees and spread them on the road. He was in the center of the procession, and the crowds all around him were shouting,

"Praise God for the Son of David!
Bless the One who comes in the name of the Lord!
Praise God in highest heaven!"

The entire city of Jerusalem was stirred as he entered. "Who is this?" they asked.

And the crowds replied, "It's Jesus, the prophet from Nazareth in Galilee." (Matthew 21:1–11, also see Psalm 118:26; Matthew 23:37–39)

Another apostle of Jesus wrote:

The next day, the news that Jesus was on the way to Jerusalem swept through the city. A huge crowd of Passover visitors took palm branches and went down the road to meet him. They shouted,

"Praise God!
Bless the one who comes in the name of the Lord!
Hail to the King of Israel!"

Jesus found a young donkey and sat on it, fulfilling the prophecy that said:

"Don't be afraid, people of Israel.
Look, your King is coming, Sitting on a donkey's colt."

His disciples didn't realize at the time that this was a fulfillment of prophecy. But after Jesus entered into his glory, they remembered that these Scriptures had come true before their eyes. Those in the crowd who had seen Jesus call Lazarus back to life were telling others all about it. That was the main reason so many went out to meet him—because they had heard about this mighty miracle. Then the Pharisees said to each other, "We've lost. Look, the whole world has gone after him!" (John 12:12–19, also refer to Genesis 49:11)

A doctor of medicine and a believer of Jesus, Luke, documented his findings from those eyewitnesses of Jesus:

Then, as He was now drawing near the descent of the Mount of Olives, the whole multitude of the disciples began to rejoice and praise God with a loud voice for all the mighty works they had seen. Saying:

"Blessed is the King who comes in the name of the Lord!
Peace in heaven and glory in the highest."

And some of the Pharisees called to Him from the crowd, "Teacher, rebuke Your disciples."

But He answered and said to them, "I tell you that if these should keep silent, the stones would immediately cry out." (Luke 19:37–40 NKJV)

Where Is the People of Israel's Own Land?

About 520 years before Christ, there was a very important prophecy made by the prophet Zechariah:

> I will strengthen Judah and save Israel; I will reestablish them because I love them. It will be as though I had never rejected them, for I am the Lord their God, who will hear their cries. The people of Israel will become like mighty warriors, and their hearts will be happy as if by wine. Their children, too, will see it all and be glad; their hearts will rejoice in the Lord. When I whistle to them, they will come running, for I have redeemed them. From the few that are left, their population will grow again to its former size. Though I have scattered them like seeds among the nations, still they will remember me in distant lands. With their children, they will survive and come home again to Israel. I will bring them back from Egypt and Assyria and resettle them in Gilead and Lebanon. There won't be enough room for them all! (Zechariah 10:6–10)

"Reestablish them" means to give them the New Covenant so that they may live again, with eternal life (see Jeremiah 31:31–33; Luke 22:20; and Hebrews 12:24).

"Will see it all"—In the last days, all the younger generation of Jews will recognize Jesus.

"Come home again to Israel" has the same meaning: "Accept Jesus as Messiah." This is the only way they may return to their own land. As soon as the Jews have accepted Jesus as their Messiah, their names are recorded in the Book of Life. There is no need for all the Jews return physically to the country of Israel! No matter whether they are sleeping or awake when Jesus returns, they will be able to enter the New Jerusalem—the permanent home for the Jews!

"They will come running" refers to a drastic change that will take place in the last days. The Jews will accept Jesus as their Messiah in an astonishing speed.

"There won't be enough room for them all" refers to the land God gave to the Jews in the Old Covenant. It will no longer be sufficient to hold all the Jews.

God has already whistled. Have you heard His whistle yet?

One day the Pharisees asked Jesus, "When will the Kingdom of God come?" Jesus replied, "The Kingdom of God isn't ushered in with visible signs. You won't be able to say, 'Here it is!' or 'It's over there!' For the Kingdom of God is among you." (Luke 17:20–21)

When the words of Jesus fill our hearts, we can enjoy happiness and complete satisfaction. Our bodies become the Temple of God. He lives within us. We should give thanks to God for what we have received from God.

We can also feel the joy that non-believers cannot experience. In the Kingdom of God, there is joy and satisfaction. Sadness, temptations and evil desires were created by Satan. Since Satan cannot enter into the Kingdom of God, sadness and temptation cannot be brought into the hearts of the people, for they have God's Spirit in them.

The New Jerusalem

About 680 before Christ, Isaiah prophesied about the New Jerusalem:

> "Look! I am creating new heavens and a new earth—so wonderful that no one will even think about the old ones anymore. Be glad; rejoice forever in my creation! And look! I will create Jerusalem as a place of happiness. Her people will be a source of joy. I will rejoice in Jerusalem and delight in my people. And the sound

> of weeping and crying will be heard no more." (Isaiah 65:17–19, also refer to Hebrews 4:8–11)

> "As surely as my new heavens and earth will remain, so will you always be my people, with a name that will never disappear," says the Lord. (Isaiah 66:22)

About 776 years after the above prophecies, the apostle John documented the visions given to him by the Resurrected Jesus at the Island of Patmos about the New Jerusalem:

> Then I saw a new heaven and a new earth, for the old heaven and the old earth had disappeared. And the sea was also gone. And I saw the holy city, the New Jerusalem, coming down from God out of heaven like a beautiful bride prepared for her husband.

> I heard a loud shout from the throne, saying, "Look, the home of God is now among His people! He will live with them, and they will be His people. God Himself will be with them. He will remove all of their sorrows, and there will be no more death or sorrow or crying or pain. For the Old World and its evils are gone forever." (Revelation 21:1–4, also see Isaiah 25:6–10)

> So he took me in spirit to a great high mountain, and he showed me the holy city, Jerusalem, descending out of heaven from God. It was filled with the glory of God and sparkled like a precious gem, crystal clear like jasper. Its walls were broad and high, with twelve gates guarded by twelve angels. And the names of the twelve tribes of Israel were written on the gates. (Revelation 21:10–12)

God confirmed that in the New Jerusalem, God will live among His people. More details about the New Jerusalem can be found in Chapters 21 and 22 of Revelation. (also refer to 2 Peter 3:13, Revelation 3:12)

About 520 years before Christ, the Spirit of Jesus spoke through Zechariah:

> Shout and rejoice, O Jerusalem, for I am coming to live among you. Many nations will join themselves to the Lord on that day and they, too, will be my people. I will live among you, and you will know that the Lord Almighty sent me to you. (Zechariah 2:10–11)

> I am returning to Mount Zion, and I will live in Jerusalem. Then Jerusalem will be called the Faithful City; the mountain of the Lord Almighty will be called the Holy Mountain. (Zechariah 8:3)

> I will bring them home again to live safely in Jerusalem. They will be my people, and I will be faithful and just toward them as their God. (Zechariah 8:8)

"I" and "me" both refer to Jesus.

"Jerusalem" refers to the New Jerusalem as being described in Revelation 21.

Approximately 30 years before John wrote the Book of Revelation, Paul also wrote a letter to the Christian Jews about the destination of believers in Jesus:

> No, you have come to Mount Zion, to the city of the living God, the heavenly Jerusalem, and to thousands of angels in joyful assembly. You have come to the assembly of God's firstborn children, whose names are written in heaven. You have come to God himself, who is the judge of all people. And you have come to the spirits of the redeemed in heaven who have now been made perfect. You have come to Jesus, the one who mediates the new covenant between god and people, and to the sprinkled

> blood, which graciously forgives instead of crying out for vengeance as the blood of Abel did.
>
> See to it that you obey God, the one who is speaking to you. For if the people of Israel did not escape when they refused to listen to Moses, the earthly messenger, how terrible our danger if we reject the One who speaks to us from heaven! When God spoke from Mount Sinai his voice shook the earth, but now he makes another promise. "Once again I will shake not only the earth but the heaven also." This means that the things on earth will be shaken, so that only eternal things will be left.
>
> Since we are receiving a kingdom that cannot be destroyed, let us be thankful and please God by worshiping him with holy fear and awe. For our God is a consuming fire. (Hebrews 12:22–29)

About 600 before Christ, Jeremiah prophesied that the Jews will start back home again:

> "Then the people of Israel and Judah will join together," says the Lord, "weeping and seeking the Lord their God. They will ask the way to Jerusalem and will start back home again. They will bind themselves to the Lord with an eternal covenant that will never again be broken." (Jeremiah 50:4–5, also see Zechariah 12:10–11)

The Jews have been weeping and seeking their God by praying at the Wall. They still haven't found their God, because God does not live inside the Wall.

They can only find their God in God's own words—the Holy Bible. By the grace of God, He gave us the New Covenant or the everlasting covenant—the words of Jesus Christ. (see Jeremiah 31:31; Luke 22:19–20; John 1:1–3; and Revelation 19:13)

There is only one way for the Jews to go to their own land, the New Jerusalem—through Jesus!

Although there is no census information today showing the total number of descendants of Jacob, it may well exceed 100 million. They are scattered all over the world, not only in North America, Europe, and Africa. According to a Chinese news publication, several hundred Jews went to China about 1,000 years ago. Today, after about 30 generations of multi-children-family tradition in China, the number can be astonishing.

There is not much land left in the geographic location of the country of Israel today, although the population is only 4 million. How can it accommodate all the Jews? (refer to Zechariah 10:10)

One morning in mid-1997, the Holy Spirit hinted to me that the Jews outside the country of Israel would accept Jesus as their Messiah first, and then at last, the Jews inside Israel would follow. I have given this information to one of the representatives of a famous evangelist who contacted me as a partner of his mission in sending Bibles to the Jews in Israel.

Not many people would believe that all the Jews will accept Jesus as their Messiah; especially since it will happen within a short period of time. This mass conversion may seem impossible, but with God, nothing is impossible!

God has never deserted His selected people, even going back to the days of Abraham. Especially, when they repented of their sins and asked God to forgive them. Each time God heard their prayers and confessions and God answered them with His kind love and forgiveness. In addition, God told Jews repeatedly that He Himself would be responsible to bring them to their own land.

When God sent His Own Son, who was born as a man to bring the Jews to their own land, He was rejected by them. Their eyes and ears were shut by God. It is only a matter of time until God opens their eyes and ears.

The time is today! This book contains the good news as prophesied in Isaiah 40:9–10. Isaiah also prophesied that everyone who can see will be looking for God and those who can hear will listen to His voice. (see Isaiah 29:18, 32:1–3) Jesus promised to heal all the Jews when they turn to Him. (refer to John 12:40; Isaiah 6:9–10; 18:3; and Matthew 13:10–17)

"Your Children Will Come Again to Their Own Land"

God's Spirit spoke through Jeremiah to the mothers of Jewish baby boys two years of age and under who would be murdered by King Herod. King Herod was jealous when he heard about the birth of a new king—Jesus:

> This is what the Lord says: "A cry of anguish is heard in Ramah—mourning and weeping unrestrained. Rachel weeps for her children, refusing to be comforted—for her children are dead."
>
> But now the Lord says, "Do not weep any longer, for I will reward you. Your children will come back to you from the distant land of the enemy. There is hope for your future," says the Lord. "Your children will come again to their own land." (Jeremiah 31:15–17)

In the New Testament, Matthew, an apostle of Jesus, wrote:

> Herod was furious when he learned that the wise men had outwitted him. He sent soldiers to kill all the boys in and around Bethlehem who were two years old and under, because the wise men had told him the star first appeared to them about two years earlier. Herod's brutal action fulfilled the prophecy of Jeremiah: "A cry of anguish is heard in Ramah—weeping and mourning unrestrained. Rachel weeps for her children, refusing to be comforted—for they are dead." (Matthew 2:16–18)

As a result of the above, God showed us His glory in the following:

> Then I [John] saw the Lamb standing on Mount Zion, and with him were 144,000 who had his name and his Father's name written on their foreheads. And I heard a sound from heaven like the roaring of a great waterfall or the rolling of mighty thunder. It was like the sound of many harpists playing together.
>
> This great choir sang a wonderful new song in front of the throne of God and before the four living beings and the twenty-four elders. And no one could learn this song except those 144,000 who had been redeemed from the earth. For they are spiritually undefiled, pure as virgins, following the Lamb wherever he goes. They have been purchased from among the people on the earth as a special offering to God and to the Lamb. No falsehood can be charged against them; they are blameless. (Revelation 14:1–5)

There are differences found between the *New Living Translation* and the *New King James Version* in Revelation 14:1–5. Here is what the *New King James Version* reports:

> Then I looked, and behold, a Lamb standing on Mount Zion, and with Him one hundred and forty-four thousand, having His Father's name written on their foreheads. And I heard a voice from heaven, like the voice of many waters, and like the voice of loud thunder. And I heard the sound of harpists playing their harps. And they sang as it were a new song before the throne, before the four living creatures, and the elders; and no one could learn that song except the hundred and forty-four thousand who were redeemed from the earth. These are the ones who were not defiled with women, for they are virgins. These are the ones who follow the Lamb wherever He goes. These were redeemed from among men, being first fruits to God and to the Lamb. And

> in their mouth was found no guile, for they are without fault before the throne of God. (Revelation 14:1–5 NKJV)

The above three sections of the Holy Bible all link to one incident—Herod's brutal murder of the young boys and God's reward to the mothers of their dead sons. The definitions are as follows: Rachel was the only woman Jacob intended to marry originally. Jacob only succeeded his dreams by marrying Rachel as his second wife. The first wife of Jacob was Rachel's elder sister Leah. Although Leah was the mother of Jacob's six out of 12 children, she was not the woman Jacob intended to marry. "Rachel" here stands for all the mothers of young boys (under two years old) in Israel who were killed by King Herod.

God promised the mothers that their children, already dead, would go back to their mothers. God also said that He would reward the mothers.

There are two important issues here: First, all the young children who died under the age of two would undoubtedly enter into the Kingdom of Heaven. Second, what God promised the mothers with eternal life (whether they were qualified by their own merits and performances) so that they might meet their children again in the New Jerusalem. The promise was made before the salvation Jesus provided.

Obviously, "their own land" stated by Jeremiah refers to the New Jerusalem, the land God gives to the Jews in the New Covenant.

The number 144,000 is God's number. It does not necessarily mean the exact number one can count up to 144,000. It means "all those . . . . . ." in their entirety. The 144,000 mentioned in Revelation 14:1–5 are not the same group of 144,000 mentioned in Revelation 7:1–8. The differences are:

- In Revelation 14:1–5, the 144,000 have Jesus' and God the Father's names written on their foreheads; Revelation 7:1–8 mentions "seal of God," but no written name of Jesus. In Revelation 7:1–5, the 144,000 are waiting to be sealed and then will enter to the New Jerusalem as described in Revelation 21. In Revelation 14:1–5, the 144,000 follow Jesus wherever Jesus goes.
- In Revelation 7:1–5, the 144,000 are composed of equal numbers of 12,000 from each tribe and a total of 12 tribes. Revelation 14:1–5 makes no mention of the number of people from each tribe; instead, "they were not defiled with women (they must be only male in gender), for they are virgins. In their mouth was found no guile and without fault."
- In Revelation 14:1–5, the 144,000 are "first fruits to God and to the Lamb" or "as a special offering to God and the Lamb." God treats the death of the young boys on earth as a special offering to God and the Lamb. They were chronologically placed before those Christians beheaded for their testimonies about Jesus (Revelation 20:4, which included the disciples of Jesus). In Revelation 7:1–5 the 144,000 are the entire family of Israel. "These were redeemed among men" means God gives something to men in order to get back this 144,000. God rewards the mothers with eternal life not based on their own merits but from God's promise (a redemption God paid to man.) This is quite different from the redemption given to us by Jesus as described in Romans 3:24–25; 1 Corinthians 6:20; Galatians 1:4; 3:13; 4:5–6; Colossians 1:14; and Titus 2:14.

"I Will Leave None of My People Behind"

God instructed Ezekiel to tell the people of Israel:

> So now the Sovereign Lord says: I will end the captivity of my people; I will have mercy on Israel, for I am jealous for my holy reputation! They will accept responsibility for their past shame and treachery against me after they come home to live in peace and safety in their own land. And then no one will bother them or make them afraid. When I bring them HOME from the lands of their enemies, my holiness will be displayed to the nations. Then my people will know that I am the Lord their God—responsible for sending them away to exile and responsible for bringing them home. I will leave none of my people behind. And I will never again turn my back on them, for I will pour out my spirit upon them, says the Sovereign Lord. (Ezekiel 39:25–29; also refer to John 6:39 and Jeremiah 23:3–4)

"Come home", "their own land" and "home" refer to the New Jerusalem. When God said: "come home", he means: "come to my home." The ultimate destination of Jews or Jews' own land is God's Rest Place. (see John 14:1–4, Hebrews 4:9 and Revelation 21:1–3)

"I will NEVER AGAIN turn my back on them"—God will only fulfill this statement when Jews have already accepted Jesus as their Messiah.

"Never again" refers to the end of this world and the time when all believers of Jesus enter into the New Jerusalem. This world is a sinful place in the presence of Satan. Satan will be cast into the lake of fire before the New Jerusalem comes down from God out of heaven. (see Revelation 20:10; 21:1–2)

"I will pour out my Spirit upon them" refers to the Counselor, whom Jesus explained to His disciples:

> And I will ask the Father, and he will give you another Counselor, who will never leave you. He is the Holy Spirit, who

> leads into all truth. The world at large cannot receive him, because it isn't looking for him and doesn't recognize him. But you do, because he lives with you now and later will be in you. (John 14:16–17)

God said many times that He is the one who sent His people (the Jews) into exile and He is also the one responsible to bring them home. The return of Jews to salvation through Jesus is unavoidable. God has never lost His promise and He never will!

Today, all the people of Israel can hear the whistle. They can also see the banner. "The people of Israel will become like mighty warriors . . . they will come running." (Zechariah 10:7–8)

The Promised Land

Moses documented what God told Abraham and Jacob about the land:

> Abram dwelt in the Land of Canaan, and Lot dwelt in the cities of the plain and pitched his tent even as far as Sodom. But the men of Sodom were exceedingly wicked and sinful against the Lord. And the Lord said to Abram, after Lot had separated from him: "Lift your eyes now and look from the place where you are—northward, southward, eastward, and westward; for all the land which you see I give to you and your descendants forever. And I will make your descendants as the dust of the earth; so that if a man could number the dust of the earth, then your descendants also could be numbered. Arise, walk in the land through its length and its width, for I give it to you." (Genesis 13:12–17 NKJV)

> Now Jacob went out from Beersheba and went toward Haran. So he came to a certain place and stayed there all night, because the sun had set. And he took one of the stones of that place and

> put it at his head, and he lay down in that place to sleep. Then he dreamed, and behold, a ladder was set up on the earth, and its top reached to heaven; and there the angels of God were ascending and descending on it. And behold, the Lord stood above it and said: "I am the Lord God of Abraham your father and the God of Isaac; the land on which you lie I will give to you and your descendants. Also your descendants shall be as the dust of the earth; you shall spread abroad to the west and the east, to the north and the south; and in you and in your seed all the families of the earth shall be blessed. Behold, I am with you and will keep you wherever you go, and will bring you back to this land; for I will not leave you until I have done what I have spoken to you." (Genesis 28:10–15 NKJV)

God keeps His promise, regardless of the difficulties and the length of time. All His promises will be fulfilled.

In the old days, dreams were not far from realities. In the case of Jacob's dream, it was in fact a similar message as God told Abram (later named Abraham). There are important issues here:

1. The land God promised both Abram (Abraham) and Jacob was located in Canaan (today's country of Israel).
2. The number of descendants of both Abram (Abraham) and Jacob will be too many to count.
3. The "ladder" is Jesus or the words of God. Jesus told Nathaniel and Philip: "The truth is, you will all see heaven open and the angels of God going up and down upon the Son of Man." (John 1:51)

   In the Old Covenant, the land God gave to Abram (Abraham) and Jacob was a physical land for them and their descendants to live while they stay in this world. Moses led the Jews out of Egypt to Canaan. God wrote the Old Covenant on stone. As the Jews could not perfect the law (the Old Covenant or the Ten Commandments), God decided to give them the New Covenant in order to save them. In the New Covenant, Jesus will lead the Jews from this world to the New Jerusalem by means of His words sealed by His Blood. This time God will write the New Covenant in their hearts. (see Jeremiah 31:31–34 and Luke 22:20)

4. God promised Jacob that He would bring him and his descendants back to this land. At that moment, God spoke to Jacob from heaven (on the top of the ladder). "This land" refers to God's Resting Place—the New Jerusalem.
5. It has been stated many times in both the Old and New Testaments that God will live among His people. (see Exodus 29:45–46; Leviticus 26:11–12; 1 Kings 6:13; Ezekiel 37:24–28; 43:7–9; Zechariah 2:10–11; 8:3, 8; and Revelation 21:3)
6. Jesus told His disciples: "There are many rooms in my Father's home, and I am going to prepare a place for you. If this were not so, I would tell you plainly. When everything is ready, I will come and get you, so that you will always be with me where I am." (John 14:2–5)

The size of the nation of Israel cannot accommodate all the world's Jews now or in the future. The physical relocation of Jews to the present Israel is not by God's instruction. For this reason, most Jews will continue to live outside Israel until the Second Coming of Jesus. Whenever the Jewish people accept Jesus as their Messiah, they have the assurance from God that they will return to "this land". As promised by God, only believers in Jesus will enter into the New Jerusalem. There is no exception for the Jews. The Resurrected Jesus promised:

> All who are victorious will become pillars in the Temple of my God, and they will never have to leave it. And I will write my God's name on them, and they will be citizens in the city of my

> God—the New Jerusalem that comes down from heaven from my God. And they will have My new name inscribed upon them. (Revelation 3:12)

There are altogether twelve gates in the New Jerusalem, and the names of the twelve tribes of Israel were written on the gates. (see Revelation 21:12) This is another confirmation by God Himself that "this land" is the "New Jerusalem".

In the last days, God will fulfill His promise to save all the "remnant few" descendants of Jacob as soon as the Gentile numbers are met. (see Isaiah 10:21–22; Romans 9:27–29; and 11:25–27) God promised that none of His people will be left behind. (see Jeremiah 23:4; Ezekiel 39:28)

Why Will All the Jews Be Saved?

As the day of Jesus' Second Coming becomes close, very close; both Jews and Gentiles should pay attention to the following statement made by Paul in his letter to the Christians in Rome:

> I want you to understand this mystery, dear brothers and sisters, so that you will not feel proud and start bragging. Some of the Jews have hard hearts, but this will last only until the complete number of Gentiles comes to Christ. And so all Israel will be saved. Do you remember what the prophets said about this? "A Deliverer will come from Jerusalem, And he will turn Israel from all ungodliness. And then I will keep my covenant with them and take away their sins." (Romans 11:25–27)

"All Israel will be saved." One day, all the Jews will accept Jesus as their Messiah. This will happen before Jesus' Second Coming, as Jesus put a condition in His promise to the Jews. (refer to Matthew 23:39)

"A Deliverer" refers, of course, to Jesus. All the people of Israel will be saved only through the salvation of Jesus. This fulfills the prophecy of Isaiah about the Redeemer who will come to Jerusalem. The Redeemer is none other than Jesus. (refer to Isaiah 59:20–21)

"My covenant" refers to the New Covenant.

Only the New Covenant can save the Jews, because they cannot keep up with the Old Covenant God gave them through Moses. The New Covenant is a fulfillment of the Old Covenant. (refer to Jeremiah 31:31–34)

Contrary to the statement made above, Paul sent the following message to the Christians in Rome:

> Concerning the Gentiles, God says in the prophecy of Hosea: "Those who were not my people, I will now call my people. And I will love those whom I did not love before." And "Once they were told, You are not my people." But now he will say: "You are children of the living God."
>
> Concerning Israel, Isaiah the prophet cried out: "Though the people of Israel are as numerous as the sand on the seashore, only a small number will be saved. For the Lord will carry out his sentence upon the earth quickly and with finality." And Isaiah said in another place: "If the Lord Almighty had not spared a few of us, we would have been wiped out as completely as Sodom and Gomorrah."
>
> Well then, what shall we say about these things? Just this: The Gentiles have been made right with God by faith, even though they were not seeking him. But the Jews, who tried so hard to get right with God by keeping the law, never succeeded. Why not? Because they were trying to get right with God by keeping the law and being good instead of by depending on faith. They

> stumbled over the great rock in their path. God warned them of this in the Scriptures when he said. "I am placing a stone in Jerusalem that causes people to stumble, And a rock that makes them fall. But anyone who believes in him will not be disappointed." (Romans 9:25–33; also refer to Isaiah 10:21–22)

For the period since Jesus was born as a man until the beginning of the generation of His Second Coming, most of the Jews have been relying on keeping the law instead of accepting Jesus as their Messiah. As one example, the Jews brought a woman to Jesus whom they had caught in the act of adultery. They asked Him for a decision. According to the law, she should be stoned to death. However, not one stone was thrown and the woman was released unpunished.

Another example, Jews complained to Jesus about the healing of sicknesses on the day of rest—the Sabbath. Jesus responded: "The Son of Man is also Lord of the Sabbath."

Because no one can be perfect under the law, God sent His Son to bring salvation to all of us. Anyone who believes in Jesus as Savior or Messiah will be saved. To the contrary, those who do not believe in Jesus but are trying their best to obey the law (the Old Covenant) cannot be saved.

Faith is created from belief. Belief is found from the presence of God's Word in our heart.

In the old days, Noah's faith in God's words led him to build the ark that saved his whole family from the Flood. God blessed Abraham because of Abraham's faith. God made David strong also because of his faith. Faith is not only important to our daily life, it is also the critical path to eternal life.

Three Stages of Relationship Between God and Man

- *From Adam to Noah:* God had been very close and friendly with man from the day He made Adam until the time Noah was 500 years old. Since there were no law established in this early period of time, man would have no difficulty gaining eternal life. This stage was terminated when God said: "My Spirit will not put up with humans for such a long time, for they are only mortal flesh." (Genesis 6:3)
- *From Noah to the Death of Jesus as a Man:* God used man as His servants (i.e., the prophets). The Ten Commandments (the Old Covenant) were given by God to Moses for the Jewish people. As no one can perfectly follow the law, sins among man escalated and accumulated. Worst of all, man became superstitious and worshiped idols. God was not pleased with what man did. However, by God's grace, He gave men in this stage a chance to receive eternal life: The Spirit of Jesus preached to the spirits in the prison. (see 1 Peter 3:19–20; 4:6)
- *From Jesus' Resurrection until His Second Coming*: Only those who believe in Jesus will be saved. For the Jews, only a small number will be saved. No matter how hard the Jews tried to obey the law, they cannot keep up with it. Most of the Jews in this stage have not accepted Jesus as their Messiah. Jesus told the Jewish leaders:

> "That is why I said that you will die in your sins; for unless you believe that I am who I say I am, you will die in your sins." (John 8:24)

This was also due to fact that the Jews who prosecuted Jesus and yelled:

"We will take responsibility for his death—we and our children!" (Matthew 27:25)

There is only one way to be saved, no other way. Jesus told Thomas and His other apostles:

"I am the way, the truth and the life. No one can come to the Father except through me." (John 14:6)

"I Will Put My Spirit in You (Dry Bones)"

About 580 before Christ, Ezekiel spoke about a vision:

The Lord took hold of me, and I was carried away by the Spirit of the Lord to a valley filled with bones. He led me around among the old, dry bones that covered the valley floor. They were scattered everywhere across the ground. Then he asked me, "Son of man, can these bones become living people again?"

"O Sovereign Lord," I replied, "you alone know the answer to that."

Then he said to me, "Speak to these bones and say, 'Dry bones, listen to the word of the Lord! This is what the Sovereign Lord says: Look! I am going to breathe into you and make you live again! I will put flesh and muscles on you and cover you with skin. I will put breath into you and you will come to life. Then you will know that I am the Lord.'"

So I spoke these words, just as he told me. Suddenly as I spoke, there was a rattling noise all across the valley. The bones of each body came together and attached themselves as they had been before. Then as I watched, muscles and flesh formed over the bones. Then skin formed to cover their bodies, but they still had no breath in them.

> Then he said to me, "Speak to the winds and say: 'This is what the Sovereign Lord says: Come, O breath, from the four winds! Breathe into these dead bodies so that they may live again.'"
>
> So I spoke as he commanded me, and the wind entered the bodies, and they began to breathe. They all came to life and stood up on their feet—a great army of them.
>
> Then he said to me, "Son of man, these bones represent the people of Israel. They are saying, 'We have become old, dry bones—all hope is gone.' Now give them this message from the Sovereign Lord: O my people, I will open your graves of exile and cause you to rise again. Then I will bring you back to the land of Israel. When this happens, O my people, you will know that I am the Lord. I will put my spirit in you, and you will live and return home to your own land. Then you will know that I am the Lord. You will see that I have done everything just as I promised. I, the Lord, have spoken!" (Ezekiel 37:1–14)

Today, God has removed all the obstacles from the Jewish people. They can now open their ears and eyes so they can hear and see their Messiah. They will no longer feel "all hope is gone." Today, they can hear and see the Word of God through Jesus.

Life is in Jesus. Everything that was created was created through Him. "Live again" and "rise again" both refer to being born again.

"Land of Israel" and "own land" both refer to the New Jerusalem.

"My Spirit" refers to the Spirit of Jesus or the Holy Spirit.

"I have done everything just as I promised" refers to God's promise to give the Jews the New Covenant to save them. All the Jewish people will be saved ONLY after they have accepted the New Covenant—Jesus as their Messiah.

"I Will Give Them Singleness of Heart"

In about 580 before Christ, God's Spirit spoke through Ezekiel:

> And I will give them singleness of heart and put a new spirit within them. I will take away their hearts of stone and give them tender hearts instead, so they will obey my laws and regulations. Then they will truly be my people, and I will be their God. (Ezekiel 11:19–20)

> Then I will sprinkle clean water on you, and you will be clean. Your filth will be washed away, and you will no longer worship idols. And I will give you a new heart with new and right desires, and I will put a new spirit in you. I will take out your stony heart of sin and give you a new obedient heart. And I will put my spirit in you so you will obey my laws and do whatever I command. (Ezekiel 36:25–27)

The Book of Ezekiel gives at least fifteen references to the Jews as rebellious. They were so, not because they did not know who was their God, but because they had a stone heart. God had made "their eyes closed and their ears shut."

"New heart"—God will replace the old stubborn heart with a new obedient heart for every Jew. He will remove the obstacles so each person can see and hear clearly. (refer to Jeremiah 31:33)

"New spirit" refers to the "representative" of Jesus, the Counselor or the Holy Spirit. (refer to John 16:13–15)

"My spirit" refers to the New Covenant or the words of God spoken through Jesus. (refer to John 6:63)

"But This Is the New Covenant"

About 600 years before Christ, God's spirit spoke through the prophet Jeremiah to the Jews that God loves the Jews as much as a husband loves his wife. He also gave them the imperative to accept the New Covenant (Jesus as their Messiah), because they had broken the Old Covenant:

> Long ago the Lord said to Israel: "I have loved you, my people, with an everlasting love. With unfailing love I have drawn you to myself. I will rebuild you, my virgin Israel." (Jeremiah 31:3–4)
>
> "The day will come," says the Lord, "when I will make a new covenant with the people of Israel and Judah. This covenant will not be like the one I made with their ancestors when I took them by the hand and brought them out of the land of Egypt. They broke that covenant, though I loved them as a husband loves his wife," says the Lord.
>
> "But this is the new covenant I will make with the people of Israel on that day," says the Lord. "I will put my laws in their minds, and I will write them on their hearts. I will be their God, and they will be my people. And they will not need to teach their neighbors, nor will they need to teach their family, saying: 'You should know the Lord.' For everyone, from the least to the greatest, will already know me," says the Lord. "And I will forgive their wickedness and will never again remember their sins." (Jeremiah 31:31–34)

The Old Covenant God gave to the people of Israel through Moses was the Ten Commandments. Although the Jewish people tried their best to keep the Ten Commandments as their law, they could not do so perfectly.

Because God wishes to save His people, He gives His people the New Covenant.

The New Covenant, or the New Testament, does not supersede the Old Covenant, it fulfills it.

"I loved them as a husband loves his wife" can also be a reference to the wedding feast in the Book of Revelation:

> Then I heard again what sounded like the shout of a huge crowd, or the roar of mighty ocean waves, or the crash of loud thunder: "Hallelujah! For the Lord our God, the Almighty, reigns. Let us be glad and rejoice and honor him. For the time has come for the wedding feast of the Lamb, and his bride has prepared herself. She is permitted to wear the finest white linen." (Fine linen represents the good deeds done by the people of God.)
>
> And the angel said, "Write this: 'blessed are those who are invited to the wedding feast of the lamb.'" And he added, "These are true words that come from God."
>
> Then I fell down at his feet to worship him, but he said, "No, don't worship me. For I am a servant of God, just like you and other brothers and sisters who testify of their faith in Jesus. Worship God. For the essence of prophecy is to give a clear witness for Jesus." (Revelation 19:6–10)

"I will put my laws in their minds"—unlike the Old Covenant, when God wrote them on stones, this time God will write them in their hearts. The Holy Spirit will remind the Jews of the words spoken by Jesus when they accept Jesus as their Messiah.

"Will already know me"—because God had already told the Jews in the Old Testament about the New Covenant. He also told them about their Messiah. Since the Jews are familiar with the Old Testament, they can easily find Jesus (their Messiah appointed by God). God will send them the Holy Spirit so that they can hear and see clearly now. They will look for their Messiah in the New Testament as well. (refer to 1 John 2:27)

In Matthew 26:26–28 NKJV we see the definition of the New Covenant:

> And as they were eating, Jesus took bread, blessed it and broke it, and gave it to the disciples and said, "Take, eat; this is my body." Then He took the cup, and gave thanks, and gave it to them, saying, "Drink from it, all of you. For this is my blood of the new covenant, which is shed for many for the remission of sins." (also see Luke 22:19–20)

Leviticus 17:11 states concerning blood: "For the life of any creature is in its blood. I have given you the blood so you can make atonement for your sins. It is the blood representing life, that brings you atonement."

God will give the new heart (softer heart instead of stubborn heart) and the new spirit (the Holy Spirit) to each of His selected people (the Jews) on the day He chooses to let them hear and see clearly. And that day is today!

Today, despite the fact that the Jews could not keep the Old Covenant, all their sins can be washed clean by the blood of Jesus in the New Covenant. The Jews only need to accept and follow Jesus as their Messiah.

Since the New Covenant is the fulfillment of the Old Covenant (refer to Matthew 5:17–19) and is already in place, all the people of Israel must familiarize themselves with it. The Ark and the Old Covenant are, therefore, no longer a source of salvation. Only the New Covenant can provide Jews the way to God and eternal life!

God said He is holy. Unless people are also holy, they cannot see God. There is no exception for Jews. Therefore, everyone must be made holy before entering the Kingdom of God. There is only one way to wash away sins and to become holy—through the Blood of Jesus!

When Will the Jews Return to Their Own Land?

Starting today, the people of Israel will begin to return to their own land. God told the Jews to return to Him:

> Ever since the days of your ancestors, you have scorned my laws and failed to obey them. Now return to me, and I will return to you. (Malachi 3:7)

When the Jews decide to return to God, they must first of all find out the way. There is only one way man may go to God. The way can only be found in the New Covenant. (refer to John 14:6) Only after the Jews accept Jesus as their Messiah, God will return to them and will live among them. (refer to Revelation 21:3)

This New Place of Rest Was Not the Land of Canaan

Our Resting Place is our home. God's Resting Place is His home, the Kingdom of God, the Kingdom of Heaven, the New Jerusalem. If we are denied entrance into His rest, the only reason is our own unbelief. The apostle Paul explained this subject in detail in a letter he wrote to Christian Jews:

> That is why the Holy Spirit says: "Today you must listen to his voice. Don't harden your hearts against him as Israel did when they rebelled, when they tested God's patience in the wilderness. There your ancestors tried my patience, even though they saw my miracles for forty years. So I was angry with them, and I said, 'Their hearts always turn away from me. They refuse to do what I tell them.' So in my anger I made a vow: 'They will never enter my place of rest.'
>
> Be careful then, dear brothers and sisters. Make sure that your own hearts are not evil and unbelieving, turning you away from the living God. You must warn each other every day, as long as it

is called "today," so that none of you will be deceived by sin and hardened against God. For if we are faithful to the end, trusting God just as firmly as when we first believed, we will share in all that belongs to Christ. But never forget the warning: "Today you must listen to his voice. Don't harden your hearts against him as Israel did when they rebelled."

And who were those people who rebelled against God, even though they heard his voice? Weren't they the ones Moses led out of Egypt? And who made God angry for forty years? Wasn't it the people who sinned, whose bodies fell in the wilderness? And to whom was God speaking when he vowed that they would never enter his place of rest? He was speaking to those who disobeyed him.

So we see that they were not allowed to enter his rest because of their unbelief. (Hebrews 3:7–19; also see Psalms 95:8–11)

God's promise of entering his place of rest still stands, so we ought to tremble with fear that some of you might fail to get there. For this Good News—that God has prepared a place of rest—has been announced to us just as it was to them. But it did them no good because they didn't believe what God told them. For only we who believe can enter his place of rest.

As for those who didn't believe, God said: "In my anger I made a vow: They will never enter my place of rest," even though His place of rest has been ready since He made the world.

We know it is ready because the Scriptures mention the seventh day, saying: "On the seventh day God rested from all his work." But in the other passage God said: "They will never enter my place of rest." So God's rest is there for people to enter. But those who formerly heard the Good News failed to enter, because they

> disobeyed God. So God set another time for entering His place of rest, and that time is today. God announced this through David a long time later in the words already quoted: "Today you must listen to his voice. Don't harden your hearts against him."
>
> This new place of rest is not the land of Canaan, where Joshua led them. If it had been, God would not have spoken later about another day of rest. So there is a special rest still waiting for the people of God. For all who enter into God's rest will find rest from their labors, just as God rested after creating the world. Let us do our best to enter that place of rest. For anyone who disobeys God, as the people of Israel did, will fall. (Hebrews 4:1–11)

Obviously, "this new place of rest" is the New Jerusalem described in Revelation 21.

Circumcision

In the Old Covenant, God ordered His selected people to circumcise all their baby boys when they were eight days old so that the mark on the body of each male would show his obedience of God's Covenant. However, God likes to read the minds of His people. He was not happy when the Jews failed to keep the law in the Old Covenant. Instead of punishing them, however, He decided to give them the New Covenant to save them. This time, He would write the Covenant on their hearts instead of on stone.

If the Jews still insist that they should follow the Old Covenant, they will have no share in the salvation God gave to them through the New Covenant—Jesus. They will die in their sins without having eternal life.

To make God happy is to keep His commandments. That is not difficult if we believe in Jesus.

About 2,000 years before Christ, God instructed Abraham regarding circumcision:

"Your part of the agreement," God told Abraham, "is to obey the terms of the covenant. You and all your descendants have this continual responsibility. This is the covenant that you and your descendants must keep: Each male child must be circumcised on the eighth day after his birth. This applies not only to members of your family, but also to the servants born in your household and the foreign-born servants whom you have purchased. All must be circumcised. Your bodies will thus bear the mark of my everlasting covenant. Anyone who refuses to be circumcised will be cut off from the covenant family for violating the covenant." (Genesis 17:9–14)

Then about 1405 before Christ, Moses documented:

But if they confess their iniquity and the iniquity of their fathers, with their unfaithfulness in which they were unfaithful to Me, and that they also have walked contrary to Me, and that I also have walked contrary to them and have brought them into the land of their enemies; if their uncircumcised hearts are humbled, and they accept their guilt—then I will remember My covenant with Jacob, and My covenant with Isaac and My covenant with Abraham I will remember; I will remember the land". (Leviticus 26:40–42 NKJV)

In about 620 before Christ, Jeremiah prophesied:

"A time is coming," says the Lord, "when I will punish all those who are circumcised in body but not in spirit—the Egyptians, Edomites, Ammonites, Moabites, the people who live in distant places, and yes, even the people of Judah. Like all these pagan nations, the people of Israel also have uncircumcised hearts." (Jeremiah 9:25–26)

Jeremiah further prophesied:

> "But this is the new covenant I will make with the people of Israel on that day," says the Lord. "I will put my laws in their minds, and I will write them on their hearts. I will be their God, and they will be my people." (Jeremiah 31:33)

The apostle Paul's letter to the Christians in Rome in about A.D. 57, talks about circumcision in detail:

> The Jewish ceremony of circumcision is worth something only if you obey God's law. But if you don't obey God's law, you are no better off than an uncircumcised Gentile. And if the Gentiles obey God's law, won't God give them all the rights and honors of being his own people? In fact, uncircumcised Gentiles who keep God's law will be much better off than you Jews who are circumcised and know so much about God's law but don't obey it.
> For you are not a true Jew just because you were born of Jewish parents or because you have gone through the Jewish ceremony of circumcision. No, a true Jew is one whose heart is right with God. And true circumcision is not a cutting of the body but a change of heart produced by God's Spirit. Whoever has that kind of change seeks praise from God, not from people. (Romans 2:25–29)

> Obviously, the law applies to those to whom it was given, for its purpose is to keep people from having excuses and to bring the entire world into judgment before God. For no one can ever be made right in God's sight by doing what His law commands. For the more we know God's law, the clearer it becomes that we aren't obeying it. (Romans 3:19–20)

> Or is He the God of the Jews only? Is He not also the God of the Gentiles? Yes, of the Gentiles also, since there is one God who will justify the circumcised by faith and the uncircumcised through faith. Do we then make void the law through faith? Certainly not! On the contrary, we establish the law. (Romans 3:29–31 NKJV)

The apostle Paul also discussed the value of circumcision in his letter to the church in Galatia:

> So Christ has really set us free. Now make sure that you stay free, and don't get tied up again in slavery to the law. Listen! I, Paul, tell you this: If you are counting on circumcision to make you right with God, then Christ cannot help you. I'll say it again. If you are trying to find favor with God by being circumcised, you must obey all the regulations in the whole law of Moses. For if you are trying to make yourselves right with God by keeping the law, you have been cut off from Christ! You have fallen away from God's grace.
>
> But we who live by the Spirit eagerly wait to receive everything promised to us who are right with God through faith. For when we place our faith in Christ Jesus, it makes no difference to God whether we are circumcised or not circumcised. What is important is faith expressing itself in love. (Galatians 5:1–6)

Wake Up, Israel!

About 700 before Christ, Isaiah had already prophesied about this book: "In that day the deaf shall hear the words of the book, and the eyes of the blind shall see out of obscurity and out of darkness." (Isaiah 29:18 NKJV)

Today, the Holy Spirit has come to the people of Israel. Their ears can now hear, and eyes can now see. (see Isaiah 18:3; 32:1–3)

All they need to do is to accept the Holy Spirit into their hearts. They will be reminded by the Holy Spirit to mourn for persecuting Jesus, the True Messiah, the Son of the Living God, and for their own sins.

About 475 years before Christ, Jesus spoke through Zechariah:

> Then I will pour out a spirit of grace and prayer on the family of David and on all the people of Jerusalem. They will look on me whom they have pierced and mourn for him as for a firstborn son who has died. The sorrow and mourning in Jerusalem on that day will be like the grievous mourning of Hadad-rimmon in the valley of Megiddo.
>
> All Israel will weep in profound sorrow, each family by itself, with the husbands and wives in separate groups. The family of David will mourn, along with the family of Nathan, the family of Levi, and the family of Shimei. Each of the surviving families from Judah will mourn separately, husbands and wives apart. (Zechariah 12:10–14)

"I," "me," and "him" are all representations of Jesus (at the time of this prophecy, Jesus was the same party with God the Father). That is another example of what Jesus said in John 10:30, "The Father and I are one."

On the island of Patmos, the apostle John documented a vision of the Resurrected Jesus: "Look! He comes with the clouds of heaven. And everyone will see him—even those who pierced him. And all the nations of the earth will weep because of him. Yes! Amen!" (Revelation 1:7)

Bless the One who comes in the name of the Lord.

chapter five

The Holy Spirit

GOD THE FATHER, THE SON JESUS, AND THE HOLY SPIRIT COMPRISE the Trinity. They are not divisible; they are united together as one God. The Holy Spirit is the Spirit of God. Jesus told a Samaritan woman: "For God is Spirit, so those who worship him must worship in spirit and in truth." (John 4:24) Jesus told His disciples: "It is the Spirit who gives eternal life. Human effort accomplishes nothing. And the very words I have spoken to you are spirit and life." (John 6:63)

The Holy Spirit is so important that we find the Holy Spirit both at the beginning and end of the Holy Bible (refer to Genesis 1:2 and Revelation 22:17). Having the Holy Spirit is a condition for entering into the Kingdom of God. This is shown by Jesus' words to Nicodemus: "Most assuredly, I say to you, unless one is born of water and the Spirit, he cannot enter the Kingdom of God." (John 3:5)

Rivers of Living Water

Jesus left Judea to return to Galilee. On the way, He went through the Samaritan village of Sychar. He met a Samaritan woman drawing water from the Jacob's well and told her He could give her 'living water':

> He had to go through Samaria on the way. Eventually he came to the Samaritan village of Sychar, near the parcel of ground that Jacob gave to his son Joseph. Jacob's well was there; and Jesus, tired from the long walk, sat wearily beside the well about noontime. Soon a Samaritan woman came to draw water, and Jesus said to her, "Please give me a drink." He was alone at the time because his disciples had gone into the village to buy some food. The woman was surprised, for Jews refuse to have anything to do with Samaritans. She said to Jesus, "You are a Jew, and I am a Samaritan woman. Why are you asking me for a drink?"
>
> Jesus replied, "If you only knew the gift God has for you and who I am, you would ask me, and I *would give you living water.*"
> "But sir, you don't have a rope or a bucket," she said, "and this is a very deep well. Where would you get this living water? And besides, are you greater than our ancestor Jacob who gave us this well? How can you offer better water than he and his sons and his cattle enjoyed?"
>
> Jesus replied, "People soon become thirsty again after drinking this water. But the water I give them takes away thirst altogether. It becomes a *perpetual spring* within them, *giving them eternal life*." (John 4:4–14; *emphasis added*)

On the last day, the climax of the festival, Jesus stood and shouted to the crowds:

> "If you are thirsty, come to me! If you believe in me, come and drink! For the Scriptures declare that rivers of living water will flow out from within." (When He said "living water," He was speaking of the Spirit, who would be given to everyone believing in him. But the Spirit had not yet been given, because Jesus had not yet entered into his glory.) (John 7:37–39)

> After Jesus told His disciples about His forthcoming departure from the world, He comforted them that He would not leave them as orphans: "And I will ask the Father, and he will give you another Counselor, who will never leave you. He is the Holy Spirit, who leads into all truth. The world at large cannot receive him, because it isn't looking for him and doesn't recognize him. But you do, because he lives with you now and later will be in you." (John 14:16–17)

"He lives with you now" refers to Jesus.

"Later will be in you"–After Jesus' resurrection, He will live within His disciples by means of the Holy Spirit–His Representative. (see 1 Corinthians 3:16 and 6:19)

At the end of the world, the Resurrected Jesus will still urge the Holy Spirit to reach out to those who are willing to accept:

> "It is done! I am the Alpha and the Omega, the Beginning and the End. I will give of the fountain of the water of life freely to him who thirsts." (Revelation 21:6 NKJV)

What Does the Holy Spirit Do?

Jesus also told His disciples that the coming Counselor would convince the world of its sins:

> "But it is actually best for you that I go away, because if I don't, the counselor won't come. If I do go away, he will come because I will send him to you. And when he comes, he will convince

> the world of its sin, and of God's righteousness, and of the coming judgment." (John 16:7–8)

Jesus emphasized the importance of the presence of the Holy Spirit. He loved His disciples. However, He preferred to send them the Holy Spirit than to stay with them in this world in flesh and blood. Spiritual life is more important than physical life. The Holy Spirit can strengthen both. The Holy Spirit leads us to the everlasting eternal life. The days in each person's life have been numbered; every person will die someday. No one can earn eternal life when sins still exist. Without the presence of the Holy Spirit, man can hardly identify and overcome sins. Flesh and blood alone cannot win over Satan's bait and traps.

All the communications between God and man are made through the Holy Spirit. It happens in both ways. When God tells us something, the Holy Spirit notifies us. When we need to communicate with God, the Holy Spirit brings our messages (praise, worship, prayers, etc.) to God. Christians cannot live without the Holy Spirit. The Holy Spirit acts as a "direct link" between God and us, and vice versa. He is the connection between God's spirit and our spirit. The contact is direct and immediate, no time is lost.

The Holy Spirit does wonderful things. He guides, strengthens, empowers us, saves our lives, prophesies, shows God's greatness, reveals God's secrets, and gives us eternal life. The Holy Spirit is a free gift from God.

Jesus fulfilled His promise to His disciples by sending the Holy Spirit to them after His resurrection:

> On the day of Pentecost, seven weeks after Jesus' resurrection, the believers were meeting together in one place. Suddenly, there was a sound from heaven like the roaring of a mighty windstorm in the skies above them, and it filled the house where they were meeting. Then, what looked like flames or tongues of

fire appeared and settled on each of them. And everyone present was filled with the Holy Spirit and began speaking in other languages, as the Holy Spirit gave them this ability. (Acts 2:1–4)

Peter replied, "Each of you must turn from your sins and turn to God, and be baptized in the name of Jesus Christ for the forgiveness of your sins. Then you will receive the gift of the Holy Spirit." (Acts 2:38)

Spiritual Gifts

In a letter the apostle Paul wrote to the church members in Corinth, Greece; he made a detailed introduction as well as explanation about the gifts of the Holy Spirit:

So I want you to know how to discern what is truly from God: No one speaking by the Spirit of God can curse Jesus, and no one is able to say, "Jesus is Lord," except by the Holy Spirit. Now there are different kinds of spiritual gifts, but it is the same Holy Spirit who is the source of them all. There are different kinds of service in the church, but it is the same Lord we are serving. There are different ways God works in our lives, but it is the same God who does the work through all of us. A spiritual gift is given to each of us as a means of helping the entire church.

To one person the Spirit gives the ability to give wise advice; to another he gives the gift of special knowledge. The Spirit gives special faith to another, and to someone else he gives the power to heal the sick. He gives one person the power to perform miracles, and to another the ability to prophecy. He gives someone else the ability to know whether it is really the Spirit of God or another spirit that is speaking. Still another person is given the ability to speak in unknown languages, and another is given the ability to interpret what is being said. It is the one and only

> Holy Spirit who distributes these gifts. He alone decides which gift each person should have. (1 Corinthians 12:3–11)

Unforgivable Sin!

Jesus gave a warning to all men regarding the most serious sin against the Holy Spirit:

> "Every sin or blasphemy can be forgiven—except blasphemy against the Holy Spirit, which can never be forgiven. Anyone who blasphemes against me, the Son of Man, can be forgiven, but blasphemy against the Holy Spirit will never be forgiven, either in this world or in the world to come." (Matthew 12:31–32; also see Mark 3:28–29 and Luke 12:10)

The Holy Bible stipulates the seriousness of the above statement at least three times. This is the only sin or offense that *cannot be forgiven* by God. Therefore, no one can become a true Christian without the Holy Spirit living inside him or her. The Holy Spirit is the Truth. (refer to John 16:13; 1 John 5:6.) Christians need the Holy Spirit to live within them each second and each minute of our life. He is the representative of the Resurrected Jesus and the counselor Jesus promised to send to His disciples through God the Father.

The Holy Spirit reminds us of the words of Jesus; verifies and tells us the truth; and strengthens our faith and spiritual life. The Holy Spirit was the one who raised Jesus from the dead. He will also be the one to raise us from the dead in the Second Coming of Jesus (the Return of Jesus). Without the presence of the Holy Spirit in our heart, we will go to the wrong place and live a miserable life; wandering around without a target or destination and never entering into the Kingdom of God.

God loves us. He does not wish us to get lost. Instead, He is expecting us to have eternal life and to live with Him in His home

(God's Resting Place or the New Jerusalem) one day. Therefore, He warned us about this *unique sin which we should never commit*.

It is not useful to merely mention the Holy Spirit during preaching, singing, or praying without giving Him an opportunity to help us. We must pursue and get hold of Him and invite Him to live within us. Without the Holy Spirit, we have no hope for eternal life.

In addition, lying to the Holy Spirit carries a serious penalty. Ananias lied to the Holy Spirit and his wife Sapphira agreed to this deception. "Then Peter said, 'Ananias, why has Satan filled your heart? You lied to the Holy Spirit, and you kept some of the money for yourself. The property was yours to sell or not sell, as you wished. And after selling it, the money was yours to give away. How could you do a thing like this? You weren't lying to us but to God.'" (Acts 5:3–4) As soon as they were told by Peter of their deception, they fell to the floor and died.

Lying is one of the most powerful tools Satan uses to enslave man. Satan is the father of lies. On the contrary, the Holy Spirit always reminds us to tell the truth.

The apostle Paul preached to the church members in Ephesus on the way to keep a close relationship with the Holy Spirit: "And do not bring sorrow to God's Holy Spirit by the way you live. Remember, he is the one who has identified you as his own, guaranteeing that you will be saved on the day of redemption." (Ephesians 4:30)

The Holy Spirit Is Powerful

God the Holy Spirit is the active force behind miracles and acts of creation. "In the beginning God created the heavens and the earth. The earth was empty, a formless mass cloaked in darkness. And the Spirit of God was hovering over its surface." (Genesis 1:1–2)

The Spirit of God is also the Alpha and the Omega, the beginning and the end. Jesus was the Spirit of God before He was born as a man. (refer to Proverb 8:22–36 and John 1:1–3)

God sent the angel Gabriel to Nazareth, a village in Galilee, to inform a virgin named Mary. At that time, she was engaged to a man named Joseph. "The angel replied, 'The Holy Spirit will come upon you, and the power of the Most High will overshadow you. So the baby born to you will be holy, and he will be called the Son of God.'" (Luke 1:35)

In about 475 before Christ, God instructed the prophet Zechariah to say the following: "Then I will pour out a spirit of grace and prayer on the family of David and on all the people of Jerusalem. They will look on me whom they have pierced and mourn for him as for an only son. They will grieve bitterly for him as for a firstborn son who has died." (Zechariah 12:10) This is another confirmation that man can find the truth via the Holy Spirit.

The Book of Romans is the first among thirteen epistles written by the apostle Paul. In that letter he wrote: "And Jesus Christ our Lord was shown to be the Son of God when God powerfully raised him from the dead by means of the Holy Spirit." (Romans 1:4)

Guides, Strengthens, Empowers

Human beings need the Holy Spirit all the time, because they are weak both physically and spiritually. Especially when they face sicknesses, financial difficulties, and challenges from others, including the temptations from Satan. However, all the weakness can be changed to strength when the Holy Spirit arrives. When the Holy Spirit comes to us, we can feel the strength of God in us. All we need to do is to trust Him and to release all our burdens to Him. Jesus said, "Come to me, all of you who are weary and carry heavy burdens, and I will give you rest." (Matthew 11:28) Jesus will give us rest by means of His representative, the Holy Spirit.

Jesus told His disciples:

> "But when the Father sends the counselor as my representative–and by the Counselor I mean the Holy Spirit–he will teach you everything and will remind you of everything I myself have told you." (John 14:26)

Jesus also told His disciples: "If I do go away, he [the Holy Spirit] will come because I will send him [the Holy Spirit] to you." (John 16:7) We may see in the above the harmonic Trinitarian relationship among God the Father, His Son Jesus, and the Holy Spirit.

Jesus told His disciples that the Holy Spirit would guide them:

> When the Spirit of truth comes, he will guide you into all truth. He will not be presenting his own ideas; he will be telling you what he has heard. He will tell you about the future. He will bring me glory by revealing to you whatever he receives from me. All that the Father has is mine; this is what I mean when I say that the Spirit will reveal to you whatever he receives from me. (John 16:13–15)

The Resurrected Jesus further described the role of the Holy Spirit to His disciples, and it applies to us even now: "But when the Holy Spirit has come upon you, you will receive power and will tell people about me everywhere—in Jerusalem, throughout Judea, in Samaria, and to the ends of the earth." (Acts 1:8) The presence of the Holy Spirit in the lives of believers shows that Jesus' statement has been fulfilled.

Paul wrote to the Christians in Rome about the guidance provided by the Holy Spirit: "And the Holy Spirit helps us in our distress. For we don't even know what we should pray for, nor how we should pray. But the Holy Spirit prays for us with groanings that cannot be expressed in words. And the Father who knows all hearts knows what the Spirit is saying, for the Spirit pleads for us believers in harmony with God's own will." (Romans 8:26–27) When the Holy Spirit prays for us, we are speaking in tongues.

In that same letter, Paul explained that man can only be made pure by the Holy Spirit: "For I am, by God's grace, a special messenger from Christ Jesus to you Gentiles. I bring you the Good News and offer you up as a fragrant sacrifice to God so that you might be pure and pleasing to him by the Holy Spirit." (Romans 15:15–16)

Produce Good Fruit in Us

Paul was disturbed by the "improper Gospel" spread among the church members in Galatia. He, therefore, emphasized the importance of the Holy Spirit's presence. The Holy Spirit has no conflict with the law as the law was made through Him:

> So I advise you to live according to your new life in the Holy Spirit. Then you won't be doing what your sinful nature craves. The old sinful nature loves to do evil, which is just opposite from what the Holy Spirit wants. And the Spirit gives us desires that are opposite from what the sinful nature desires. These two forces are constantly fighting each other, and your choices are never free from this conflict. But when you are directed by the Holy Spirit, you are no longer subject to the law.
>
> When you follow the desires of your sinful nature, your lives will produce these evil results: sexual immorality, impure thoughts, eagerness for lustful pleasure, idolatry, participation in demonic activities, hostility, quarreling, jealousy, outbursts of anger, selfish ambition, divisions, the feeling that everyone is wrong except those in your own little group, envy, drunkenness, wild parties, and other kinds of sin. Let me tell you again, as I have before, that anyone living that sort of life will not inherit the Kingdom of God.

> But when the Holy Spirit controls our lives, he will produce this kind of fruit in us: love, joy, peace, patience, kindness, goodness, faithfulness, gentleness, and self-control. Here there is no conflict with the law.
>
> Those who belong to Christ Jesus have nailed the passions and desires of their sinful nature to his cross and crucified them there. If we are living now by the Holy Spirit, let us follow the Holy Spirit's leading in every part of our lives. Let us not become conceited, or irritate one another, or be jealous of one another. (Galatians 5:16–26)

What He Teaches Is True

Before Jesus sent His disciples to preach the Gospel and heal the sick, He warned them about oppositions from non-believers, but He also told them the support they might receive from the Holy Spirit under adverse situations:

> "When you are arrested, don't worry about what to say in your defense, because you will be given the right words at the right time. For it won't be you doing the talking–it will be the Spirit of your Father speaking through you." (Matthew 10:19–20)

The apostle Peter also explained to his fellow church members that the Holy Spirit will help those who was being arrested or persecuted for being a follower of Jesus:

> Dear friends, don't be surprised at the fiery trials you are going through, as if something strange were happening to you. Instead, be very glad–because these trials will make you partners with Christ in his suffering, and afterward you will have the wonderful joy of sharing his glory when it is displayed to all the world. Be happy if you are insulted for being a Christian,

> for then the glorious Spirit of God will come upon you. (1 Peter 4:12–14)

The apostle John shared his understandings about the Holy Spirit with other Christians:

> But you have received the Holy Spirit, and he lives within you, so you don't need anyone to teach you what is true. For the Spirit teaches you all things, and what he teaches is true–it is not a lie. So continue in what he has taught you, and continue to live in Christ. (1 John 2:27)

Speaking for God and Revealing God's Secrets

True prophets of God cannot prophesy by their own wisdom or imagination. Instead, they were all speaking what God told them to say via the Holy Spirit. The famous prophet Isaiah made it clear: "The Spirit of the Sovereign Lord is upon me, because the Lord has appointed me to bring good news to the poor. He has sent me to comfort the brokenhearted and to announce that captives will be released and prisoners will be freed." (Isaiah 61:1)

In about 800 before Christ, God's Spirit spoke through the prophet Joel:

> I will pour out my Spirit upon all people. Your sons and daughters will prophesy. Your old men will dream dreams. Your young men will see visions. In those days, I will pour out my Spirit even on servants, men and women alike. (Joel 2:28–29)

God sent His Spirit to Jesus without limit: "After his baptism, as Jesus came up out of the water, the heavens were opened and he saw the Spirit of God descending like a dove and settling on him." (Matthew 3:16) Jesus and the Holy Spirit work as one. Jesus told

His disciples one important task of the Holy Spirit is to remind them about Jesus—the Word of God (see John 15:26–27).

In a letter Paul sent to the church in Corinth, he mentioned some exceptional capabilities of the Holy Spirit:

> But we know these things because God has revealed them to us by his Spirit, and his Spirit searches out everything and shows us even God's deep secrets. No one can know what anyone else is really thinking except that person alone, and no one can know God's thoughts except God's own Spirit. And God has actually given us his Spirit (not the world's spirit) so we can know the wonderful things God has freely given us. When we tell you this, we do not use words of human wisdom. We speak words given to us by the Spirit, using the Spirit's words to explain spiritual truths. But people who aren't Christians can't understand these truths from God's Spirit. It all sounds foolish to them because only those who have the Spirit can understand what the Spirit means. We who have the Spirit understand these things, but others can't understand us at all. How could they? For: "Who can know what the Lord is thinking? Who can give him counsel?" But we can understand these things, for we have the mind of Christ. (1 Corinthians 2:10–16)

The Resurrected Jesus instructed His eleven disciples to spread the Gospel and to baptize the new disciples: "Therefore, go and make disciples of all the nations, baptizing them in the name of the Father and the Son and the Holy Spirit." (Matthew 28:19) No one can be considered as born again without being baptized in the name of the Father, the Son, and the Holy Spirit. Baptism is a way in which a new believer in Jesus confirms that he or she has repented of his/her sins and believed in Jesus as his/her Savior in front of God and man. It also outwardly shows that he/she chooses to give up the old way of living and to begin with a new life by following the Christ. Repentance followed by baptism allows one to receive the gift of the Holy Spirit. (see Acts 2:38)

Christians Have the Spirit of Christ Living in Them

Paul advised the Christians in Rome about the relationship between Christians and the Holy Spirit. He also explained about the power of the Holy Spirit, which God gives us in the New Covenant:

> So now there is no condemnation for those who belong to Christ Jesus. For the power of the life-giving Spirit has freed you through Christ Jesus from the power of sin that leads to death. The law of Moses could not save us, because of our sinful nature. But God put into effect a different plan to save us. He sent his own Son in a human body like ours, except that ours are sinful. God destroyed sin's control over us by giving his Son as a sacrifice for our sins. He did this so that the requirement of the law would be fully accomplished for us who no longer follow our sinful nature but instead follow the Spirit.
>
> Those who are dominated by the sinful nature think about sinful things, but those who are controlled by the Holy Spirit think about things that please the Spirit. If your sinful nature controls your mind, there is death. But if the Holy Spirit controls your mind, there is life and peace. For the sinful nature is always hostile to God. It never did obey God's laws, and it never will. That's why those who are still under the control of their sinful nature can never please God.
>
> But you are not controlled by your sinful nature. You are controlled by the Spirit if you have the Spirit of God living in you. (And remember that those who do not have the Spirit of Christ living in them are not Christians at all.) Since Christ lives within you, even though your body will die because of sin, *your spirit is alive* because you have been made right with God. The spirit of

> God, who raised Jesus from the dead, lives in you. And just as he raised Christ from the dead, he will give life to your mortal body by this same spirit living within you. So, dear brothers and sisters, you have no obligation whatsoever to do what your sinful nature urges you to do. For if you keep on following it, you will perish. But if through the power of the Holy Spirit you turn from it and its evil deeds, you will live. For all who are led by the Spirit of God are children of God. So you should not be like cowering, fearful slaves. You should behave instead like God's very own children, adopted into his family—calling him "Father, dear Father." For his Holy Spirit speaks to us deep in our hearts and tells us that we are God's children. (Romans 8:1–16; *emphasis added*)

The Unique Way to Eternal Life

Jesus told Nicodemus, a Pharisee and a Jewish religious leader, the conditions required for entering into the Kingdom of God:

> After dark one evening, a Jewish religious leader named Nicodemus, a Pharisee, came to speak with Jesus. "Teacher," he said, "we all know that God has sent you to teach us. Your miraculous signs are proof enough that God is with you."
>
> Jesus replied, "I assure you, unless you are born again, you can never see the Kingdom of God."
>
> "What do you mean?" exclaimed Nicodemus. "How can an old man go back into his mother's womb and be born again?"
>
> Jesus replied, "The truth is, no one can enter the Kingdom of God without being born of water and the spirit. Humans can reproduce only human life, but the Holy Spirit gives new life from heaven. So don't be surprised at my statement that you must be born again. Just as you can hear the wind but can't tell

where it comes from or where it is going, so you can't explain how people are born of the Spirit." (John 3:1–8)

When we have been born again, we may *see* the Kingdom of God by reading God's words, but if we wish to *enter into* the Kingdom of God, we must be baptized in water and the Holy Spirit. Baptism in water is a demonstration of one's will in accepting Jesus as his/her Savior in front of witnesses, including God. To be baptized or filled by the Holy Spirit is an important and necessary step in a Christian's life. Only when we have been filled with the Holy Spirit, Satan will not be able to find room to come into our hearts. With the presence of the Holy Spirit in our hearts, we will have sufficient power to overcome Satan.

In a letter Paul sent to Titus, a young pastor at Crete, an island in the Mediterranean, he emphasized that the Holy Spirit would lead Christians to eternal life:

> But then God our Savior showed us his kindness and love. He saved us, not because of the good things we did, but because of his mercy. He washed away our sins and gave us a new life through the Holy Spirit. He generously poured out the Spirit upon us because of what Jesus Christ our Savior did. He declared us not guilty because of his great kindness. And now we know that we will inherit eternal life. (Titus 3:4–7)

How to Distinguish the Holy Spirit

The apostle John taught Christians how to distinguish the Holy Spirit:

> Dear friends, do not believe everyone who claims to speak by the Spirit. You must test them to see if the spirit they have comes from God. For there are many false prophets in the world. This is the way to find out if they have the Spirit of God: If a prophet

> acknowledges that Jesus Christ became a human being, that person has the Spirit of God. If a prophet does not acknowledge Jesus, that person is not from God. Such a person has the spirit of the antichrist. You have heard that he is going to come into the world, and he is already here.
>
> But you belong to God, my dear children. You have already won your fight with these false prophets, because the Spirit who lives in you is greater than the spirit who lives in the world. These people belong to this world, so they speak from the world's viewpoint, and the world listens to them. But we belong to God; that is why those who know God listen to us. If they do not belong to God, they do not listen to us. That is how we know if someone has the Spirit of truth or the spirit of deception. (1 John 4:1–6)

Tongues-Speaking and Miracle-Healing

When a person has been filled by the Holy Spirit, he/she may give up control of his/her prayer or singing to the Holy Spirit and thereby speaks or sings in words or language that the speaker doesn't know. This is called "speaking in tongues."

Several years ago, I saw a miracle healing program on the television. I told my family: "This is the most important event in a Christian's life, as God heals the sick through the Holy Spirit!" We should not miss any such program. In addition, we had attended miracle healing services monthly in different locations. Most of them were being held far away from home.

We went there because we were seeking God's healing of ourselves, bringing others who needed miracle healing, and also praying for others who needed to be healed.

Perhaps there were many people who shared my belief that miracle healing was the most important event that they must participate in. Each time, we had to arrive at least three hours before the service to get a seat.

Now I feel both tongues-speaking and miracle-healing are not as important as I have thought of in the past. The most important desire or challenge of a Christian is to earn and to be rewarded with eternal life not just for oneself but for many.

Gifts of the Holy Spirit

In the letter Paul wrote to the church members in Corinth, he made an introduction of different kinds of gifts sent to us by God through the Holy Spirit. He further ranked their priorities:

> Now all of you together are Christ's body, and each one of you is a separate and necessary part of it. Here is a list of some of the members that God has placed in the body of Christ: first are apostles, second are prophets, third are teachers, then those who do miracles, those who have the gift of healing, those who can help others, those who can get others to work together, those who speak in unknown languages. Is everyone an apostle? Of course not. Is everyone a prophet? No. Are all teachers? Does everyone have the power to do miracles? Does everyone have the gift of healing? Of course not. Does God give all of us the ability to speak in unknown languages? Can everyone interpret unknown languages? No! And in any event, you should desire the most helpful gifts. (1 Corinthians 12:27–31)

Some Christians can be filled with the Holy Spirit very easily. After the initial experience, they may be filled by the Holy Spirit as soon as they start to sing, pray, or just raise their hands. On the other hand, there are many people who wish to be filled with Holy Spirit but are unsuccessful. No matter how hard they try, they are not successful. Not everyone can speak in tongues or perform miracles through the power of the Holy Spirit.

My mother was a devoted and faithful Christian. She desired and prayed to be given the gift of prophecy ever since her youth. She was not given what she had repeatedly asked for. When she was in her eighties, although she felt disappointed, she continued her request to God. Until the last few days of her life, she was happy as she knew God answered her prayers in another way. God instead gave the gift to her younger generation through the Holy Spirit, even more than what she had asked for. In fact, God takes care of us more than we can think of. Sometimes, we may only find out long after His grace.

An Honorable Guest

The Holy Spirit is an honorable guest. He will not come into us unless we invite Him to do so with all out heart, i.e., to empty our hearts as we wash a drinking glass and put it upside down before we invite Him. When the Holy Spirit comes to us, He will stay in us as long as we desire. However, we may send Him away by our own wish.

For those who have not yet been filled with the Holy Spirit and wish to be filled, here is a list of suggestions:

- GIVE priority in our mind to Jesus above all our wealth, people we love, and everything the world can offer us.
- SPEAK to Jesus only the truth. For God is a Spirit, He knows everything in our heart.
- THANK Jesus for giving us life and all our needs.
- CONFIRM to Jesus that nothing is more valuable to us than His salvation.
- MAINTAIN direct contact with Jesus. Do not let anyone or anything come to our mind at the moment we are inviting the Holy Spirit to come.
- GLORIFY Jesus for bringing us God's words—the New Covenant to save us.
- ADMIT AND CONFESS all our sins to God, and ask Him to forgive and wash us clean with the blood of Jesus.
- DON'T STOP the tears when they start.

- HUMBLE ourself. Call Jesus our Creator, Master, Redeemer and Savior.
- TELL Jesus we love Him with all our heart.
- PRAISE God by singing or praying as loud as we can, with 100 percent devotion.*
- PRAY "Jesus, Jesus, Jesus . . ." (the Jesus Prayer) **. Raise both hands high (aiming to reach Jesus) with head facing the sky (aiming to face Jesus) and eyes closed.
- MOURN for Jesus who was God, came to this world as a man, and died for our sins. Pray aloud the words in Isaiah 53:4–8.
- SHOUT for Jesus as a man, who triumphed over Satan. (Jesus freed us from being the slaves of Satan to become the children of God. He was resurrected on the third day following His death.)
- TELL Jesus we have *no more shame* to face Him if He comes again now.
- CONTINUE to maintain direct contact as if the world has Jesus and "me" only!
- PROMISE Jesus that "I" will try "my" best to avoid sin from now on and request Him to send the Holy Spirit to strengthen "my" faith.
- INVITE sincerely the Holy Spirit to stay in our heart. Once He comes:
- RELEASE ourself completely to Him. Let Him take control.
- DO NOT think of any other thing at this moment. One hundred percent concentration is needed.
- ASK Jesus to do His will in us and to give the most helpful gift through the Holy Spirit.***
- THANK Jesus for giving us the Holy Spirit (if already received).

- KEEP ON praising the Father and thanking Jesus for guiding us the way to eternal life.

* Based on my experience, the following hymns are helpful:

How Great Thou Art
When I Survey the Wondrous Cross
Jesus, Keep Me Near the Cross
Just As I Am
He Touched Me
Alleluia
(The second verse may be changed to "Thank You, Jesus")
I Pledge Allegiance to The Lamb

We should also raise both of our hands high, close our eyes, *and sing aloud with all our heart*. We may need to practice singing so that we can memorize the words. As a start, one may wish to choose one or two easy hymns; i.e., "Just As I Am" and "Alleluia." The reason the words change in the second verse of "Alleluia" to "Thank You Jesus" is to enable our worship to be made directly to Jesus instead of to a third party; i.e., "He or Him."

** Jesus is the Creator for everything. He is the Beginning and the End.

We can worship Him by praying only His name repeatedly. You will find each time we call His name in our "Jesus prayer," there is a different meaning. It can be a very powerful prayer as the Holy Spirit may take over the prayer right from the beginning.

*** Read 1 Corinthians 12:27–31 for details.

"Father, please send us the Holy Spirit without limit!"

chapter six

Rebuilding God's Temple

EVER SINCE I WAS THREE OR FOUR YEARS OF AGE, I AND MY SIBLINGS were taught by our mother to watch for the Jewish people to begin rebuilding their temple. Once the rebuilding of their temple starts, it will not be long until the Second Coming of Jesus and the end of the world.

In the early 1990s, I suggested to my wife that we should take a trip to Israel. If God needs us to relocate to Israel to participate in the rebuilding of the temple, we should have no other alternative but to follow His instructions. This trip did not occur, first because of my poor health; but later because I was not convinced that I needed to do so after reading the words of God under the guidance of the Holy Spirit.

In about 592–570 before Christ, Ezekiel described in detail a vision of the rebuilding of God's temple (see Ezekiel 40–48). The instructions from God were to build a temple under the Old Covenant. He outlined the duties of the priest and the offerings of animal blood for the remission of sins (see Ezekiel 40:38–43; 43:18–27;

and 44:11,15). The distribution of land among the 12 tribes of Israel was also described in detail (see Ezekiel 47 and 48). These instructions were good only until the day Jesus started to preach as a man about 2,000 years ago.

The blood of Jesus, in His one-time offering of Himself, completed the salvation (removal of sins) for all mankind. Therefore, if we still insist on reestablishing the practices used in the days of the Old Covenant, we are in fact denying the New Covenant God gave us. Jesus cannot be crucified for us again!

It is clear that the Jews cannot depend on the Old Covenant to save them, because no one can keep it. God, therefore, promised to save them by giving them the New Covenant (see Jeremiah 31:31–34). "Rebuilding God's Temple," therefore, means that God will change the unbelievers to become the believers of Jesus Christ.

God also redefined the land He gave to His people in Jeremiah 31:15–17 and Revelation 21. The land God promised His people in the New Covenant is the New Jerusalem, not Canaan or today's nation of Israel, which God gave to His people after He brought them out of Egypt in the Old Covenant.

Will God Live in a Temple Built by Man?

The following are the answers from God's own words:

As part of King Solomon's prayer:

> But will God really live on earth? Why, even the highest heavens cannot contain you. How much less this Temple I have built! (1 Kings 8:27)

> This is what the Lord says: "Heaven is my throne, and the earth is my footstool. Could you ever build me a temple as good as that? Could you build a dwelling place for me? My hands have made both heaven and earth, and they are mine. I, the Lord, have spoken!" (Isaiah 66:1–2, also see Acts 7:48–50)

> He is the God who made the world and everything in it. Since he is Lord of heaven and earth, he doesn't live in man-made temples, and human hands can't serve his needs for he has no needs. He himself gives life and breath to everything, and he satisfies every need there is. From one man he created all the nations throughout the whole earth. He decided beforehand which should rise and fall, and he determined their boundaries. (Acts 17:24–26)

Jesus Is God's Temple

About 580 before Christ, Ezekiel prophesied that in an everlasting covenant, the New Covenant, God would put His temple among His people:

> And I will make a covenant of peace with them, an everlasting covenant. I will give them their land and multiply them, and I will put my temple among them forever. I will make my home among them. I will be their God, and they will be my people. And since my temple will remain among them forever, the nations will know that I, the Lord, have set Israel apart for myself to be holy. (Ezekiel 37:26–28; also see Revelation 21:3)

"I will put" and "I will make" show a strong statement by God that His decision will remain until it is fulfilled.

Jesus referred to Himself as the new covenant:

> After supper he took another cup of wine and said, "This wine is the token of God's new covenant to save you—an agreement sealed with the blood I will pour out for you." (Luke 22:20)

Again, the apostle Paul wrote in a letter to the Christian Jews that Jesus is called the everlasting covenant:

> Jesus is the great Shepherd of the sheep by an everlasting covenant, signed with his blood. To him be glory forever and ever. Amen! (Hebrews 13:21)

John recorded a self-explanatory statement Jesus made to the Jews about the Temple:

> It was time for the annual Passover celebration, and Jesus went to Jerusalem. In the Temple area he saw merchants selling cattle, sheep, and doves for sacrifices; and he saw money changers behind their counters. Jesus made a whip from some ropes and chased them all out of the Temple. He drove out the sheep and oxen, scattered the money changers' coins over the floor, and turned over their tables. Then, going over to the people who sold doves, he told them, "Get these things out of here. Don't turn my Father's house into a marketplace!"
>
> Then his disciples remembered this prophecy from the Scriptures: "Passion for God's house burns within me"
>
> "What right do you have to do these things?" the Jewish leaders demanded. "If you have this authority from God, show us a miraculous sign to prove it."
>
> "All right," Jesus replied. "Destroy this temple, and in three days I will raise it up."
>
> "What!" they exclaimed. "It took forty-six years to build this Temple, and you can do it in three days?"
>
> But by "this temple," Jesus meant His body. After he was raised from the dead, the disciples remembered that he had said this. And they believed both Jesus and the Scriptures. (John 2:13–22)

"I will raise it up"—The resurrection of Jesus was made by the power of God through the Holy Spirit. When Jesus said, "I will raise it up," He meant that He would be resurrected by His own power. This can be confirmed by Jesus in His preaching to the Jews immediately following His description of Himself as a good shepherd: "No one can take my life from me. I lay down my life voluntarily. For I have the right to lay it down when I want to and also the power to take it again. For my Father has given me this command." (John 10:18)

John also described Jesus as the temple: "No temple could be seen in the city for the Lord God Almighty and the Lamb are its temple." (Revelation 21:22)

About 520 before Christ, Zechariah prophesied about the building of the Lord's Temple:

> The Lord Almighty says: "Here is the man called the Branch. He will branch out where he is and build the Temple of the Lord. He will build the Lord's Temple, and he will receive royal honor and will rule as king from his throne. He will also serve as priest from his throne, and there will be perfect harmony between the two." (Zechariah 6:12–13)

"Here is the man called the Branch" refers to none other than Jesus.

"Branch out" means to spread the Gospel to others and help them to become Christians.

"Build the Lord's Temple" means that Christians together are the Temple of the Lord.

About 700 before Christ, Isaiah prophesied this about Jesus as a branch:

> Out of the stump of David's family will grow a shoot, yes, a new branch bearing fruit from the old root. And the Spirit of the Lord will rest on him, the Spirit of wisdom and understanding, the Spirit of counsel and might, the Spirit of knowledge and the fear of the Lord. (Isaiah 11:1–2)

About 600 before Christ, Jeremiah also prophesied Jesus as a Branch—Righteous Branch:

> "For the time is coming", says the Lord, "when I will place a Righteous Branch on King David's throne. He will be a king who rules with wisdom. He will do what is just and right throughout the land. And this is his name: The Lord is our righteousness! In that day Judah will be saved, and Israel will live in safety." (Jeremiah 23:5–6, also refer to Revelation 22:16)

Christians Together Are God's Temple

Zechariah also prophesied that Gentiles (not the Jewish people) would also accept Jesus as their Savior to become Christians (Temple of the Lord):

> Many will come from distant lands to rebuild the Temple of the Lord. And when this happens, you will know my messages have been from the Lord Almighty. (Zechariah 6:15)

The apostle Paul emphasized the importance of keeping the Temple of God holy to the church in Corinth:

> Don't you realize that all of you together are the temple of God and that the Spirit of God lives in you? God will bring ruin upon anyone who ruins this temple. For God's temple is holy, and you Christians are that temple. (1 Corinthians 3:16–17)

> Or don't you know that your body is the temple of the Holy Spirit, who lives in you and was given to you by God? You do not belong to yourself, for God bought you with a high price. So you must honor God with your body. (1 Corinthians 6:19–20)

> And what union can there be between God's temple and idols? For we are the temple of the living God. As God said: "I will

> live in them and walk among them. I will be their God, and they will be my people. Therefore, come out from them and separate yourselves from them, says the Lord. Don't touch their filthy things, and I will welcome you. And I will be your Father, and you will be my sons and daughters, says the Lord Almighty." (2 Corinthians 6:16–18)

About four years after Paul wrote those letters to the church in Corinth, he also wrote a letter to the church in Ephesus regarding the Holy Temple for the Lord:

> Now all of us, both Jews and Gentiles, may come to the Father through the same Holy Spirit because of what Christ has done for us. So now you Gentiles are no longer strangers and foreigners. You are citizens along with all of God's holy people. You are members of God's family. We are his house, built on the foundation of the apostles and the prophets. And the cornerstone is Christ Jesus himself. We who believe are carefully joined together, becoming a holy temple for the Lord. Through him you Gentiles are also joined together as part of this dwelling where God lives by his Spirit. (Ephesians 2:18–22)

About 30 years after the resurrection of Jesus, the apostle Peter preached to the Christians that all Christians are God's spiritual temple:

> Come to Christ, who is the living cornerstone of God's temple. He was rejected by the people, but he is precious to God who chose him. And now God is building you, as living stones, into his spiritual temple. What's more, you are God's holy priests, who offer the spiritual sacrifices that please him because of Jesus Christ. (1 Peter 2:4–5, also see Psalm 118:22)

God Lives Among His People

One of Jesus first disciples, Peter, told a young follower named Mark the facts about Jesus. Mark then wrote the gospel of Mark. As Peter had been very close to Jesus when Jesus was teaching, Mark had special information other disciples might not be aware of. Nevertheless, the following event described by Mark was not unique:

> Then Jesus uttered another loud cry and breathed his last. And the curtain in the temple was torn in two, from top to bottom. (Mark 15:37–38)

This is a very important message, since it signified the beginning of the New Covenant. It appears in Luke's Gospel as well in more detail:

> By this time it was noon, and darkness fell across the whole land until three o'clock. The light from the sun was gone. And suddenly, the thick veil hanging in the temple was torn apart. Then Jesus shouted, 'Father, I entrust my spirit into your hands!' and with those words he breathed his last. (Luke 23:44–46)

With the sacrifice of Jesus for all of us, once for all, the barrier (the curtain or the veil inside the Temple) between God and man has been torn apart by God Himself. The Ark of the Covenant and the priest in the Temple are no longer a necessity—God will put the New Covenant and the Everlasting Covenant "in their minds" and "on their hearts" of the people of Israel (see Jeremiah 31:31–33). Therefore, Christians can worship God and remove their sins at any time and any place they wish. Thanks to the sacrifice of Jesus!

About 63 years after the resurrection of Jesus, the Resurrected Jesus told Apostle John in a vision that God will live with His people in the New Jerusalem:

> I heard a loud shout from the throne, saying, 'Look, the home of God is now among his people! He will live with them, and they will be his people. God himself will be with them. (Revelation 21:3)

God does not live among His people the same way as a person with flesh and blood. Instead, God lives inside the hearts of His people.

In fact, God mentioned many times in the Old Testament that He would live among His people. In the New Covenant God will continue to live with His people. Zechariah prophesied also about the New Jerusalem:

> I will live among the people of Israel and be their God. (Exodus 29:45)

> I will live among you, and I will not despise you. I will walk among you; I will be your God, and you will be my people. (Leviticus 26:11–12)

> You will eat it for a whole month until you gag and are sick of it. For you have rejected the Lord, who is here among you, and you have complained to him, "Why did we ever leave Egypt?" (Numbers 11:20)

> You must not defile the land where you are going to live, for I live there myself. I am the Lord, who lives among the people of Israel. (Numbers 35:34)

> I will live among the people of Israel and never forsake my people. (1 Kings 6:13)

> I will put my Temple among them forever. I will make my home among them. I will be their God, and they will be my people.

> And since my temple will remain among them forever, the nations will know that I, the Lord, have set Israel apart for myself to be holy. (Ezekiel 37:26–28)

> And the Lord said to me, "Son of man, this is the place of my throne and the place where I will rest my feet. I will remain here forever, living among the people of Israel." (Ezekiel 43:7)

> The Lord says, "Shout and rejoice, O Jerusalem, for I am coming to live among you. Many nations will join themselves to the Lord on that day, and they, too, will be my people. I will live among you, and you will know that the Lord Almighty sent me to you." (Zechariah 2:10–11, also see John 14:2–4; Revelation 21:3,12)

> And now the Lord says: "I am returning to Mount Zion, and I will live in Jerusalem. Then Jerusalem will be called the Faithful City; the mountain of the Lord Almighty will be called the Holy Mountain." (Zechariah 8:3)

> I will bring them home again to live safely in Jerusalem. They will be my people, and I will be faithful and just toward them as their God. (Zechariah 8:8)

In the New Testament, Jesus told His disciples: "All those who love me will do what I say. My Father will love them, and we will come to them and live with them." (John 14:23)

Has the Rebuilding Started?

Christians are the Temple of God! Have you seen buds on the fig tree and other trees become tender and their leaves begin to sprout? Because there are more and more people, in unprecedented numbers, accepting Jesus as their Savior or Messiah nowadays, we can see with our own eyes that the rebuilding of God's Temple has begun.

The time for God's harvest is approaching. He needs more people like you to participate in the rebuilding of His Temple. (see Matthew 9:37–38)

"Father, You are invited to live in the Temple we are building for you!"

chapter seven

The Eternal Life

Eternal life is a reward for belief in Jesus. Jesus Christ was the first man raised from the dead by means of the Holy Spirit to eternal life. He created the way for Christians to follow Him as sheep follow their shepherd.

There is nothing more precious than eternal life—the everlasting life. Our present life cannot compare with eternal life, since our present life must end one day. In addition, problems, sadness, and evil temptations will not be found in eternal life.

The most important reason God sent Jesus to this world as a man was to defeat death and Satan. God does not die. Only as a man could Jesus die. Jesus made eternal life possible through His own death and resurrection.

"Everyone Who Believes in Me Will Have Eternal Life"

When Nicodemus, a Jewish religious leader, asked Jesus about eternal life, Jesus answered:

> For only I, the Son of Man, have come to earth and will return to heaven again. And as Moses lifted up the bronze snake on a pole in the wilderness, so I, the Son of Man, must be lifted up on a pole, so that everyone who believes in me will have eternal life. (John 3:13–15)

In the same way, all Christians who have died will be resurrected one day. They will live with God in the New Jerusalem (also known as "My Father's House", the Heavenly Jerusalem, The New Heaven and the New Earth, the Kingdom of Heaven and God's Resting Place).

The Kingdom of Heaven

Jesus made comparisons to teach His disciples about the Kingdom of Heaven:

> "The Kingdom of Heaven is like a treasure that a man discovered hidden in a field. In his excitement, he hid it again and sold everything he owned to get enough money to buy the field—and to get the treasure, too!
>
> Again, the Kingdom of Heaven is like a pearl merchant on the lookout for choice pearls. When he discovered a pearl of great value, he sold everything he owned and bought it!
>
> Again, the Kingdom of Heaven is like a fishing net that is thrown into the water and gathers fish of every kind. When the net is full, they drag it up unto the shore, sit down, sort the good fish into crates, and throw the bad ones away. That is the way it will be at the end of the world. The angels will come and separate the wicked people from the godly, throwing the wicked into the fire. There will be weeping and gnashing of teeth. Do you understand?"

> "Yes," they said, "we do."
>
> Then he added, "Every teacher of religious law who has become a disciple in the Kingdom of Heaven is like a person who brings out of the storehouse the new teachings as well as the old." (Matthew 13:44–52)

The Life and the Death

Jesus preached to the Jews: "Anyone who obeys my teaching will never die." (John 8:51)

Before Jesus raised Lazarus from the dead, He told Martha, a sister of Lazarus:

> I am the resurrection and the life. Those who believe in me, even though they die like everyone else, will live again. They are given eternal life for believing in me and will never perish." (John 11:25–26, also see Isaiah 26:19)

Not long before Jesus' crucifixion, He answered the apostle Thomas in front of His other disciples: "Jesus told him, 'I am the way, the truth and the life, no one can come to the father except through me.'" (John 14:6)

On the other hand, Jesus also told the Jews: "Therefore I said to you that you will die in your sins; for if you do not believe that I am He, you will die in your sins." (John 8:24 NKJV)

When Jesus said: "I am He," He meant He is the Messiah and the God Almighty. No one can have eternal life without Jesus, with sins still existing. The blood of Jesus is the only means for the sins of man to be cleansed.

Paul wished to make clear to the Christians in Corinth that there is indeed eternal life: "If the dead do not rise, 'Let us eat and drink, for tomorrow we die.'" (1 Corinthians 15:32 NKJV)

Jesus told the Jews the importance of real life:

> "Beware! Don't be greedy for what you don't have. Real life is not measured by how much we own."
>
> And he gave an illustration: "A rich man had a fertile farm that produced fine crops. In fact, his barns were full to overflowing. So he said, 'I know! I'll tear down my barns and build bigger ones. Then I'll have room enough to store everything. And I'll sit back and say to myself, My friend, you have enough stored away for years to come. Now take it easy! Eat, drink, and be merry!'"
>
> "But God said to him, 'You fool! You will die this very night. Then who will get it all?'"
>
> "Yes, a person is a fool to store up earthly wealth but not have a rich relationship with God." (Luke 12:15–21; see also Matthew 16:26)

Everyone Is Responsible for His/Her Own Deeds

The prophet Ezekiel documented a message given to him by God that everyone is responsible for his/her own performance in order to be saved:

> Son of man, suppose the people of a country were to sin against me, and I lifted my fist to crush them, cutting off their food supply and sending a famine to destroy both people and animals alike. Even if Noah, Daniel, and Job were there, their righteousness would save no one but themselves, declares the Sovereign Lord.
>
> Or suppose I were to send an invasion of dangerous wild animals to devastate the land and kill the people. Even if these

> three men were there, the Sovereign Lord swears that it would do no good—it wouldn't save the people from destruction. Those three alone would be saved, but the land would be devastated.
>
> Or suppose I were to bring war against the land, and I told enemy armies to come and destroy everything. Even if these three men were in the land, the Sovereign Lord swears that they could not save the people. They alone would be saved.
>
> Or suppose I were to pour out my fury by sending an epidemic of disease into the land, and the plague killed people and animals alike. Even if Noah, Daniel, and Job were living there, the Sovereign Lord swears that they could not save the people. They alone would be saved by their righteousness. (Ezekiel 14:13–20)

The four cases above represent all types of disasters. God will only save those by their own righteousness. Ezekiel continued:

> Then another message came to me [Ezekiel] from the Lord: "Why do you quote this proverb in the land of Israel: 'The parents have eaten sour grapes, but their children's mouths pucker at the taste?' As surely as I live," says the Sovereign Lord, "you will not say this proverb anymore in Israel. For all people are mine to judge—both parents and children alike. And this is my rule: The person who sins will be the one who dies." (Ezekiel 18:1–4)

Jeremiah also prophesied that no one, even the righteous persons can save others:

> Then the Lord said to me, "Even if Moses and Samuel stood before me pleading for these people, I wouldn't help them. Away with them! Get them out of my sight!" (Jeremiah 15:1)

James, one of the younger brothers of Jesus emphasized the importance of "proper behaviors":

> "Dear brothers and sisters, what's the use of saying you have faith if you don't prove it by your actions? That kind of faith can't save anyone. Suppose you see a brother or sister who needs food or clothing, and you say, 'Well, good-bye and God bless you; stay warm and eat well'—but then you don't give that person any food or clothing. What good does that do?
>
> So you see, it isn't enough just to have faith. Faith that doesn't show itself by good deeds is no faith at all—it is dead and useless.
>
> Just as the body is dead without a spirit, so also faith is dead without good deeds." (James 2:14–17, 26)

The apostle John documented the important teaching as well as an answer made by Jesus to Nicodemus: "For God so loved the world that he gave his only Son, so that everyone who believes in him will not perish but have eternal life. God did not send his Son into the world to condemn it, but to save it." (John 3:16–17, also see John 6:37–40)

Jesus said: "The decisive issue is whether they obey my Father in Heaven." (Matthew 7:21) He also said: "If you love me, obey my commandments." (John 14:15) Eternal life is in fact a reward for individual performances. More details can be found in Matthew 13, and Revelation 2–3. In the last chapter of the Bible, the Resurrected Jesus said: "See, I am coming soon, and my reward is with me, to repay all according to their deeds." (Revelation 22:12)

Is Eternal Life Easy to Earn?

As Jesus was being crucified between two criminals, the following conversations took place among them:

> One of the criminals hanging beside him scoffed, "So you're the Messiah, are you? Prove it by saving yourself—and us, too, while you're at it!"
>
> But the other criminal protested, "Don't you fear God even when you are dying? We deserve to die for our evil deeds, but this man hasn't done anything wrong." Then he said, "Jesus, remember me when you come into your Kingdom."
>
> And Jesus replied, "I assure you, today you will be with me in paradise." (Luke 23:39–43)

We know Jesus was resurrected on the third day after His death. When Jesus said: "today you will be with me in paradise," He did not mean: "today you will be resurrected." Resurrection to eternal life for all Christians will be made by God (by means of the Holy Spirit) at the Second Coming of Jesus. Paradise is a waiting room. (see 1 Thessalonians 4:14–17 and Revelation 20:4–6)

Jesus preached to the Jews on the following day after He fed over 5,000 people with two fish and five barley loaves: "Anyone who believes in me already has eternal life." (John 6:47)

Jesus also preached to the Jews: "I assure you, those who listen to my message and believe in God who sent me have eternal life. They will never be condemned for their sins, but they have already passed from death into life." (John 5:24)

John the Baptist told his disciples about Jesus: "The Father loves his Son, and he has given him authority over everything. And all who believe in God's son have eternal life. Those who don't obey the Son will never experience eternal life, but the wrath of God remains upon them." (John 3:35–36)

In the first epistle among the 13 Paul wrote, he taught the Christians in Rome the way they could be saved:

> For if you confess with your mouth that Jesus is Lord and believe in your heart that God raised him from the dead, you will be saved. For it is by believing in your heart that you are made right with God, and it is by confessing with your mouth that you are saved. As the Scriptures tell us, 'Anyone who believes in him will not be disappointed.' Jew and Gentile are the same in this respect. They all have the same Lord, who generously gives his riches to all who ask for them. For 'Anyone who calls on the name of the Lord will be saved.' (Romans 10:9–13)

Paul also advised the Christians in Rome the difference between being the slaves of Satan and the slaves of God:

> But now you are free from the power of sin and have become slaves of God. Now you do those things that lead to holiness and result in eternal life. For the wages of sin is death, but the free gift of God is eternal life through Christ Jesus our Lord. (Romans 6:22–23)

A religious lawyer, who intended to test Jesus, asked Him about eternal life:

> One day an expert in religious law stood up to test Jesus by asking him this question: "Teacher, what must I do to receive eternal life?"
>
> Jesus replied, "What does the law of Moses say? How do you read it?"
>
> The man answered, "You must love the Lord your God with all your heart, all your soul, all your strength, and all your mind." And, "Love your neighbor as yourself."
>
> "Right!" Jesus told him. "Do this and you will live!" (Luke 10:25–28; see also Matthew 22:37–40)

In his second letter to Timothy, Paul emphasized that it is Jesus who provides us with the Good News through which we may have everlasting life:

> "It is God who saved us and chose us to live a holy life. He did this not because we deserve it, but because that was his plan long before the world began—to show his love and kindness to us through Christ Jesus. And now he has made all of this plain to us by the coming of Christ Jesus, our Savior, who broke the power of death and showed us the way to everlasting life through the Good News." (2 Timothy 1:9–10)

Is Eternal Life Difficult to Earn?

The apostle Matthew documented the conversations between Jesus and an almost perfect rich young man:

> Someone came to Jesus with this question: "Teacher, what good things must I do to have eternal life?"
>
> "Why ask me about what is good?" Jesus replied. "Only God is good. But to answer your question, you can receive eternal life if you keep the commandments."
>
> "Which ones?" the man asked.
>
> And Jesus replied: "Do not murder. Do not commit adultery. Do not steal. Do not testify falsely. Honor your father and mother. Love your neighbor as yourself."
>
> "I've obeyed all these commandments," the young man replied. "What else must I do?"
>
> Jesus told him, "If you want to be perfect, go and sell all you have and give the money to the poor, and you will have treasure in heaven. Then come, follow me."

> But when the young man heard this, he went sadly away because he had many possessions. (Matthew 19:16–22, also see Mark 10:17–22 and Luke 18:18–23)

Difficulties of the Rich

God sees our hearts. Many rich people believe money is the most important thing in life. Therefore they are not willing to give up money for eternal life. Jesus said: "Wherever your treasure is, there your heart and thoughts will also be." (Matthew 6:21)

> Then Jesus said to his disciples: "I tell you the truth, it is very hard for a rich person to get into the Kingdom of Heaven. I say it again—It is easier for a camel to go through the eye of a needle than for a rich person to enter the Kingdom of God!" (Matthew 19:23–24)

Jesus also said the following to John the Baptist's disciples:

> Go back to John and tell him about what you have heard and seen—the blind see, the lame walk, the lepers are cured, the deaf hear, the dead are raised to life, and the good news is being preached to the poor. (Matthew 11:4–5)

Can a Rich Man Have Eternal Life?

Would you rather be poor instead of rich? Matthew 19:26 reports: "Jesus looked at them [His disciples] intently and said, 'Humanly speaking, it is impossible. But with God everything is possible.'"

There have been many faithful and rich Christians in the past as well as in the present. The decisive issue is whether the rich man sees his wealth as more important than the words of Jesus. If he treats the Good News as more important than his money—provided he can humble himself, believe in Jesus, and accept Him as his Savior, ask Jesus to cleanse him whenever he commits a sin, and tries his best to prevent sins from recurring—then he will receive eternal life as promised by Jesus. Of course, this is no small challenge to a rich man. He cannot be successful if he hasn't invited the Holy Spirit to live in him.

Luke, an associate of Paul, described a rich man who humbled himself when he met Jesus:

> Jesus entered Jericho and made his way through the town. There was a man there named Zacchaeus. He was one of the most influential Jews in the Roman tax-collecting business, and he had become very rich. He tried to get a look at Jesus, but he was too short to see over the crowds. So he ran ahead and climbed a sycamore tree beside the road, so he could watch from there.
>
> When Jesus came by, he looked up at Zacchaeus and called him by name. "Zacchaeus!" he said. "Quick, come down! For I must be a guest in your home today."
>
> Zacchaeus quickly climbed down and took Jesus to his house in great excitement and joy. But the crowds were displeased. "He has gone to be the guest of a notorious sinner," they grumbled.
>
> Meanwhile, Zacchaeus stood there and said to the Lord, "I will give half my wealth to the poor, Lord, and if I have overcharged people on their taxes, I will give them back four times as much!"
>
> Jesus responded, "Salvation has come to this home today, for this man has shown himself to be a son of Abraham. And I, the Son of Man, have come to seek and save those like him who are lost." (Luke 19:1–10)

Always Give God the Top Priority

Jesus taught His disciples the priorities in life and the necessary qualifications to become His true disciples:

> Your enemies will be right in your own household! If you love your father or mother more than you love me, you are not worthy of being mine; or if you love your son or daughter more than me, you are not worthy of being mine. If you refuse to take up your cross and follow me, you are not worthy of being mine. If you cling to your life, you will lose it; but if you give it up for me, you will find it. (Matthew 10:36–39)

Jesus is not asking us to fight against our family members as enemies. However, He wishes to know if, when there is a choice or dispute between two or more of the family members regarding God and man, who comes first? The important issue is on which side do you choose to stand? Do you refuse or accept to take up your own cross (hardships) and to follow Jesus?

Be Decisive! Stay Away from Sin

Jesus taught His disciples the important criteria needed in order to enter heaven:

> So if your hand or foot causes you to sin, cut it off and throw it away. It is better to enter heaven crippled or lame than to be thrown into the unquenchable fire with both of your hands and feet. And if your eye causes you to sin, gouge it out and throw it away. It is better to enter heaven half blind than to have two eyes and be thrown into hell. (Matthew 18:8–9)

Jesus emphasized how valuable eternal life is. Everyone must prepare to make a critical decision or sacrifice when there is a time he or she has to choose to give in to temptations and sins offered by Satan or to follow Jesus and obey the words of God.

Although sinful habits and sinful behaviors may prove to be difficult and/or costly to remove, God always looks at the lost one.

Christians have the Holy Spirit sent to us by Jesus. He will strengthen us when we are weak either physically, spiritually or both.

Obey God the Father in Heaven

Jesus told His disciples there was only one condition for entering the Kingdom of God:

> Not all people who sound religious are really godly. They may refer to me as "Lord," but they still won't enter the Kingdom of Heaven. The decisive issue is whether they obey my Father in heaven. On judgment day many will tell me, "Lord, Lord, we prophesied in your name and cast out demons in your name and performed many miracles in your name." But I will reply, "I never knew you. Go away, the things you did were unauthorized." (Matthew 7:21–23)

How do we obey the Father in Heaven? To obey the Father in heaven we must read and obey the words of God found in the Holy Bible. Good behavior is also important as described by the younger brother of Jesus: "Just as the body is dead without a spirit, so also faith is dead without good deeds." (James 2:26)

Jesus told His disciples the rigorous condition for entering into the Kingdom of Heaven: "But I warn you—unless you obey God better than the teachers of religious law and the Pharisees do, you can't enter the Kingdom of Heaven at all!" (Matthew 5:20)

As described in the New Testament (Matthew 23 in detail), the teachers of religious law always emphasized the importance of the law and how to follow the law, but they had no love. The Pharisees had many criticisms but seldom took the necessary actions to do what was good. Both the teachers of religious law and Pharisees were well-educated people. They always relied on and showed off their human wisdom and academic qualifications. Salvation will not go to them, because God stays with humble people.

Jesus summarized how to obey God the Father as recorded in Matthew 5 and 6:

> You have heard that the law of Moses says, Love your neighbor and hate your enemy. But I say, love your enemies! Pray for those who persecute you! In that way, you will be acting as true children of your Father in heaven. For he gives his sunlight to both the evil and the good, and he sends rain on the just and on the unjust, too. If you love only those who love you, what good is that? Even corrupt tax collectors do that much. If you are kind only to your friends, how are you different from anyone else? Even pagans do that. But you are to be perfect, even as your Father in heaven is perfect. (Matthew 5:43–48)

Christians Need Faith

A simple message from Jesus about faith was documented three times in the New Testament. No one can enter into the Kingdom of God unless accompanied by undoubting faith:

> One day some parents brought their little children to Jesus so he could touch them and bless them, but the disciples told them not to bother him. Then Jesus called for the children and said to the disciples, "Let the children come to me. Don't stop them! For the Kingdom of God belongs to such as these. I assure you, anyone who doesn't have their kind of faith will never get into the Kingdom of God." (Luke 18:15–17, also see Matthew 19:13–15 and Mark 10:13–16)

Children accept more often than they refuse. They do not have much skepticism or preconceived ideas in their minds. In order to enter into the Kingdom of God, adults also need to accept Jesus and the Gospel with undoubting faith.

Sacrifices for God Will Be Rewarded

Jesus told His disciples whoever sacrificed for Him and the Good News will be rewarded with eternal life:

> And Jesus replied, "I assure you that everyone who has given up house or brothers or sisters or mother or father or children or property, for my sake and for the Good News, will receive now in return, a hundred times over, houses, brothers, sisters, mothers, children, and property—with persecutions. And in the world to come they will have eternal life." (Mark 10:29–30)

"Good News" refers to the Gospel, the Words of God, the New Testament and the New Covenant.

"In the world to come" refers to the New Jerusalem coming down from God out of heaven. This is a place for eternal life. God will live among His people.

Only Those Who Endure to the End Will Be Saved

Many people who accepted Jesus as their Savior, for one reason or another, can neither be found in the church nor do they behave like Christians anymore. In short, they walked away from God. They have not been able to decline the temptations given to them by Satan. They also did not ask the Holy Spirit to stay in them. They may feel ashamed (for sins committed as Adam and Eve did in the Garden of Eden) but did not have the courage to come back as a "lost sheep." No matter what good works they had done, they are no longer saved (see Matthew 24:13).

For those who do not wish to be cast into the lake of fire, don't hesitate, come back to Jesus and He will forgive all your sins. All Jesus wants from us is a sincerely repentant heart.

Will it be hard to follow Jesus? Certainly, it is a struggle, but others have suffered—and still suffer—for their faith in Christ. Early believers were persecuted, imprisoned, tortured, and killed for their faith. But those who endure to the end will be saved. (Matthew 10:22)

When John was sent into exile to the island of Patmos, the Holy Spirit sent this message through him to the church members in Smyrna:

> Don't be afraid of what you are about to suffer. The Devil will throw some of you into prison and put you to the test. You will be persecuted for '10 days'. Remain faithful even when facing death, and I will give you the crown of life. (Revelation 2:10)

Most servants appointed by God, both the prophets in the Old Testament and the apostles of Jesus, were persecuted and executed. Nobody should afraid of death, because no one can avoid it ever since God created the first man. It is sin that causes us to die. It is the Holy Spirit who gives eternal life. We only need to follow Jesus in order to achieve the reward of eternal life.

Thirty years after Jesus' resurrection, the apostle Peter wrote a letter to Christians in the lands of Pontus, Galatia, and Cappadocia to give them encouragement to face the trials so that they would be rewarded by trusting Jesus:

> All honor to the God and Father of our Lord Jesus Christ, for it is by his boundless mercy that God has given us the privilege of being born again. Now we live with a wonderful expectation because Jesus Christ rose again from the dead. For God has reserved a priceless inheritance for his children. It is kept in heaven

for you, pure and undefiled, beyond the reach of change and decay. And God, in his mighty power, will protect you until you receive this salvation, because you are trusting him. It will be revealed on the last day for all to see. So be truly glad! There is wonderful joy ahead, even though it is necessary for you to endure many trials for a while.

These trials are only to test your faith, to show that it is strong and pure. It is being tested as fire tests and purifies gold—and your faith is far more precious to God than mere gold. So if your faith remains strong after being tried by fiery trials, it will bring you much praise and glory and honor on the day when Jesus Christ is revealed to the whole world.

You love him even though you have never seen him. Though you do not see him, you trust him; and even now you are happy with a glorious, inexpressible joy. Your reward for trusting him will be the salvation of your souls.

This salvation was something the prophets wanted to know more about. They prophesied about this gracious salvation prepared for you, even though they had many questions as to what it all could mean. They wondered what the Spirit of Christ within them was talking about when he told them in advance about Christ's suffering and his great glory afterward. They wondered when and to whom all this would happen.

They were told that these things would not happen during their lifetime, but many years later, during yours. And now this Good News has been announced by those who preached to you in the power of the Holy Spirit sent from heaven. It is all so wonderful that even the angels are eagerly watching these things happen. (1 Peter 1:3–12)

The Water and the Spirit

Jesus disclosed two important steps needed for entering into the Kingdom of God to a Jewish religious leader named Nicodemus:

> I assure you, unless you are born again, you can never see the Kingdom of God. (John 3:3)

> The truth is, no one can enter the Kingdom of God without being born of water and the spirit. (John 3:5)

To be born again means a person who believes that Jesus is the Son of God and died for our sins, and he or she has accepted Jesus as Savior. He or she also crucifies all his/her sins on the cross, and asks Jesus for forgiveness and to wash the sins clean by the blood of Jesus. From that time on, the "new Christian" maintains close contact with God, puts the words of God deep in his/her heart, and tries his/her very best to avoid sins.

Being born again is not a guarantee of eternal life or entry into the Kingdom of God. It allows that one may see the Kingdom of God only.

The phrase "born of water and the spirit," refers to a person who accepts Jesus as his Savior and is baptized in water, witnessed by others; and then invites the Holy Spirit to stay inside him. Only with the presence of the Holy Spirit staying inside us may we overcome Satan and enter into the Kingdom of God. The Holy Spirit always reminds us the truth and the words of God. He can also strengthen our spiritual weakness. Man cannot defeat Satan without the company of the Holy Spirit!

The True Bread from Heaven

Jesus surprised the Jews when He preached to them that they could not have eternal life if they did not eat His flesh and drink His blood:

> However, the bread from heaven gives eternal life to everyone who eats it. I am the living bread that came down out of heaven. Anyone who eats this bread will live forever, this bread is my flesh, offered so the world may live. (John 6:50–51)

> So Jesus said again, "I assure you, unless you eat the flesh of the Son of Man and drink his blood, you cannot have eternal life within you. But those who eat my flesh and drink my blood have eternal life, and I will raise them at the last day. For my flesh is the true food, and my blood is the true drink. All who eat my flesh and drink my blood remain in me, and I in them. I live by the power of the living Father who sent me; in the same way, those who partake of me will live because of me. I am the true bread from heaven. Anyone who eats this bread will live forever and not die as your ancestors did, even though they ate the manna." (John 6:53–58)

To "eat the flesh of the Son of Man" means to read, understand, remember and keep the words of Jesus in our heart. To "drink his blood" refers again to the blood of Jesus shed for the forgiveness of our sins.

In John 1:1, the apostle John described Jesus: "In the beginning the Word already existed. He was with God, and he was God." In Revelation 19:13, John described the Resurrected Jesus: "He was clothed with a robe dipped in blood, and his title was the Word of God."

In Luke 22:19–20, In the Last Supper of Jesus and His disciples before His crucifixion:

> Then he took a loaf of bread; and when he had thanked God for it, he broke it in pieces and gave it to the disciples, saying, "This is my body, given for you. Do this in remembrance of me."

> After supper he took another cup of wine and said, "This wine is the token of God's new covenant to save you—an agreement sealed with the blood I will pour out for you." (see also Matthew 26:28 and Mark 14:24)

A part of Jesus' prayer to God the Father in the night before His crucifixion:

> When Jesus had finished saying all these things, he looked up to heaven and said, "Father, the time has come. Glorify your Son so he can give glory back to you. For you have given him authority over everyone in all the earth. He gives eternal life to each one you have given him. And this is the way to have eternal life—to know you, the only true God, and Jesus Christ, the one you sent to earth." (John 17:1–3)

Whoever Has God's Son Has Life

The apostle John described the importance of the three witnesses: the spirit, the water, and the blood. He also warned that no one may have eternal life without accepting Jesus in his or her heart:

> For every child of God defeats this evil world by trusting Christ to give the victory. And the ones who win this battle against the world are the ones who believe that Jesus is the Son of God.

> And Jesus Christ was revealed as God's Son by his baptism in water and by shedding his blood on the cross—not by water only, but by water and blood. And the Spirit also gives us the testimony that this is true. So we have these three witnesses—the Spirit, the water, and the blood—and all three agree. Since we believe human testimony, surely we can believe the testimony that comes from God. And God has testified about his

> Son. All who believe in the Son of God know that this is true. Those who don't believe this are actually calling God a liar because they don't believe what God has testified about his Son.
>
> And this is what God has testified: He has given us eternal life, and this life is in his Son. So whoever has God's Son has life; whoever does not have his Son does not have life. (1 John 5:4–12, also see John 6:37–40)

In a letter Paul wrote to Titus, a young pastor at Crete, Paul also pointed out the important relationship between the Holy Spirit and eternal life:

> But then God our Savior showed us his kindness and love. He saved us, not because of the good things we did, but because of his mercy. He washed away our sins and gave us a new life through the Holy Spirit. He generously poured out the Spirit upon us because of what Jesus Christ our Savior did. He declared us not guilty because of his great kindness. And now we know that we will inherit eternal life. (Titus 3:4–7)

Loving God Means Keeping His Commandments

Over 50 years after Jesus' resurrection, the apostle John confirmed what Jesus had told His disciples about 60 years before:

> Everyone who believes that Jesus is the Christ is a child of God. And everyone who loves the Father loves his children, too. We know we love God's children if we love God and obey his commandments. Loving God means keeping his commandments, and really, that isn't difficult. For every child of God defeats this evil world by trusting Christ to give the victory. And the ones who win this battle against the world are the ones who believe that Jesus is the Son of God. (1 John 5:1–5)

Jesus told His disciples:

> Not all people who sound religious are really godly. They may refer to me as 'Lord,' but they still won't enter the Kingdom of Heaven. The decisive issue is whether they obey my Father in heaven. (Matthew 7:21)

> Then he called his disciples and the crowds to come over and listen. "If any of you wants to be my follower," he told them, "you must put aside your selfish ambition, shoulder your cross, and follow me. If you try to keep your life for yourself, you will lose it. But if you give up your life for my sake and for the sake of the Good News, you will find true life. And how do you benefit if you gain the whole world but lose your own soul in the process? Is anything worth more than your soul?" (Mark 8:34–37)

This World Is Fading Away

The apostle John advised the younger generations of Christians when he was about 90 years old. He told them the importance of eternal life that would last forever as compared with our present life offered by the world—a temporary one that would soon fade away:

> Stop loving this evil world and all that it offers you, for when you love the world, you show that you do not have the love of the Father in you. For the world offers only the lust for physical pleasure, the lust for everything we see, and pride in our possessions. These are not from the Father. They are from this evil world. And this world is fading away, along with everything it craves. But if you do the will of God, you will live forever. (1 John 2:15–17)

The First Resurrection

The apostle John described a vision of the first resurrection when he was being exiled to the Island of Patmos:

> Then I saw thrones, and the people sitting on them had been given the authority to judge. And I saw the souls of those who had been beheaded for their testimony about Jesus, for proclaiming the word of God. And I saw the souls of those who had not worshiped the beast or his statue, nor accepted his mark on their forehead or their hands. They came to life again, and they reigned with Christ for a thousand years. This is the first resurrection. (The rest of the dead did not come back to life until the thousand years had ended.) Blessed and holy are those who share in the first resurrection. For them the second death holds no power, but they will be priests of God and of Christ and will reign with him a thousand years. (Revelation 20:4–6; also refer to 1 Thessalonians 4:14–17)

To Meet the Lord in the Air

The apostle Paul described the destination of Christians—the First Resurrection—in a letter addressed to the church in Thessalonica (a prominent seaport and the capital of the Roman province of Macedonia at that time):

> And now, brothers and sisters, I want you to know what will happen to the Christians who have died so you will not be full of sorrow like people who have no hope. For since we believe that Jesus died and was raised to life again, we also believe that when Jesus comes, God will bring back with Jesus all the Christians who have died.
>
> I can tell you this directly from the Lord: We who are still living when the Lord returns will not rise to meet him ahead of those who are in their graves. For the Lord himself will come down from heaven with a commanding shout, with the call of the archangel, and with the trumpet call of God. First, all the Christians who have died will rise from their graves. Then, together with them, we who are still alive and remain on the earth will be caught up in the clouds to meet the Lord in the air and

remain with him forever. (1 Thessalonians 4:13–17, also refer to Revelation 20:4–6; Isaiah 52:8–9)

Transformed into Heavenly Bodies

The apostle Paul wished to strengthen the faith among the church members in Corinth, he describes "a wonderful secret" in his letter to them:

> What I am saying, dear brothers and sisters, is that flesh and blood cannot inherit the Kingdom of God. These perishable bodies of ours are not able to live forever.
>
> But let me tell you a wonderful secret God has revealed to us. Not all of us will die, but we will all be transformed. It will happen in a moment, in the blinking of an eye, when the last trumpet is blown. For when the trumpet sounds, the Christians who have died will be raised with transformed bodies. And then we who are living will be transformed so that we will never die. For our perishable earthly bodies must be transformed into heavenly bodies that will never die.
>
> When this happens—when our perishable earthly bodies have been transformed into heavenly bodies that will never die—then at last the Scriptures will come true:
>
> "Death is swallowed up in victory. O death, where is your victory? O death, where is your string?" (1 Corinthians 15:50–55, also refer to John 6:63; Revelation 20:4–6, 14–15)

"I Will Raise Them from the Dead"

After Jesus fed more than 5,000 people with two fish and five barley loaves, He continued to preach to the Jews:

> "For people can't come to me unless the Father who sent me draws them to me, and at the last day I will raise them from the dead." (John 6:44)

The phrase, "For people can't come to me," is not restricted to only those who went to Jesus preaching about 2,000 years ago; it also refers to whoever accepts Jesus as his/her Savior or Messiah today.

"I Will Come and Get You"

Jesus comforted His disciples as they were very sad after they heard that He would go away:

> "There are many rooms in my Father's home, and I am going to prepare a place for you. If this were not so, I would tell you plainly. When everything is ready, I will come and get you, so that you will always be with me where I am. And you know where I am going and how to get there." (John 14:2–4)

"I am going" means Jesus knew He would die and be resurrected on the third day (i.e. going to the home of God the Father).

"I will come to get you" means the disciples of Jesus will also be resurrected at the Second Coming of Jesus.

With the phrase, "So that you will always be with me where I am," Jesus promised all His disciples (except Judas who betrayed Jesus who subsequently hanged himself) and His believers (Christians) that they would have eternal life in the Kingdom of God or the New Jerusalem. This also fulfills the prophesies in the Old Testament that God would raise a Shepherd from the descendants of David. He would be the King of the Jews forever, and also the one who will bring the Jews back to their own land, the land God promised their ancestors.

Dead Will Rise Again

After He healed a lame man lying sick for thirty-eight years, Jesus continued His preaching to the Jews:

> "Don't be so surprised! Indeed, the time is coming when all the dead in their graves will hear the voice of God's Son, and they will rise again. Those who have done good will rise to eternal life, and those who have continued in evil will rise to judgment." (John 5:28–29)

Jesus prophesied that in the last day (the Third Stage of the Second Coming of Jesus, details can be found in Chapter One) that all the dead will rise again. This refers to the Second Resurrection (the final resurrection). Everyone resurrected in the Second Resurrection is subject to judgment. There are two destinations: the eternal life in the New Jerusalem or the everlasting lake of fire.

The Final Resurrection and the Judgment

The apostle John described what he saw in a vision of the judgment and the end of this world:

> And I saw a great white throne, and I saw the one who was sitting on it. The earth and sky fled from his presence, but they found no place to hide. I saw the dead, both great and small, standing before God's throne. And the books were opened, including the Book of Life. And the dead were judged according to the things written in the books, according to what they had done. The sea gave up the dead in it, and death and the grave gave up the dead in them. They were all judged according to their deeds. And death and the grave were thrown into the lake of fire. This is the second death—the lake of fire. And anyone

> whose name was not found recorded in the book of life was thrown into the lake of fire. (Revelation 20: 11–15)

Only Christians who obeyed the words of God will not be judged or condemned:

> There is no judgment awaiting those who trust him. But those who do not trust him have already been judged for not believing the only Son of God. (John 3:18, also see Romans 8:1)

> Jesus said: "I assure you, those who listened to my message and believe in God who sent me have eternal life. They will never be condemned for their sins, but they have already passed from death into life." (John 5:24)

The Home of God Is Now Among His People!

The apostle John described a vision in which he saw the New Jerusalem—the destination for all the Christians and the place for eternal life. It is also the Kingdom of God as God will live there among His people forever:

> Then I saw a new heaven and a new earth, for the old heaven and the old earth had disappeared. And the sea was also gone. And I saw the holy city, the New Jerusalem, coming down from God out of heaven like a beautiful bride prepared for her husband.

> I heard a loud shout from the throne, saying, "Look, the home of God is now among his people! He will live with them, and they will be his people. God himself will be with them. He will remove all of their sorrows, and there will be no more death or sorrow or crying or pain. For the old world and its evils are gone forever." (Revelation 21:1–4, also see Isaiah 65:17–19, 66:22)

The Resurrected Jesus who sat on the throne said:

> "All who are victorious will inherit all these blessings, and I will be their God, and they will be my children. But cowards who turn away from me, and unbelievers, and the corrupt, and murderers, and the immoral, and those who practice witchcraft, and idol worshipers, and all liars—their doom is in the lake that burns with fire and sulfur. This is the second death." (Revelation 21:7–8)

"All who are victorious" refers to those Christians who endure to the end. (refer to Matthew 10:22; 24:13; Mark 13:13)

"Jesus, thank you for showing us the way to the New Jerusalem."

chapter eight

Defeat Satan

SATAN, ALSO KNOWN AS THE DEVIL, THE SERPENT AND THE DRAGON, is an evil spirit; the source of sins and the father of liars. When Adam sinned, Satan took control of the world. Since man became slaves of Satan, man must die for the sins they committed. Satan is destined to die in the lake of fire (the second death, permanent death). All his followers, the angels who followed him and people who failed to refuse his temptations, cannot escape the fate of permanent death. There is only one way that we can avoid the permanent death—by following Jesus instead of Satan.

Who Is Satan?

Satan was originally Lucifer, the most beautiful and powerful angel in heaven, but his pride drove him to rebel against God. The prophet Isaiah described where Satan came from, his evil desire and prophesied his fate:

> How you are fallen from heaven, O shining star, son of the morning! You have been thrown down to the earth, you who destroyed the nations of the world. For you said to yourself, "I will ascend to heaven and set my throne above God's stars. I will preside on the mountain of the gods far away in the north. I will climb to the highest heavens and be like the Most High." But instead, you will be brought down to the place of the dead, down to its lowest depths. Everyone there will stare at you and ask, "Can this be the one who shook the earth and the kingdoms of the world? Is this the one who destroyed the world and made into a wilderness? Is this the king who demolished the world's greatest cities and had no mercy on his prisoners?"
>
> The kings of the nations lie in stately glory in their tombs, but you will be thrown out of your grave like a worthless branch. Like a corpse trampled underfoot, you will be dumped into a mass grave with those killed in battle. You will descend to the pit. You will not be given a proper burial, for you have destroyed your nation and slaughtered your people. Your son will not succeed you as king. (Isaiah 14:12–20)

God's Spirit also spoke through the prophet Ezekiel to Satan about his creation, his rebellion and the penalty for his rebellion:

> You were the perfection of wisdom and beauty. You were in Eden, the garden of God. Your clothing was adorned with every precious stone—red carnelian, chrysolite, white moonstone, beryl, onyx, jasper, sapphire, turquoise, and emerald—all beautifully crafted for you and set in the finest gold. They were given to you on the day you were created. I ordained and anointed you as the mighty angelic guardian. You had access to the holy mountain of God and walked among the stones of fire.
>
> You were blameless in all you did from the day you were created until the day evil was found in you. Your great wealth filled you

> with violence, and you sinned. So I banished you from the mountain of God. I expelled you, O mighty guardian, from your place among the stones of fire. Your heart was filled with pride because of all your beauty. You corrupted your wisdom for the sake of your splendor. So I threw you to the earth and exposed you to the curious gaze of kings. You defiled your sanctuaries with your many sins and your dishonest trade. So I brought fire from within you, and it consumed you. I let it burn you to ashes on the ground in the sight of all who were watching. All who knew you are appalled at your fate. You have come to a terrible end, and you are no more. (Ezekiel 28:14–19)

Never Fight Satan Alone

Based merely on the strength of man, no one can win the war against Satan except Jesus.

Satan interferes with our thinking by sending messages to us with ambiguities, skepticism and/or with conditions attached to his bribes or temptations. He can see us, but we cannot see him. We can feel his presence when we find something in our mind telling us to go away from God or leading us to the opposite way from what God told us to go. All Satan's slaves or sinners are trying their best to stay away from God. It is mostly because they feel ashamed, like how Adam felt after taking the forbidden fruit offered by Eve.

The only way to defeat Satan is to borrow the power from Jesus. He wins over Satan all the time. Confrontations with Satan exist every minute of our life. All we need to do is to admit we are sinners, humble ourselves, pray for Jesus' salvation, and ask Him to send His representative, the Holy Spirit to us.

Jesus gave us an example of what might happen if we try to fight Satan alone:

> When an evil spirit leaves a person, it goes into the desert, seeking rest but finding none. When it says, 'I will return to the

> person I came from.' So it returns and finds its former home empty, swept, and clean. Then the spirit finds seven other spirits more evil than itself, and they all enter the person and live there. And so that person is worse off than before. That will be the experience of this evil generation. (Matthew 12:43–45; see also Luke 11:24–26)

To avoid dangerous situations such as the one Jesus spoke of, we should always pray and be filled with the Holy Spirit. This is especially important for those who have just accepted Jesus as their Savior. We must never leave our heart empty when Jesus has taken the sins and the evil spirits away from us. We must have faith and be decisive, never allow any slightest flexibility or room for Satan coming into us.

Satan's World

The world became Satan's colony since God threw him from heaven down to the earth. Jesus told His disciples: "I will no longer talk much with you, for the ruler of this world is coming, and he has nothing in Me." (John 14:30 NKJV) Jesus also told His disciples they did not belong to the world:

> When the world hates you, remember it hated me before it hated you. The world would love you if you belonged to it, but you don't. I chose you to come out of the world, and so it hates you. Do you remember what I told you? "A servant is not greater than the master." Since they persecuted me, naturally they will persecute you. And if they had listened to me, they would listen to you! The people of the world will hate you because you belong to me, for they don't know God who sent me. They would not be guilty if I had not come and spoken to them. But now they have no excuse for their sin. Anyone who hates me hates my Father, too. If I hadn't done such miraculous signs

> among them that no one else could do, they would not be counted guilty. But as it is, they saw all that I did and yet hated both of us—me and my Father. This has fulfilled what the Scriptures said: "They hated me without cause." But I will send you the Counselor—the Spirit of Truth. He will come to you from the Father and will tell you all about me. And you must also tell others about me because you have been with me from the beginning. (John 15:18–27)

The night before His crucifixion, Jesus prayed to keep His disciples safe from Satan:

> I have given them your word. And the world hates them because they do not belong to the world, just as I do not. I'm not asking you to take them out of the world, but to keep them safe from the evil one. They are not part of this world any more than I am. Make them pure and holy by teaching them your words of truth. (John 17:14–17)

This is part of the prayer Jesus prayed immediately before His arrest. Jesus was more concerned about the spiritual life and the eternal life of His disciples than their physical life in the world. He prayed that God would not allow any of His disciples to be tempted away from God by Satan.

Satan has tremendous power in the world, not because God is weak; instead, it is a way God chooses to show His glory when the time has come. It will come sooner than most of us have expected.

Jesus replied to Pontius Pilate, the Governor of Judea, when the Jews brought Jesus to him for judgment: "Then Jesus answered, 'I am not an earthly king. If I were, my followers would have fought when I was arrested by the Jewish leaders. But my kingdom is not of this world.'" (John 18:36)

When we are still living in this world, we face temptations and threats from Satan in each minute of our life. Christians are facing a lifelong battle against Satan. Of course, the winner is always Jesus. He has neither been defeated nor will He be defeated by Satan. Since we believe and trust Jesus as our Savior, He will fight the battle with us by sending His representative, the Holy Spirit, to us. That's why Jesus said: "but those who endure to the end will be saved." (Matthew 10:22) Only those who have the Holy Spirit in their hearts can endure to the end.

Satan's Bondage Can Only Be Released by Trusting Jesus

Satan knew very well that Paul was an obedient servant of God. Without exception, Satan challenged him more strongly as Satan does to all those who go closer to God. Satan grabs every opportunity to seduce man.

Paul told the Christians in Rome:

> But sin took advantage of this law and aroused all kinds of forbidden desires within me! If there were no law, sin would not have that power.
>
> I felt fine when I did not understand what the law demanded. But when I learned the truth, I realized I had broken the law and was a sinner, doomed to die. So the good law, which was supposed to show me the way of life, instead gave me the death penalty. Sin took advantage of the law and fooled me; it took the good law and used it to make me guilty of death. But still, the law itself is holy and right and good.
>
> But how can that be? Did the law, which is good, cause my doom? Of course not! Sin used what was good to bring about my condemnation. So we can see how terrible sin really is. It uses God's good commandment for its own evil purposes.

> The law is good, then. The trouble is not with the law but with me [Paul], because I am sold into slavery, with sin as my master. I don't understand myself at all, for I really want to do what is right, but I don't do it. Instead, I do the very thing I hate. I know perfectly well that what I am doing is wrong, and my bad conscience shows that I agree that the law is good. But I can't help myself, because it is sin inside me that makes me do these evil things.
>
> I know I am rotten through and through so far as my old sinful nature is concerned. No matter which way I turn, I can't make myself do right. I want to, but I can't. When I want to do good, I don't. And when I try not to do wrong, I do it anyway. But if I am doing what I don't want to do, I am not really the one doing it; the sin within me is doing it.
>
> It seems to be a fact of life that when I want to do what is right, I inevitably do what is wrong. I love God's law with all my heart. But there is another law at work within me that is at war with my mind. This law wins the fight and makes me a slave to the sin that is still within me. Oh, what a miserable person I am! Who will free me from this life that is dominated by sin? Thank God! The answer is in Jesus Christ our Lord. (Romans 7:8–25)

Only the presence of the Holy Spirit in our hearts can provide us with the necessary power to overcome sin. In a letter Paul addressed to the church in Ephesus, he described God's love and mercy to His children by giving eternal life and raised them from the dead along with Jesus:

> Once you were dead, doomed forever because of your many sins. You used to live just like the rest of the world, full of sin, obeying Satan, the mighty prince of the power of the air. He is the spirit at work in the hearts of those who refuse to obey

> God. All of us used to live that way, following the passions and desires of our evil nature. We were born with an evil nature, and we were under God's anger just like everyone else.
>
> But God is so rich in mercy, and he loved us so very much, that even while we were dead because of our sins, he gave us life when he raised Christ from the dead. (It is only by God's special favor that you have been saved!) For he raised us from the dead along with Christ, and we are seated with him in the heavenly realms—all because we are one with Christ Jesus. And so God can always point to us as examples of the incredible wealth of his favor and kindness toward us, as shown in all he has done for us through Christ Jesus.
>
> God saved you by his special favor when you believed. And you can't take credit for this; it is a gift from God. Salvation is not a reward for the good things we have done, so none of us can boast about it. For we are God's masterpiece. He has created us anew in Christ Jesus, so that we can do the good things he planned for us long ago. (Ephesians 2:1–10)

Satan wishes to have as many people as possible to follow him. He wants us to become his slaves so that he wishes he can become more powerful than God. When we are moving closer to God, that is the moment Satan puts more skeptical ideas and temptations into our minds. He will try his very best to confuse us. He also likes us to believe that what we know God did for us is untrue; or at least makes us doubtful about the truth and God's love. We can easily find out whether the idea is from Satan by praying to God as soon as we have received a doubtful input. A doubtful input is a message that comes into our mind persuading us to do something we did not anticipate.

The Holy Spirit is always faithful; He will tell us what is the truth and what is the false. Contrary to what God gives us free and clear, the offers made by Satan always accompanied with conditions or temptations and ambiguous.

Avoid Being a Victim

Never underestimate the challenges or temptations from Satan. We can see so many people once were close to God but have become entangled with Satan. Many people have been defeated by Satan, including pastors, evangelists, and God's servants. The main factors that caused their defeat are:

- They fought the battle against Satan in their own strength.
- They gave way to Satan just a little at the beginning and underestimated the consequences.

The only way we will not lose the battle against Satan is to ask Jesus to help us and request the Holy Spirit to live within ourselves. If we give only a small opportunity to Satan, we can hardly stand firm again. So, stand firm and give Satan no opportunity!

After all, Satan does not even consider people as his enemies. He knows very well that man carries flesh and blood. Man is therefore very weak and vulnerable by nature. He will definitely be the winner if we fail to retain God's Word and the Holy Spirit in our hearts at all times. Satan is jealous of God. His only enemy is God.

Although Satan may not treat man as his enemy, Christians must treat Satan as their enemy, because Satan will target them as enemies. Because Satan is a spirit, he can see us from inside out. He will start to attack us because we chose God instead of him. But Satan fears God as he knows that he cannot win over God in direct confrontations. Therefore, Satan's best tactics are cheating, lying, scaring, threatening, tormenting and/or tempting people with lust as his bait.

The only time we do not wish to have God's help to fight against Satan is when we still love our sinful life and are unwilling to give it up. Although we may feel ashamed of our sins, we are reluctant to humble ourselves before God to confess our sins and request His forgiveness. As such, we become an easy prey for Satan, like a newborn gazelle being hunted by a lioness. One sided! No fight! What a pitiful victim! On the other hand, those who have been born into God's family do not sin, because God's life is in them. So they cannot keep on sinning, because they have been born of God. (see 1 John 3:9)

Satan Is the Father of Lies

Jesus denounced the Jewish leaders:

> For you are the children of your father the Devil, and you love to do the evil things he does. He was a murderer from the beginning and has always hated the truth. There is no truth in him. When he lies, it is consistent with his character; for he is a liar and the father of lies. (John 8:44)

The Father of Lies is worse than a liar himself. He teaches others to lie so that more people will be condemned together with him.

Satan's Temptations

Judas, one of the twelve disciples of Jesus betrayed Jesus for 30 pieces of silver. The bribe was offered to Judas by the Jewish High Priest. Obviously, Judas was motivated by money—it was greed that led him to death. "It was time for supper, and the Devil had already enticed Judas, son of Simon Iscariot, to carry out his plan to betray Jesus." (John 13:2)

The Serpent enticed man to disobey God. Man ignored the warning from God and acted the way the Serpent seduced. The outcome was death:

> Now the serpent was the shrewdest of all the creatures the Lord God had made. "Really?" he asked the woman. "Did God really say you must not eat any of the fruit in the garden?"
>
> "Of course we may eat it," the woman told him. "It's only the fruit from the tree at the center of the garden that we are not allowed to eat. God says we must not eat it or even touch it, or we will die."
>
> "You won't die!" the serpent hissed. "God knows that your eyes will be opened when you eat it. You will become just like God, knowing everything, both good and evil."
>
> The woman was convinced. The fruit looked so fresh and delicious, and it would make her so wise! So she ate some of the fruit. She also gave some to her husband, who was with her. Then he ate it, too. At that moment, their eyes were opened, and they suddenly felt shame at their nakedness. So they strung fig leaves together around their hips to cover themselves. (Genesis 3:1–7)

The serpent is also known as the dragon, the Devil and Satan:

> This great dragon—the ancient serpent called the Devil, or Satan, the one deceiving the whole world—was thrown down to the earth with all his angels. (Revelation 12:9)

Satan is very clever. He first confused Eve and then enticed her to act according to his planned plot.

Satan is both abusive and aggressive. When Jesus was led to the wilderness by the Holy Spirit to be tempted, Satan tried to use three different strategies: necessity, pride and lust.

Necessities: For 40 days and nights Jesus had not eaten anything. The Devil started to tempt Jesus with bread, as he knew Jesus was very hungry because Jesus had flesh and blood. The Devil failed.

Pride: He then suggested that Jesus jump from the highest point of the Temple in order to prove He was the Son of God, showing His personal pride. Again, Satan failed.

Lust: After he tempted Jesus twice without any success, the Devil used lust as his bait. This is the most serious temptation, because he knows men are commonly known to have greed in their mind:

> Next the Devil took him to the peak of a very high mountain and showed him the nations of the world and all their glory. "I will give it all to you," he said, "if you will only kneel down and worship me."
>
> "Get out of here, Satan," Jesus told him. "For the scriptures say, 'You must worship the Lord your God; serve only him.'"
>
> Then the Devil went away, and angels came and cared for Jesus. (Matthew 4:8–11)

Notice that Jesus always responded to Satan's temptations with the Word of God. Jesus knew that was His most effective weapon against temptation.

Tormentor

Satan has no mercy on man. He knows man was created by God and God treated His believers as His own children. Satan always uses man as his tool to challenge God. In the end, God will be the winner with all the glory.

There is no exception, including the case of Job:

> Then the Lord asked Satan, "Have you noticed my servant Job? He is the finest man in all the earth—a man of complete integrity. He fears God and will have nothing to do with evil. And he

> has maintained his integrity, even though you persuaded me to harm him without cause."
>
> Satan replied to the Lord, "Skin for skin—he blesses you only because you bless him. A man will give up everything he has to save his life. But take away his health, and he will surely curse you to your face!"
>
> "All right, do with him as you please," the Lord said to Satan. "But spare his life." So Satan left the Lord's presence, and he struck Job with a terrible case of boils from head to foot.
>
> Then Job scraped his skin with a piece of broken pottery as he sat among the ashes. His wife said to him "Are you still trying to maintain your integrity? Curse God and die."
>
> But Job replied, "You talk like a godless woman. Should we accept only good things from the hand of God and never anything bad?" So in all this, Job said nothing wrong. (Job 2:3–10)

Although Satan tortured Job, Job maintained his faith in God. By doing so, he gave God the glory He originally expected from man. Of course, by his faith, Job was then rewarded by God. If we are not greedy and not afraid to stand firm for Jesus or the Gospel, then Satan will gain nothing from us.

Luke wrote about a crippled woman tortured by an evil spirit. She was healed by Jesus purely based on His love and mercy:

> One Sabbath day as Jesus was teaching in a synagogue, he saw a woman who had been crippled by an evil spirit. She had been bent double for eighteen years and was unable to stand up straight. When Jesus saw her, he called her over and said, "Woman, you are healed of your sickness!" Then he touched

her, and instantly she could stand straight. How she praised and thanked God! (Luke 13:10–13)

In another case Satan tortured man:

Then a demon–possessed man, who was both blind and unable to talk, was brought to Jesus. He healed the man so that he could both speak and see. (Matthew 12:22)

Fight Satan

Jesus taught His disciples not to fear the death of the body: "Don't be afraid of those who want to kill you. They can only kill your body, they cannot touch your soul. Fear only God, who can destroy both soul and body in hell." (Matthew 10:28)

In Paul's letter to the Church in Ephesus, he outlined a detailed strategy to fight against Satan:

Put on all of God's armor so that you will be able to stand firm against all strategies and tricks of the Devil. For we are not fighting against people made of flesh and blood, but against the evil rulers and authorities of the unseen world, against those mighty powers of darkness who rule this world, and against wicked spirits in the heavenly realms.

Use every piece of God's armor to resist the enemy in the time of evil, so that after the battle you will still be standing firm. Stand your ground, putting on the sturdy belt of truth and the body armor of God's righteousness. For shoes, put on the peace that comes from the Good News, so that you will be fully prepared. In every battle you will need faith as your shield to stop the fiery arrows aimed at you by Satan. Put on salvation as your helmet, and take the sword of the spirit, which is the word of God. Pray at all times and on every occasion in the power of the Holy Spirit.

> Stay alert and be persistent in your prayers for all Christians everywhere. (Ephesians 6:11–18)

When the Holy Spirit arrives, He will remind us of the Word of God. He will also give us the necessary strength to resist the challenge of Satan. On the other hand, we must read the words of God every day and obey His commands.

Humble Ourselves Before God

Among the advice given to us by the younger brother of Jesus is to humble ourselves before God. It is only in this way we may receive help from God.

> So humble yourselves before God. Resist the Devil, and he will flee from you. Draw close to God, and God will draw close to you. Wash your hands, you sinners; purify your hearts, you hypocrites. Let there be tears for the wrong things you have done. Let there be sorrow and deep grief. Let there be sadness instead of laughter, and gloom instead of joy. When you bow down before the Lord and admit your dependence on him, he will lift you up and give you honor. (James 4:7–10)

Peter was not a stranger to the attacks of Satan. On one occasion, he was defeated by Satan when he denied Jesus three times because he failed to stay alert and pray. In his advice to younger Christians, he also emphasized the importance of being humble in front of God:

> So humble yourselves under the mighty power of God, and in his good time he will honor you. Give all your worries and cares to God, for he cares about what happens to you.
>
> Be careful! Watch out for attacks from the Devil, your great enemy. He prowls around like a roaring lion, looking for some

> victim to devour. Take a firm stand against him, and be strong in your faith. Remember that your Christian brothers and sisters all over the world are going through the same kind of suffering you are.
>
> In his kindness God called you to his eternal glory by means of Jesus Christ. After you have suffered a little while, he will restore, support, and strengthen you, and he will place you on a firm foundation. (1 Peter 5:6–10)

The Defeat of Satan

We do not have a choice. We must defeat Satan, or he will defeat us. We can only defeat Satan when we have the Word of God and the Holy Spirit living in us. We cannot fight him in our own power or with our own words. Only Jesus has overcome the world (the power of Satan). Believers in Jesus may also overcome the world by trusting in Him: "I have told you all this so that you may have peace in me. Here on earth you will have many trials and sorrows. But take heart, because I have overcome the world." (John 16:33)

More than 50 years following the resurrection of Jesus, the apostle John offered his recommendations to younger Christians for defeating Satan: "For every child of God defeats this evil world by trusting Christ to give the victory. And the ones who win this battle against the world are the ones who believe that Jesus is the Son of God." (1 John 5:4–5) He continued: "We know that those who have become part of God's family do not make a practice of sinning, for God's Son holds them securely, and the evil one cannot get his hands on them. We know that we are children of God and that the world around us is under the power and control of the evil one." (1 John 5:18–19)

The disciples of Jesus were happy as they had a successful mission after they followed the instructions given to them by Jesus:

> When the seventy-two disciples returned, they joyfully reported to him, "Lord, even the demons obey us when we use your name!"
>
> "Yes," he told them, "I saw Satan falling from heaven as a flash of lightning! And I have given you authority over all the power of the enemy, and you can walk among snakes and scorpions and crush them. Nothing will injure you. But don't rejoice just because evil spirits obey you; rejoice because your names are registered as citizens of heaven." (Luke 10:17–20)

About 60 years later, John documented his vision about the defeat of Satan by the Christians because of their testimonies and the blood of Jesus:

> Then there was war in heaven. Michael and the angels under his command fought the dragon and his angels. And the dragon lost the battle and was forced out of heaven. This great dragon—the ancient serpent called the Devil, or Satan, the one deceiving the whole world—was thrown down to the earth with all his angels.
>
> Then I heard a loud voice shouting across the heavens: "It has happened at last—the salvation and power and kingdom of our God, and the authority of his Christ! For the Accuser has been thrown down to earth—the one who accused our brothers and sisters before our God day and night. And they have defeated him because of the blood of the Lamb and because of their testimony. And they were not afraid to die. Rejoice, O heavens! And you who live in the heavens, rejoice! But terror will come on the earth and the sea. For the Devil has come

> down to you in great anger, and he knows that he has little time." (Revelation 12:7–12)

> Together they will wage war against the Lamb, but the Lamb will defeat them because he is Lord over all lords and King over all kings, and his people are the called and chosen and faithful ones. (Revelation 17:14)

John also documented his vision about the arrest of Satan and his being locked away for a thousand years:

> Then I [John] saw an angel come down from heaven with the key to the bottomless pit and a heavy chain in his hand. He seized the dragon—that old serpent, the Devil, Satan—and bound him in chains for a thousand years. The angel threw him into the bottomless pit, which he then shut and locked so Satan could not deceive the nations anymore until the thousand years were finished. Afterward he would be released again for a little while. (Revelation 20:1–3)

In the same vision, John saw the final fate of Satan and his followers—being thrown into the lake of fire where they would suffer forever:

> When the thousand years end, Satan will be let out of his prison. He will go out to deceive the nations from every corner of the earth, which are called Gog and Magog. He will gather them together for battle—a mighty host, as numberless as sand along the shore. And I saw them as they went up on the broad plain of the earth and surrounded God's people and the beloved city. But fire from heaven came down on the attacking armies and consumed them.

Then the Devil, who betrayed them, was thrown into the lake of fire that burns with sulfur, joining the beast and the false prophet. There they will be tormented day and night forever and ever. (Revelation 20:7–10)

"Thank you, Father for giving us the victory in Christ Jesus!"

chapter nine

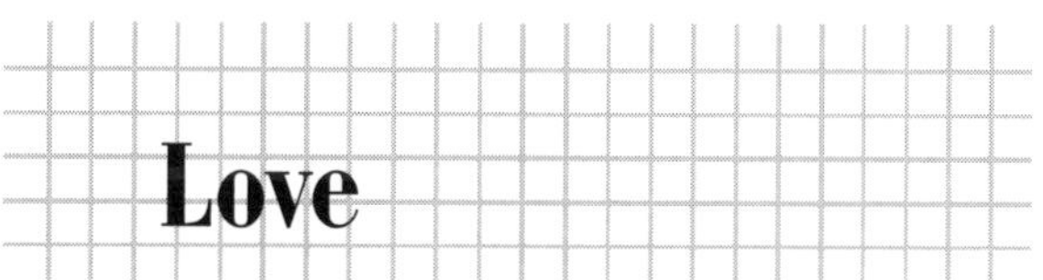

Love

GOD IS LOVE. GOD LOVES US FIRST. GOD COMMANDS US TO LOVE Him. Besides loving Him, He also commands us to love others. In the New Covenant, Jesus explained that all the commandments are based on love: "Love God, and also love others."

Paul brought up a lot of important issues that would lead to an ideal standard for Christians regarding love. In his first letter to the church members in Corinth, he pointed out love should become a basic criterion among Christians:

> If I could speak in any language in heaven or on earth but didn't love others, I would only be making meaningless noise like a loud gong or a clanging cymbal. If I had the gift of prophecy, and if I knew all the mysteries of the future and knew everything about everything, but didn't love others, what good would I be? And if I had the gift of faith so that I could speak to a mountain and make it move, without love I would be no good

> to anybody. If I gave everything I have to the poor and even sacrificed my body, I could boast about it; but if I didn't love others, I would be of no value whatsoever. (1 Corinthians 13:1–3)

The Definition of Love

In 1 Corinthians 13:4–8, Paul further defined what love is, and what love isn't:

- Love is patient and kind.
- Love is not jealous or boastful or proud or rude.
- Love does not demand its own way.
- Love is not irritable, and it keeps no record of when it has been wronged.
- It is never glad about injustice but rejoices whenever the truth wins out.
- Love never gives up, never loses faith, is always hopeful, and endures through every circumstance.
- Love will last forever

Love, he said, is the top priority among Christians: "There are three things that will endure—faith, hope, and love—and the greatest of these is love." (1 Corinthians 13:13)

The Most Important Commandment

Jesus answered the question of a teacher of religious law regarding the most important commandment:

> But when the Pharisees heard that he had silenced the Sadducees with his reply, they thought up a fresh question of their own to ask him. One of them, an expert in religious law, tried to trap him with this question: "Teacher, which is the most important commandment in the law of Moses?"

> Jesus replied, "'You must love the Lord your God with all your heart, all your soul, and all your mind.' This is the first and greatest commandment. A second is equally important: 'Love your neighbor as yourself.' All the other commandments and all the demands of the prophets are based on these two commandments." (Matthew 22:34–40; also see Luke 10:25–28 and Mark 12:28–31)

"I Command You to Love Each Other"

We cannot become the disciples of Jesus if we do not love one another. Jesus gave a new commandment to His disciples: "So now I am giving you a new commandment: love each other. Just as I have loved you, you should love each other. Your love for one another will prove to the world that you are my disciples." (John 13:34–35)

Jesus pointed out to His disciples the importance of love:

> I have loved you even as the Father has loved me. Remain in my love. When you obey me, you remain in my love, just as I obey my Father and remain in his love. I have told you this so that you will be filled with my joy. Yes, your joy will overflow! I command you to love each other in the same way that I love you. And here is how to measure it—the greatest love is shown when people lay down their lives for their friends. You are my friends if you obey me. I no longer call you servants, because a master doesn't confide in his servants. Now you are my friends, since I have told you everything the Father told me. You didn't choose me. I chose you. I appointed you to go and produce fruit that will last, so that the Father will give you whatever you ask for, using my name. I command you to love each other. (John 15:9–17)

More than 50 years after the resurrection of Jesus, John confirmed again that Jesus commanded His disciples to love each other: "And this is his commandment: We must believe in the name of his Son, Jesus Christ, and love one another, just as he commanded us. Those who obey God's commandments live in fellowship with him, and he with them. And we know he lives in us because the Holy Spirit lives in us." (1 John 3:23–24)

God's Love

God loved us first. God's love for man can be found throughout the entire Holy Bible—from Genesis to Revelation. The greatest love from God to man is that He gives us His only begotten Son, Jesus Christ, so that whoever believes in Him will have eternal life. No matter from which angle we look at God's words, we can find only one answer: God is love. Psalm 136 is a wonderful chapter in the Holy Bible having 26 verses. Every verse describes how God loves His people. Each verse ends with: "His faithful love endures for ever."

In a letter sent to the Christians in Rome, Paul emphasized that Jesus died for us because of God's great love: "When we were utterly helpless, Christ came at just the right time and died for us sinners. Now, no one is likely to die for a good person, though someone might be willing to die for a person who is especially good. But God showed his great love for us by sending Christ to die for us while we were still sinners." (Romans 5:6–8)

The love of God for us has no conditions, no limits and no end. God's love is greater than parents' love for their children. How many parents die for their children because their children sinned? In Paul's letter to the Christians in Rome, he challenged that nothing can separate us from God's love:

> Can anything ever separate us from Christ's love? Does it mean he no longer loves us if we have trouble or calamity, or are persecuted, or are hungry or cold or in danger or threatened with death? (Even the Scriptures say, "For your sake we are killed every day; we are being slaughtered like sheep.") No,

> despite all these things, overwhelming victory is ours through Christ, who loved us.
>
> And I am convinced that nothing can ever separate us from his love. Death can't, and life can't. The angels can't, and the demons can't. Our fears for today, our worries about tomorrow, and even the powers of hell can't keep God's love away. Whether we are high above the sky or in the deepest ocean, nothing in all creation will ever be able to separate us from the love of God that is revealed in Christ Jesus our Lord. (Romans 8:35–39)

Paul described that God's love is so great that no man can measure it:

> And I pray that Christ will be more and more at home in your hearts as you trust in him. May your roots go down deep into the soil of God's marvelous love. And may you have the power to understand, as all God's people should, how wide, how long, how high, and how deep his love really is. May you experience the love of Christ, though it is so great you will never fully understand it. Then you will be filled with the fullness of life and power that comes from God. (Ephesians 3:17–19)

Love God

If we love God, we listen to His words and obey His commands. Only by doing so we can have a happy and healthy life. In addition, we can be rewarded with eternal life. To use a negative approach: What may go wrong if we listen and obey God's words? The answer is we will lose nothing and nothing will go wrong.

John recorded what Jesus told the Jews when they did not believe Jesus and wanted to kill Him: "Jesus told them, 'If God were your Father, you would love me, because I have come to you from God. I am not here on my own, but he sent me.'" (John 8:42)

John later pointed out to the church members that it is a necessity for Christians to show our love for God by obeying His commandments: "Everyone who believes that Jesus is the Christ is a child of God. And everyone who loves the Father loves his children, too. We know we love God's children if we love God and obey his commandments. Loving God means keeping his commandments, and really, that isn't difficult." (1 John 5:1–3, also see John 14:15)

When John said that it was not difficult to keep God's commandments, he was referring to a statement made by Jesus: "For my yoke fits perfectly, and the burden I give you is light." (Matthew 11:30) The secret behind this is that Christians should unload all their burdens on Jesus. He will give us rest. (refer to Matthew 11:28)

A Christian's duty is to love God, and to love others.

Love Others

In a letter Paul sent to the Christians in Rome, he explained why loving others is so important:

> Pay all your debts, except the debt of love for others. You can never finish paying that! If you love your neighbor, you will fulfill all the requirements of God's law. For the commandments against adultery and murder and stealing and coveting—and any other commandment—are all summed up in this one commandment: 'Love your neighbor as yourself.' Love does no wrong to anyone, so love satisfies all of God's requirements. (Romans 13:8–10)

In his letter to the church in Ephesus, Paul suggested that Christians should follow the example of Jesus' love for others: "Live a life filled with love for others, following the example of Christ, who loved you and gave himself as a sacrifice to take away your sins. And God was pleased, because that sacrifice was like sweet perfume to him." (Ephesians 5:2)

Paul also stressed that Christians have no reason not to love each other:

> Since God chose you to be the holy people whom he loves, you must clothe yourselves with tenderhearted mercy, kindness, humility, gentleness, and patience. You must make allowance for each other's faults and forgive the person who offends you. Remember, the Lord forgave you, so you must forgive others. And the most important piece of clothing you must wear is love. Love is what binds us all together in perfect harmony. And let the peace that comes from Christ rule in your hearts. For as members of one body you are all called to live in peace. And always be thankful. (Colossians 3:12–15)

John urged Christians to really show their love for each other:

> This is the message we have heard from the beginning: We should love one another. We must not be like Cain, who belonged to the evil one and killed his brother. And why did he kill him? Because Cain had been doing what was evil, and his brother had been doing what was right. So don't be surprised, dear brothers and sisters, if the world hates you.
>
> If we love our Christian brothers and sisters, it proves that we have passed from death to eternal life. But a person who has no love is still dead. Anyone who hates another Christian is really a murderer at heart. And you know that murderers don't have eternal life within them. We know what real love is because Christ gave up his life for us. And so we also ought to give up our lives for our Christian brothers and sisters. But if anyone has enough money to live well and sees a brother or sister in need and refuses to help—how can God's love be in that person?

> Dear children, let us stop just saying we love each other; let us really show it by our actions. It is by our actions that we know we are living in the truth, so we will be confident when we stand before the Lord. (1 John 3:11–19)

John further elaborated about the importance of love among Christians. Since love comes from God and God is love, there is no reason for Christians not to love each other if they have God's Spirit living in them:

> Dear friends, let us continue to love one another, for love comes from God. Anyone who loves is born of God and knows God. But anyone who does not love does not know God—for God is love.
>
> God showed how much he loved us by sending his only Son into the world so that we might have eternal life through him. This is real love. It is not that we loved God, but that he loved us and sent his Son as a sacrifice to take away our sins.
>
> Dear friends, since God loved us that much, we surely ought to love each other. No one has ever seen God. But if we love each other, God lives in us, and his love has been brought to full expression through us.
>
> And God has given us his Spirit as proof that we live in him and he in us. Furthermore, we have seen with our own eyes and now testify that the Father sent his Son to be the Savior of the world. All who proclaim that Jesus is the Son of God have God living in them, and they live in God. We know how much God loves us, and we have put our trust in him.
>
> God is love, and all who live in love live in God, and God lives in them. And as we live in God, our love grows more perfect. So we will not be afraid on the day of judgment, but we can face him with confidence because we are like Christ here in this world.

> Such love has no fear because perfect love expels all fear. If we are afraid, it is for fear of judgment, and this shows that his love has not been perfected in us. We love each other as a result of his loving us first.
>
> If someone says, "I love God," but hates a Christian brother or sister, that person is a liar, for if we don't love people we can see, how can we love God, whom we have not seen? And God himself has commanded that we must love not only him but our Christian brothers and sisters, too. (1 John 4:7–21)

Love Your Enemies

One day, on a mountainside, Jesus taught His disciples to "love your enemies." When Jesus was being crucified, He prayed to God the Father to forgive those who persecuted and crucified Him. He did it so that His disciples may follow His example.

> You have heard that the law of Moses says, "Love your neighbor" and hate your enemy. But I say, love your enemies! Pray for those who persecute you! In that way, you will be acting as true children of your Father in heaven. For he gives his sunlight to both the evil and the good, and he sends rain on the just and on the unjust, too. If you love only those who love you, what good is that? Even corrupt tax collectors do that much. If you are kind only to your friends, how are you different from anyone else? Even pagans do that. But you are to be perfect, even as your Father in heaven is perfect. (Matthew 5:44–48)

The early Christian leader Stephen also prayed for his enemies as they killed him: "'Lord Jesus, receive my spirit.' And he fell to his knees, shouting, 'Lord, don't charge them with this sin!' And with that, he died." (Acts 7:59–60)

Besides those teachings made by apostles Paul and John concerning the necessity of love among the Christians, there are additional merits: In about 950 before Christ, King Solomon offered the words of wisdom: "Hatred stirs up strife, but love covers all sins." (Proverbs 10:12) In about A.D. 63, Peter also echoed King Solomon's statement by saying: "Most important of all, continue to show deep love for each other, for love covers a multitude of sins." (1 Peter 4:8)

Mutual Love

Paul told the church members in Corinth that love is a basic requirement that God gives to Christians: "It is love that really builds up the church. Anyone who claims to know all the answers doesn't really know very much. But the person who loves God is the one God knows and cares for." (1 Corinthians 8:1–3)

Jesus told His disciples that those who love Him and obey His commandments will be rewarded: "Those who obey my commandments are the ones who love me. And because they love me, my Father will love them, and I will love them. And I will reveal myself to each one of them." (John 14:21) Jesus continued: "All those who love me will do what I say. My Father will love them, and we will come to them and live with them." (John 14:23)

In the second letter Paul sent to Corinth, he said that those who were born again should live in their new life in Jesus and to please Jesus. To please Jesus is to obey His commandments. To obey His commandments are to love God and others.

> Whatever we do, it is because Christ's love controls us. Since we believe that Christ died for everyone, we also believe that we have all died to the old life we used to live. He died for everyone so that those who receive his new life will no longer live to please themselves. Instead, they will live to please Christ, who died and was raised for them. (2 Corinthians 5:14–15)

"Father, we love you because you loved us first."

chapter ten

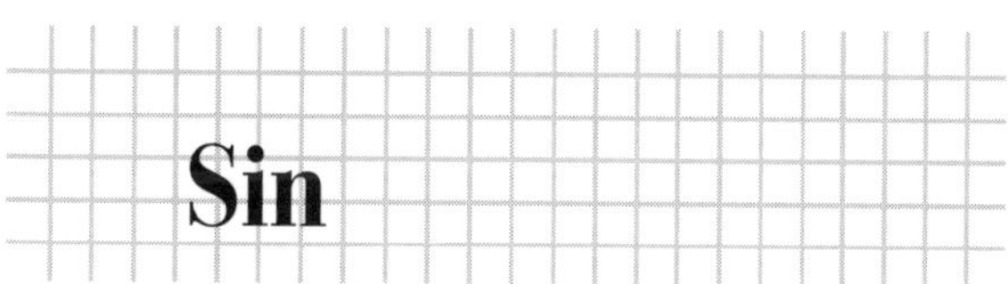

Sin

OTHER THAN JESUS, NO MAN HAS LIVED WITHOUT SIN SINCE THE VERY beginning. Because of our sin nature, we all have to deal with sin. "For all have sinned; all fall short of God's glorious standard." (Romans 3:23) And although Jesus has taken the punishment for our sins, we must first of all, accept Him as our Savior or Messiah and then still deal with sin in every minute of our life.

God Accepts Humble Confessions

Because God is holy, we cannot see Him when we have unconfessed sins. Although Jesus died for our sins, we must repent and confess our sins as soon as we know they were committed. And, rather than a blanket confession, we should confess to God what, where, when, how and against whom we have sinned. In addition to confessing our sins, we must also ask for His forgiveness. It is an important privilege among Christians to be able to confess in our prayers to God directly.

No matter how powerful or rich he became, King David never forgot to confess his own sins frequently and regularly. No matter how far he strayed from God, no matter how terrible his sins, he always repented and asked God to forgive him. With such a close relationship, David certainly set a good example for all Christians to follow. God was happy for what David did. He said many times in advance that the Messiah would come out of David's family (descendants).

Once David prayed: "Finally, I confessed all my sins to you and stopped trying to hide them. I said to myself, 'I will confess my rebellion to the Lord.' And you forgave me! All my guilt is gone." (Psalms 32:5)

Another time, David made this humble confession to God:

> For I recognize my shameful deeds—they haunt me day and night. Against you, and you alone, have I sinned; I have done what is evil in your sight. You will be proved right in what you say, and your judgment against me is just. For I was born a sinner —yes, from the moment my mother conceived me. (Psalms 51:3–5)

The apostle John warned Christians to be honest and humble in making their confessions. Only in this way the sins can be forgiven. This is what John said:

> So we are lying if we say we have fellowship with God but go on living in spiritual darkness. We are not living in the truth. But if we are living in the light of God's presence, just as Christ is, then we have fellowship with each other, and the blood of Jesus, His Son, cleanses us from every sin.
>
> If we say we have no sin, we are only fooling ourselves and refusing to accept the truth. But if we confess our sins to him, he is faithful and just to forgive us and to cleanse us from every wrong.

> If we claim we have not sinned, we are calling God a liar and showing that his word has no place in our hearts. (1 John 1:6–10)

Stay Away from Sin

Of course it's far better to avoid sin rather than continually live in the cycle of sin, confess, and repent. But very often, we find it difficult to resist sins. That is the time we need God's help. God always lets us have our own choice. If we deliberately sin, He will not stop us. However, if we pray to Him earnestly and ask for His help, He will not hesitate to help us by sending us the Holy Spirit to strengthen our mind's weaknesses.

King David knew this secret blessing very well—he always prayed for God's help when he was weak spiritually or physically or both. As King David knew he carried a body of flesh and blood that was vulnerable to temptations, he prayed for God's help to overcome himself: "Keep me from deliberate sins! Don't let them control me. Then I will be free of guilt and innocent of great sin." (Psalms 19:13)

"Now You Are Free from Sin"

Paul emphasized in detail the importance and need to commit ourselves fully to the new life Jesus gives us:

> Our old sinful selves were crucified with Christ so that sin might lose its power in our lives. We are no longer slaves to sin. For when we died with Christ we were set free from the power of sin. And since we died with Christ, we know we will also share his new life. We are sure of this because Christ rose from the dead, and he will never die again. Death no longer has any power over him. He died once to defeat sin, and now he lives for the glory of God. So you should consider yourselves dead to sin and able to live for the glory of God through Christ Jesus.

> Do not let sin control the way you live; do not give in to its lustful desires. Do not let any part of your body become a tool of wickedness, to be used for sinning. Instead, give yourselves completely to God since you have been given new life. And use your whole body as a tool to do what is right for the glory of God. Sin is no longer your master, for you are no longer subject to the law, which enslaves you to sin. Instead, you are free by God's grace.
>
> So since God's grace has set us free from the law, does this mean we can go on sinning? Of course not! Don't you realize that whatever you choose to obey becomes your master? You can choose sin, which leads to death, or you can choose to obey God and receive his approval. Thank God! Once you were slaves of sin, but now you have obeyed with all your heart the new teaching God has given you. Now you are free from sin, your old master, and you have become slaves to your new master, righteousness.
>
> I speak this way, using the illustration of slaves and masters, because it is easy to understand. Before, you let yourselves be slaves of impurity and lawlessness. Now you must choose to be slaves of righteousness so that you will become holy.
>
> In those days, when you were slaves of sin, you weren't concerned with doing what was right. And what was the result? It was not good, since now you are ashamed of the things you used to do, things that end in eternal doom. But now you are free from the power of sin and have become slaves of God. Now you do those things that lead to holiness and result in eternal life. For the wages of sin is death, but the free gift of God is eternal life through Christ Jesus our Lord. (Romans 6:6–23)

Only Jesus Can Free Us from Sin

Still, Paul testified that he struggled with sin:

> The law is good, then. The trouble is not with the law but with me, because I am sold into slavery, with sin as my master. I don't understand myself at all, for I really want to do what is right, but I don't do it. Instead, I do the very thing I hate. I know perfectly well that what I am doing is wrong, and my bad conscience shows that I agree that the law is good. But I can't help myself, because it is sin inside me that makes me do these evil things.
>
> I know I am rotten through and through so far as my old sinful nature is concerned. No matter which way I turn, I can't make myself do right. I want to, but I can't. When I want to do good, I don't. And when I try not to do wrong, I do it anyway. But if I am doing what I don't want to do, I am not really the one doing it; the sin within me is doing it.
>
> It seems to be a fact of life that when I want to do what is right, I inevitably do what is wrong. I love God's law with all my heart. But there is another law at work within me that is at war with my mind. This law wins the fight and makes me a slave to the sin that is still within me. Oh, what a miserable person I am! Who will free me from this life that is dominated by sin? Thank God! The answer is in Jesus Christ our Lord. So you see how it is: In my mind I really want to obey God's law, but because of my sinful nature I am a slave to sin. (Romans 7:14–25)

Christians should never underestimate the power of our sin nature. There is a constant battle for each and every Christian to resist sin. Do not tolerate any sin, regardless of size and nature. Keep your heart open to God and closed to sin (Satan). Never accumulate sins. Always ask God for forgiveness of our sins so that we may stay away from sins and close to God at all times. Pray as often as needed and ask God's help as necessary.

Returning to Sin

In one of Peter's teachings, he warned about the danger of becoming sin's slave again once a Christian has known God's forgiveness:

> For you are a slave to whatever controls you. And when people escape from the wicked ways of the world by learning about our Lord and Savior Jesus Christ and then get tangled up with sin and become its slave again, they are worse off than before. It would be better if they had never known the right way to live than to know it and then reject the holy commandments that were given to them. They make these proverbs come true: "A dog returns to its vomit," and "A washed pig returns to the mud." (2 Peter 2:19–22)

Once our sins have been cleansed by Jesus, we should live in a new life and depart from our old life. We must do three steps preventing ourselves from going back to our old life:

1. We must read the Holy Bible every day. Without the Word of God in our heart, we are empty!
2. We must maintain close communications with God and pray regularly, at least once each time when waking up in the morning, before meals and before sleeping every night. Ask God's forgiveness of our sins as often as needed.
3. We must invite the Holy Spirit to live inside our heart—all the time.

If shame or something in our mind prevents our communications with God, then we need to confess to God all our problems and wrongdoings until we have nothing in our mind to hide from Him. Let's take the necessary steps now! Don't wait until it is too late!

Paul warned the Jews who turned from Judaism to Christianity not to nail Jesus to the cross again by turning away from God:

> For it is impossible to restore to repentance those who were once enlightened—those who have experienced the good things of heaven and shared in the Holy Spirit, who have tasted the goodness of the word of God and the power of the age to come—and who then turn away from God. It is impossible to bring such people to repentance again because they are nailing the Son of God to the cross again by rejecting him, holding him up to public shame.
>
> When the ground soaks up the rain that falls on it and bears a good crop for the farmer, it has the blessing of God. But if a field bears thistles and thorns, it is useless. The farmer will condemn that field and burn it. (Hebrews 6:4–8)

One of Satan's most powerful weapons is to cast doubts into the minds of Christians (especially those faithful and devoted Christians) about their relationship with God. Sometimes, it seems as we are approaching to a road junction. If we turned to the wrong way, we may risk not being able to return to the right way again.

The best solution is for us to invite the Holy Spirit into our heart by praying to God in Jesus' name. We need to ask Him to tell us the correct and proper way we should take. The Holy Spirit is the Truth. He will show us the right way before we go wrong. That is the reason Jesus warned that all sins can be forgiven except the sin of blasphemy against the Holy Spirit (see Matthew 12:31).

Paul also warned there would be no hope of salvation if we deliberately continue sinning:

> Dear friends, if we deliberately continue sinning after we have received a full knowledge of the truth, there is no other sacrifice that will cover these sins. There will be nothing to look forward to but the terrible expectation of God's judgment and the raging

> fire that will consume his enemies. Anyone who refused to obey the law of Moses was put to death without mercy on the testimony of two or three witnesses. Think how much more terrible the punishment will be for those who have trampled on the Son of God and have treated the blood of the covenant as if it were common and unholy. Such people have insulted and enraged the Holy Spirit who brings God's mercy to his people. For we know the one who said: "I will take vengeance, I will repay those who deserve it." He also said: "The Lord will judge his own people." It is a terrible thing to fall into the hands of the living God. (Hebrews 10:26–31; see also Deuteronomy 32:35–36)

Obey God's Words and Commandments

John, as an elder in the church, wrote to younger Christians to avoid sins by obeying God's commandments:

> My dear children, I am writing this to you so that you will not sin. But if you do sin, there is someone to plead for you before the Father. He is Jesus Christ, the one who pleases God completely. He is the sacrifice for our sins. He takes away not only our sins but the sins of all the world.
>
> And how can we be sure that we belong to him? By obeying his commandments. If someone says, 'I belong to God,' but doesn't obey God's commandments, that person is a liar and does not live in the truth. (1 John 2:1–4)

John said that Christians should avoid the sin by bringing God's Words into their hearts:

> Those who sin are opposed to the law of God, for all sin opposes the law of God. And you know that Jesus came to take away our sins, for there is no sin in him. So if we continue to live in him,

> we won't sin either. But those who keep on sinning have never known him or understood who he is.
>
> Dear children, don't let anyone deceive you about this: When people do what is right, it is because they are righteous, even as Christ is righteous. But when people keep on sinning, it shows they belong to the Devil, who has been sinning since the beginning. But the Son of God came to destroy these works of the Devil. Those who have been born into God's family do not sin, because God's life is in them. So they can't keep on sinning, because they have been born of God. So now we can tell who are children of God and who are children of the Devil. Anyone who does not obey God's commands and does not love other Christians does not belong to God. (1 John 3:4–10)

Responsible for Own Sins

If we work as employees in a large organization, we're judged by our own performances for the purpose of salary adjustments, promotions or terminations. In the relationship between God and man, we have a similar situation: everyone will be judged for one's own performances. God will then determine whether our name should appear in the Book of Life. Christians should always obey God's commandments. In order to stay strong, we must be alert and pray at all times.

Jeremiah prophesied that all people will die for their own sins:

> The people will no longer quote this proverb: "The parents eat sour grapes, but their children's mouths pucker at the taste." All people will die for their own sins—those who eat the sour grapes will be the ones whose mouths will pucker. (Jeremiah 31:29–30, also refer to Ezekiel 18:1–4)

God likes to hear prayers of confessions from each person directly. In particular, He likes to hear from the sinners:

> The word of the Lord came again to me, saying: "Son of man, when a land sins against Me by persistent unfaithfulness, I will stretch out My hand against it; I will cut off its supply of bread, send famine on it, and cut off man and beast from it. Though these three men, Noah, Daniel, and Job, were in it, they would deliver only themselves by their righteousness," says the Lord God. "If I cause wild beasts to pass through the land, and they empty it, and make it so desolate that no man may pass through because of the beasts, even though these three men were in it, as I live," says the Lord God, "they would deliver neither sons nor daughters; only they would be delivered, and the land would be desolate. Or if I bring a sword on that land, and say "sword, go through the land," and I cut off man and beast from it, "even though these three men were in it, as I live," says the Lord God, "they would deliver neither sons nor daughters, but only they themselves would be delivered. Or if I send a pestilence into that land and pour out My fury on it in blood, and cut off from it man and beast, even though Noah, Daniel, and Job were in it, as I live," says the Lord God, "they would deliver neither son nor daughter, they would deliver only themselves by their righteousness." (Ezekiel 14:12–20 NKJV)

Ezekiel prophesied four types of disasters that God used as punishments. Any one of them is sufficient to cause death to man. The four together can represent all the disasters man may suffer if they do not obey God. Only those who demonstrated their own righteousness would be saved. It is a common practice that Christian parents pray for their children regularly. Although God listens to all prayers, parents cannot confess the sins of their children. The children must confess their own sins and they must ask forgiveness for their own sins from God directly. Therefore, no one should rely on others. Everyone should look upon God directly.

Look at the case of Sodom and Gomorrah. Abraham, a righteousness man in the eyes of God, begged God not to destroy Sodom and Gomorrah. He failed, though, as the people in these two cities had committed too many sins without remorse. However, God agreed to save Lot and his family. Lot and his daughters were saved but not his wife, as she did not obey God's instructions completely. When she disobeyed God and turned back to look, she became a salt pillar. (see Genesis 18 and 19)

Warn Others

It's not enough to merely obey God ourselves. God gave an obligation to everyone to warn others about the consequences of their sins:

> If I [God] warn the wicked, saying, "You are under the penalty of death," but you [Ezekiel] fail to deliver the warning, they will die in their sins. And I will hold you responsible, demanding your blood for theirs. If you warn them and they keep on sinning and refuse to repent, they will die in their sins. But you will have saved your life because you did what you were told to do. If good people turn bad and don't listen to my warning, they will die. If you did not warn them of the consequences, then they will die in their sins. Their previous good deeds won't help them, and I will hold you responsible, demanding your blood for theirs. But if you warn them and they repent, they will live, and you will have saved your own life, too. (Ezekiel 3:18–21)

Jesus' brother James pointed out the reward when we help a lost sheep find his way back to the Shepherd: "My dear brothers and sisters, if anyone among you wanders away from the truth and is brought back again, you can be sure that the one who brings that person back will save that sinner from death and bring about the forgiveness of many sins." (James 5:19–20)

Forgive Others

It is important to emphasize at this point: dealing with our own sin also means forgiving others when they sin against us. Part of the prayer Jesus taught His disciples to pray says: "and forgive us our sins, just as we have forgiven those who have sinned against us." (Matthew 6:12)

Why? Because our unforgiveness will keep God from forgiving our own sins. Jesus told His disciples: "If you forgive those who sin against you, your heavenly Father will forgive you. But if you refuse to forgive others, your Father will not forgive your sins." (Matthew 6:14–15)

Jesus told His disciples that no one should set any limit in forgiving others: "Then Peter came to Him [Jesus] and said, 'Lord, how often shall my brother sin against me, and I forgive him? Up to seven times?' Jesus said to him, 'I do not say to you, up to seven times, but up to seventy times seven.'" (Matthew 18:21–22 NKJV)

Although seventy times seven equals four hundred and ninety, Jesus meant to forgive his brother without any limit. Since God did not set any limit in forgiving us, He expects us to follow Him as well.

Paul advised the Christians in Ephesus: "Instead, be kind to each other, tenderhearted, forgiving one another, just as God through Christ has forgiven you." (Ephesians 4:32)

Although there's no restriction on what we should or shouldn't include in our prayers, the most important part of each prayer occurs when we ask God's forgiveness of our sins. But first, before we pray, we should always ask ourselves whether we have forgiven others. Jesus taught His disciples: "But when you are praying, first forgive anyone you are holding a grudge against, so that your Father in heaven will forgive your sins, too." (Mark 11:25)

Luke recorded what Jesus taught His disciples regarding forgiving others: "I am warning you! If another believer sins, rebuke him; then if he repents, forgive him. Even if he wrongs you seven times a day and each time turns again and asks forgiveness, forgive him." (Luke 17:3–4)

Jesus prayed to God the Father to forgive the people who crucified Him: "Jesus said, 'Father, forgive these people, because they don't know what they are doing.'" (Luke 23:34)

Jesus taught His disciples to love their enemies. If we go deeper to define its meaning, we may find wisdom in it. (refer to Matthew 5:38–48)

Let the Holy Spirit Control Our Minds

Paul described clearly how living in the power of the Holy Spirit keeps us from sinning:

> When we were controlled by our old nature, sinful desires were at work within us, and the law aroused these evil desires that produced sinful deeds, resulting in death. But now we have been released from the law, for we died with Christ, and we are no longer captive to its power. Now we can really serve God, not in the old way by obeying the letter of the law, but in the new way, by the Spirit. (Romans 7:5–6)

> So now there is no condemnation for those who belong to Christ Jesus. For the power of the life-giving Spirit has freed you through Christ Jesus from the power of sin that leads to death. The law of Moses could not save us, because of our sinful nature. But God put into effect a different plan to save us. He sent his own Son in a human body like ours, except that ours are sinful. God destroyed sin's control over us by giving his son as a sacrifice for

our sins. He did this so that the requirement of the law would be fully accomplished for us who no longer follow our sinful nature but instead follow the Spirit.

Those who are dominated by the sinful nature think about sinful things, but those who are controlled by the Holy Spirit think about things that please the Spirit. If your sinful nature controls your mind, there is death. But if the Holy Spirit controls your mind, there is life and peace. For the sinful nature is always hostile to God. It never did obey God's laws, it never will. That's why those who are still under the control of their sinful nature can never please God.

But you are not controlled by your sinful nature. You are controlled by the Spirit if you have the Spirit of God living in you. (And remember that those who do not have the Spirit of Christ living in them are not Christians at all.) Since Christ lives within you, even though your body will die because of sin, your spirit is alive because you have been made right with God. The spirit of God, who raised Jesus from the dead, lives in you. And just as he raised Christ from the dead, he will give life to your mortal body by this same Spirit living within you.

So, dear brothers and sisters, you have no obligation whatsoever to do what your sinful nature urges you to do. For if you keep on following it, you will perish. But if through the power of the Holy Spirit you turn from it and its evil deeds, you will live. For all who are led by the Spirit of God are children of God. (Romans 8:1–14)

"Thank you, Father, for giving us the power over sin through the Holy Spirit!"

chapter eleven

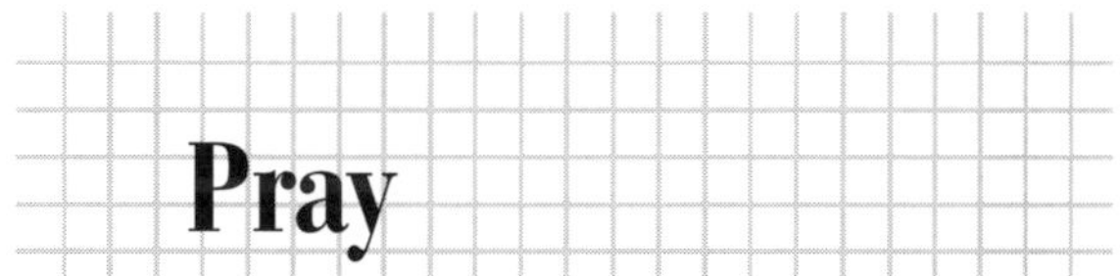

Pray

God made David a king from a shepherd boy. He remained in power for forty years. Without exception, for many times in his life, he experienced both physical and spiritual weaknesses like any other man. The difference between King David and others was that he always gained power from God through his prayers.

Regardless whether his enemies were foreign powers or his own family members, he did not fight his battles alone. He always relied on God's company.

In his prayers, he was humble and willing to confess his sins. He always gave praise and glory to God. Therefore, whenever he prayed to God for help, God did not ignore him. Many of his prayers can be found in the Psalms.

One of the most important criteria which may lead us to eternal life is our faith. Jesus said: "Only those who endure to the end will be saved." (Matthew 10:22) It is not easy for us to endure to the end unless we have strong faith. Faith comes out from trust. We cannot have trust if we do not believe. We do not believe if we have not heard or seen it. If we still haven't seen or heard about it, we must ask for it. Therefore, let us all pray God to give us the wisdom to know Him so that we can build up our faith.

God Strengthens Our Faith

Sometimes God does something to us we do not understand. One question that came to my mind recently concerned the relationship between God and my mother. She had been faithful to God all her life. She had never stopped spreading the Gospel, praying for others, and making testimonies for God. When her eyesight was left with less than one percent, due to advanced glaucoma in the last three years of her life, she still managed to complete her "Summary of Memories," documenting God's miracles given her in the past.

Since she was diagnosed with a gastric cancer and knew her days were numbered, she spent more time spreading the Gospel to others. Although we also prayed for the healing of her sicknesses, she was not healed. God let her live 15 months instead of three to six months as her doctor predicted. In the last three weeks of her life, she could not accept any food or drink while she was suffering from severe pain, thirst and agony. It gave me the impression that the torture she experienced was worse than any punishment I could imagine!

About one week before my mother left us, I had a question: *Why would God allow my mother to have such sickness and to suffer for such a long time?* She did not deserve this! On the same day, the Holy Spirit reminded me the case of a man who was blind from birth. Jesus told His disciples: "He was born blind so the power of God could be seen in him." (John 9:3) The Holy Spirit also reminded me of this: "Much is required from those to whom much is given, and much more is required from those to whom much more is given." (Luke 12:48) And this: "Don't be afraid of those who want to kill you. They can only kill your body; they cannot touch your soul. Fear only God, who can destroy both soul and body in hell." (Matthew 10:28) And last, I was reminded: "Remain faithful even when facing death, and I will give you the crown of life." (Revelation 2:10)

Then I realized that God was giving us, the younger generations, a lesson for our faith. When I trusted that God would reward my mother with the crown of life in the New Jerusalem one day, I felt proud of my mother and gave all the glory to God.

A Model Prayer

We may learn from King David in the structure of his prayer: "O Lord, you are so good, so ready to forgive, so full of unfailing love for all who ask your aid. Listen closely to my prayer, O Lord; hear my urgent cry. I will call to you whenever trouble strikes, and you will answer me." (Psalm 86:5–7)

- David, first of all, asked forgiveness from God.
- Secondly, he praised God so that he believed God would listen to his prayer closely.
- Thirdly, he showed God that he was so desperate and earnest.
- Finally, he showed his faith in God and was fully confided of God's response.

Unload Our Burdens to God in Prayers

As long as we live in this world, we cannot avoid problems, weariness and burdens, because it's not our permanent residence. That is why God sent Jesus to us so that we may overcome the world and be rewarded with eternal life in the New Jerusalem. As Christians, we should unload all our spiritual burdens to Jesus.

Spiritual burdens are confined to this world only. We did not carry them here when we were born, nor we may carry them away with us when we die. They are merely another "local produce" of this world. Burdens will remain in this world until this world fades away. Since we do not belong to this world just as Jesus does not, then we have no obligation whatsoever to carry these burdens. We only need to trust Jesus. "Then Jesus said, 'Come to me, all of you who are weary and carry heavy burdens, and I will give you rest.'" (Matthew 11:28)

God's commandments are not difficult to keep because Jesus is willing to carry all our heavy burdens. For this reason, Jesus told His disciples: "For My yoke is easy, and My burden is light." (Matthew 11:30 NKJV)

Pray for Each Other

It is important for Christians to get together. Together, we can praise God, share the experiences of each other, comfort and pray for each other when sick or weak both physically and spiritually. In addition, we have an added bonus from God, because Jesus promised to be among us when we gather together. With Jesus among us, we shall have God's super power. That is why Christians must gather together and go to church on a regular basis. Jesus told His disciples: "I also tell you this: 'If two of you agree down here on earth concerning anything you ask, my Father in heaven will do it for you. For where two or three gather together because they are mine, I am there among them.'" (Matthew 18:19–20)

Be Persistent

He told His disciples to have faith in God: "If you believe, you will receive whatever you ask for in prayer." (Matthew 21:22; also see Mark 11:24)

Jesus told a story to His disciples regarding a man asking his friend to lend him three loaves of bread at midnight:

> And He said to them, "which of you shall have a friend, and go to him at midnight and say to him, 'friend, lend me three loaves; for a friend of mine has come to me on his journey, and I have nothing to set before him'; and he will answer from within and say, 'Do not trouble me; the door is now shut, and my children are with me in bed; I cannot rise and give to you'"?
>
> "I say to you, though he will not rise and give to him because he is his friend, yet because of his persistence he will rise and give him as many as he needs. And I say to you, ask, and it will be given to you; seek, and you will find; knock, and it will be opened to you. For everyone who asks receives, and he who seeks finds, and to him who knocks it will be opened. If a son asks for bread from any father among you, will he give him a stone? Or if he asks for a fish, will he give him a serpent instead of a fish? Or if he asks for an egg, will he offer him a scorpion? If you then, being evil, know how to give good gifts to your children, how much more will your heavenly Father give the Holy Spirit to those who ask Him!" (Luke 11:5–13 NKJV)

If our prayer has not been answered by God, we should not be disappointed, but continue to pray with faith, and we will be given:

> One day Jesus told his disciples a story to illustrate their need for constant prayer and to show them that they must never give up. "There was a judge in a certain city," he said, "who was a godless man with great contempt for everyone. A widow of that city came to him repeatedly, appealing for justice against someone who had harmed her. The judge ignored her for a while, but eventually she wore him out. 'I fear neither God nor man,' he

> said to himself, 'but this woman is driving me crazy. I'm going to see that she gets justice, because she is wearing me out with her constant requests!'"
>
> Then the Lord said, "Learn a lesson from this evil judge. Even he rendered a just decision in the end, so don't you think God will surely give justice to his chosen people who plead with him day and night? Will he keep putting them off? I tell you, he will grant justice to them quickly! But when I, the Son of Man, return, how many will I find who have faith?" (Luke 18:1–8)

"Ask Anything in My Name, and I Will Do It"

Jesus told His disciples there would be power with no limit if they believed in Him:

> The truth is, anyone who believes in me will do the same works I have done, and even greater works, because I am going to be with the Father. You can ask for anything in my name, and I will do it, because the work of the Son brings glory to the Father. Yes, ask anything in my name, and I will do it! (John 14:12–14)

If the power comes from God, there is no limit. Jesus is God. He is the Father (see Isaiah 9:6 and John 10:30). Jesus said twice "I will do it!" The Resurrected Jesus can bring more power to His believers as He had been a man carrying flesh and blood. He knows the burdens, problems and weakness of man. As such, He can give us more than we asked for. We only need to believe in Him.

Pray About Everything

There is nothing we cannot tell God. In fact, God likes to hear prayers from those who are straightforward and who do not like to cut corners. In a letter Apostle Paul sent to the Christians in Philippi, he explained: "Don't worry about anything; instead, pray about everything. Tell God what you need, and thank him for all he has done." (Philippians 4:6)

James, the younger brother of Jesus, emphasized the importance of faith and how to pray for others among Christians:

> Are any among you sick? They should call for the elders of the church and have them pray over them, anointing them with oil in the name of the Lord. And their prayer offered in faith will heal the sick, and the Lord will make them well. And anyone who has committed sins will be forgiven. Confess your sins to each other and pray for each other so that you may be healed. The earnest prayer of a righteous person has great power and wonderful results. Elijah was as human as we are, and yet when he prayed earnestly that no rain would fall, none fell for the next three and a half years! Then he prayed for rain, and down it poured. The grass turned green, and the crops began to grow again. (James 5:14–18)

God Will Give Us More Than We Prayed for

God likes to hear humble prayers, but not greedy demands. King Solomon prayed in his dreams. His prayer was answered. God gave him not only wisdom as he asked, but also riches and honor. (For details refer to 1 Kings 3:5–13) King Solomon also prayed about his people. God accepted his prayer and granted him what he had been praying for. (For details refer to 1 Kings 8:22–53 and 9:2–3.)

Whenever we pray, we should think of David's recommendation to "call on Him sincerely:"

> The Lord is righteous in everything he does; he is filled with kindness. The Lord is close to all who call on him, yes, to all who call on him sincerely. He fulfills the desires of those who fear him; he hears their cries for help and rescues them. The

> Lord protects all those who love him, but he destroys the wicked. I will praise the Lord, and everyone on earth will bless his holy name forever and forever. (Psalms 145:17–21)

Don't Pray with a Doubtful Mind

James pointed out that a doubtful mind should not expect God's response:

> If you need wisdom–if you want to know what God wants you to do—ask him, and he will gladly tell you. He will not resent your asking. But when you ask him, be sure that you really expect him to answer, for a doubtful mind is as unsettled as a wave of the sea that is driven and tossed by the wind. People like that should not expect to receive anything from the Lord. (James 1:5–7)

God hears earnest and disciplined prayers. He does not like people doing evil. The apostle Peter warned the Christians: "The eyes of the Lord watch over those who do right, and his ears are open to their prayers. But the Lord turns his face against those who do evil." (1 Peter 3:12) He further advised: "The end of the world is coming soon. Therefore, be earnest and disciplined in your prayers." (1 Peter 4:7)

Direct Communications

Praying is the most important "direct communication" between man and God. It is like a free cellular telephone God gives us so that we may call Him any time we wish. Of course, there is an unique exception: God's line will never have a busy signal and it is readily available at all times. Neither battery recharge nor repair work will ever be needed.

Over the past year, whenever I suggested to one of my brothers that he should have daily prayer with his family, I always heard the same reply from him: "My brother, I do confess to God every night!"

Prayers are not restricted to confessions alone. In fact, we can say whatever we wish in our prayers. In Mark 11:24, Jesus told His disciples: "Listen to me! You can pray for anything, and if you believe, you will have it."

Praying Guidelines

Prayers should include, but are not limited to the following:

- Praising God
- Worshiping God
- Confessing our sins and asking God to forgive
- Asking for God's healing for others and ourselves
- Telling God our problems and requesting His help
- Releasing all our burdens to God
- Inviting God (the Holy Spirit) to live within us

We should always remember to pray for others first. As we pray for others, God grants His mercy to us.

In addition to the Psalms, there are several prayers in the Holy Bible we should read and keep in mind:

1. King David's Prayer : 1 Chronicles 17:16–27
2. King Solomon's Dream Prayer: 1 Kings 3:4–14
3. King Solomon's Prayer: 1 Kings 8:22–61
4. God's answer to King Solomon: 1 Kings 9:1–9
5. Jesus' Prayer: John 17

Lift Hands When Worshipping God

In speaking of prayer, I wish to share my experiences with you on the practice of raising hands in prayer. Whenever I raised both my hands high in worshiping God, I can feel the Holy Spirit much stronger in me instantly. I can gain total concentration by doing so. I also can feel a direct contact, no barrier, just between God and myself. I feel I have spoken everything I need to tell God with all my heart and without any reservation. I can also gain the feeling as if my messages have been well received by God.

Praying with hands raised are mentioned in the Holy Bible many times. It means to pray whole hearted, obedient to God, offering God all the glory, reaching God and getting His blessings. Under two occasions God responded to the prayers favorably when Moses and King Solomon prayed with their hands raised. God sends His power through the Holy Spirit to those who raised their hands with total devotion. The following is a list of examples:

> "All right," Moses replied. "As soon as I leave the city, I will lift my hands and pray to the Lord. Then the thunder and hail will stop. This will prove to you that the earth belongs to the Lord." (Exodus 9:29)

> So Moses left Pharaoh and went out of the city. As he lifted his hands to the Lord, all at once the thunder and hail stopped, and the downpour ceased. (Exodus 9:33)

> Then Solomon stood with his hands lifted toward heaven before the altar of the Lord in front of the entire community of Israel. He prayed... (1 Kings 8:22)

> At the time of the sacrifice, I stood up from where I had sat in mourning with my clothes torn. I fell to my knees, lifted my hands to the Lord my God. I prayed . . . (Ezra 9:5)

> Listen to my prayer for mercy as I cry out to you for help, as I lift my hands toward your holy sanctuary. (Psalm 28:2)

> I will honor you as long as I live, lifting up my hands to you in prayer. (Psalm 63:4)

I cry out to God without holding back. Oh, that God would listen to me! When I was in deep trouble, I searched for the Lord. All night long I pray, with hands lifted toward heaven, pleading. There can be no joy for me until he acts. (Psalm 77:1–2)

My eyes are blinded by my tears. Each day I beg for your help, O Lord; I lift my pleading hands to you for mercy. (Psalm 88:9)

Lift your hands in holiness, and bless the Lord. (Psalm 134:2)

Accept my prayer as incense offered to you, and my upraised hands as an evening offering. (Psalm 141:2)

I spread out my hands to you; My soul longs for You like a thirsty land. (Psalm 143:6)

From now on, when you lift up your hands in prayer, I will refuse to look. Even though you offer many prayers, I will not listen. For your hands are covered with the blood of your innocent victims. (Isaiah 1:15)

Rise during the night and cry out. Pour out your hearts like water to the Lord. Lift up your hands to him in prayer. Plead for your children as they faint with hunger in the streets. (Lamentations 2:19)

Let us lift our hearts and hands to God in heaven and say… (Lamentations 3:41)

So wherever you assemble, I want men to pray with holy hands lifted up to God, free from anger and controversy. (1 Timothy 2:8)

It is important when we worship God, to worship Him wholly from our heart, not partially. Hence, whenever we feel need to raise our hands in prayers or worship, make sure to raise both hands, not a single hand. We may see from all the above examples that both hands were raised when praying.

How to Pray

Jesus taught His disciples how to pray:

> And now about prayer. When you pray, don't be like the hypocrites who love to pray publicly on street corners and in the synagogues where everyone can see them. I assure you, that is all the reward they will ever get. But when you pray, go away by yourself, shut the door behind you, and pray to your Father secretly. Then your Father, who knows all secrets, will reward you.
>
> When you pray, don't babble on and on as people of other religions do. They think their prayers are answered only by repeating their words again and again. Don't be like them, because your Father knows exactly what you need even before you ask him! Pray like this:
>
> Our Father in heaven, may your name be honored. May your Kingdom come soon. May your will be done here on earth, just as it is in heaven. Give us our food for today, and forgive us our sins, just as we have forgiven those who have sinned against us. And don't let us yield to temptation, but deliver us from the evil one.
>
> If you forgive those who sin against you, your heavenly Father will forgive you. But if you refuse to forgive others, your Father will not forgive your sins. (Matthew 6:5–15; see also Luke 11:2–4)

Remember, it is always the top priority in each prayer that we confess our sins and ask for God's forgiveness first, before we pray for anything else:

> Come and listen, all you who fear God, and I will tell you what he did for me. For I cried out to him for help, praising him as I spoke. If I had not confessed the sin in my heart, my Lord would not have listened. But God did listen! He paid attention to my prayer. Praise God, who did not ignore my prayer and did not withdraw his unfailing love from me. (Psalm 66:16–20)

We cannot see our own sins without being humble. We cannot get close to God unless we are humble:

> Then Jesus told this story to some who had great self-confidence and scorned everyone else: "Two men went to the Temple to pray. One was a Pharisee, and the other was a dishonest tax collector. The proud Pharisee stood by himself and prayed this prayer: 'I thank you, God, that I am not a sinner like everyone else, especially like that tax collector over there! For I never cheat, I don't sin, I don't commit adultery, I fast twice a week, and I give you a tenth of my income.'
>
> "But the tax collector stood at a distance and dared not even lift his eyes to heaven as he prayed. Instead, he beat his chest in sorrow, saying, 'O God, be merciful to me, for I am a sinner.' I tell you, this sinner, not the Pharisee, returned home justified before God. For the proud will be humbled, but the humble will be honored." (Luke 18:9–14)

When we are praying alone, praying in tongues will certainly strengthen our faith. However, when we pray with others, we should avoid praying in tongues. Paul explained the reason:

> For if I pray in tongues, my spirit is praying, but I don't understand what I am saying. Well then, what shall I do? I will do both. I will pray in the spirit, and I will pray in words I understand.

> I will sing in the spirit, and I will sing in words I understand. For if you praise God only in the spirit, how can those who don't understand you praise God along with you? How can they join you in giving thanks when they don't understand what you are saying? (1 Corinthians 14:14–16)

Power

Jesus showed His disciples the power from God when praying. God let the disciples see the Kingdom of God when Jesus prayed. Jesus said: "And I assure you that some of you standing here right now will not die before you see the Kingdom of God" (Matthew 16:28).

> About eight days later Jesus took Peter, James, and John to a mountain to pray. And as he was praying, the appearance of his face changed, and his clothing became dazzling white . . . (Luke 9:28–29; also see Matthew 17:1–8)

Jesus raised Lazarus from the dead after He prayed:

> So they rolled the stone aside. Then Jesus looked up to heaven and said, "Father, thank you for hearing me. You always hear me, but I said it out loud for the sake of all these people standing here, so they will believe you sent me." Then Jesus shouted, "Lazarus, come out!" And Lazarus came out, bound in graveclothes, his face wrapped in a headcloth. Jesus told them, "Unwrap him and let him go!" (John 11:41–44)

By prayer, the apostle Peter raised a woman from the dead after the resurrection of Jesus:

> There was a believer in Joppa named Tabitha (which in Greek is Dorcas). She was always doing kind things for others and

> helping the poor. About this time she became ill and died. Her friends prepared her for burial and laid her in an upstairs room. But they had heard that Peter was nearby at Lydda, so they sent two men to beg him, "Please come as soon as possible!"
>
> So Peter returned with them; and as soon as he arrived, they took him to the upstairs room. The room was filled with widows who were weeping and showing him the coats and other garments Dorcas had made for them. But Peter asked them all to leave the room; *then he knelt and prayed*. Turning to the body he said, "Get up, Tabitha." And she opened her eyes! When she saw Peter, she sat up! He gave her his hand and helped her up. Then he called in the widows and all the believers, and he showed them that she was alive. (Acts 9:36–41; *emphasis added*)

God is happy when listening to our prayers for others. The prayers from many do convince God to respond more promptly. This is an example for the need to pray for others:

> But while Peter was in prison, the church prayed very earnestly for him. The night before Peter was to be placed on trial, he was asleep, chained between two soldiers, with others standing guard at the prison gate. Suddenly, there was a bright light in the cell, and an angel of the Lord stood before Peter. The angel tapped him on the side to awaken him and said, "Quick! Get up!" And the chains fell off his wrists. Then the angel told him, "Get dressed and put on your sandals." And he did. "Now put on your coat and follow me," the angel ordered.
>
> So Peter left the cell, following the angel. But all the time he thought it was a vision. He didn't realize it was really happening. They passed the first and second guard posts and came to the iron gate to the street, and this opened to them all by itself.

> So they passed through and started walking down the street, and then the angel suddenly left him.
>
> Peter finally realized what had happened. 'It's really true!' he said to himself. 'The Lord has sent his angel and saved me from Herod and from what the Jews were hoping to do to me!' (Acts 12:5–11)

Pray Patiently Alone

It definitely strengthens one's spiritual life when one prays alone in a quiet place. It may enable one to gain concentration, devotion, focus, and the feeling of getting closer to God. If we have not received God's response to our prayers, we must be patient and pray again. God likes people to have patience.

On many occasions, Jesus was found praying alone at a quiet place. His disciples followed His example! A few samples are taken from the New Testament in the sequence of the Holy Bible:

> Afterward he went up into the hills by himself to pray. (Matthew 14:23)
>
> Then Jesus brought them to an olive grove called Gethsemane, and he said, "Sit here while I go on ahead to pray." (Matthew 26:36)
>
> The next morning Jesus awoke long before daybreak and went out alone into the wilderness to pray. (Mark 1:35)
>
> Immediately after this, Jesus made his disciples get back into the boat and head out across the lake to Bethsaida, while he sent the people home. Afterward he went up into the hills by himself to pray. (Mark 6:45–46)

> But Jesus often withdrew to the wilderness for prayer. (Luke 5:16)

> One day soon afterward Jesus went to a mountain to pray, and he prayed to God all night. (Luke 6:12)

> One day as Jesus was alone, praying, he came over to his disciples and asked them, "Who do people say I am?" (Luke 9:18)

> Once when Jesus had been out praying, one of his disciples came to him as he finished and said, "Lord, teach us to pray, just as John taught his disciples." (Luke 11:1)

> Then, accompanied by the disciples, Jesus left the upstairs room and went as usual to the Mount of Olives. There he told them, "Pray that you will not be overcome by temptation." He walked away, about a stone's throw, and knelt down and prayed. (Luke 22:39–41)

> The next day as Cornelius's messengers were nearing the city, Peter went up to the flat roof to pray. (Acts 10:9)

"Keep on Praying"

In a letter the apostle Paul sent to the church in Thessalonica, he encouraged them:

> Always be joyful. Keep on Praying. No matter what happens, always be thankful, for this is God's will for you who belong to Christ Jesus. (1 Thessalonians 5:16–18)

James, a younger brother of Jesus, also encouraged Christians to "keep on praying" and "praise God."

> Are any among you suffering? They should keep on praying about it. And those who have reason to be thankful should continually sing praises to the Lord. (James 5:13)

Timothy was a close and young associate of Paul. He experienced heavy burdens when he became the pastor of a church in Ephesus. Paul was concerned about his situation and gave him a lot of recommendations, including a recommendation to pray for "all people."

> I urge you, first of all, to pray for all people. As you make your requests, plead for God's mercy upon them, and give thanks. Pray this way for kings and all others who are in authority, so that we can live in peace and quietness, in godliness and dignity. This is good and pleases God our Savior, for he wants everyone to be saved and to understand the truth. For there is only one God and one Mediator who can reconcile God and People. He is the man Christ Jesus. (1 Timothy 2:1–5)

Pray in Line with God's Will

The apostle John (at about 80 years of age) gave encouragement to the younger generation Christians so that they might have confidence in their prayers:

> And we can be confident that he will listen to us whenever we ask him for anything in line with his will. And if we know he is listening when we make our requests, we can be sure that he will give us what we ask for. (1 John 5:14–15)

Be Alert and Pray to Overcome the Weakness in the Flesh

Jesus told His disciples to keep alert and pray in the night before His crucifixion: "Keep alert and pray. Otherwise temptation will overpower you. For though the spirit is willing enough, the body is weak!" (Matthew 26:41; also see Mark 14:38) The disciples failed to keep alert and pray as they went to sleep—a weakness of the body. Perhaps the young apostle John was the only disciple who did not fall into sleep, and he heard the prayer of Jesus.

Immediately following the arrest of Jesus, the disciples either ran away or stayed far away from Jesus. Their physical and spiritual weaknesses were mainly caused by their failing to keep alert and pray as Jesus instructed them. Satan is watching us on our weakness. We are weak whenever our hearts are empty. We need the words of God and the Holy Spirit to fill in our hearts at all times so that Satan will have no chance to come in. The Holy Spirit will only come to us when we pray and invite Him.

Luke documented what Jesus prayed the night before His arrest:

> There he told them, "Pray that you will not be overcome by temptation."
>
> He walked away, about a stone's throw, and knelt down and prayed, "Father, if you are willing, please take this cup of suffering away from me. Yet I want your will, not mine."
>
> Then an angel from heaven appeared and strengthened him. He prayed more fervently, and he was in such agony of spirit that his sweat fell to the ground like great drops of blood. At last he stood up again and returned to the disciples, only to find them asleep, exhausted from grief. "Why are you sleeping?" he asked. "Get up and pray. Otherwise temptation will overpower you." (Luke 22:40–46)

Our body of flesh and blood can cause weakness in our spiritual life. Jesus knew very well that His mission from God the Father was to suffer and die for the sin of all mankind. However, He asked

God the Father: "If you are willing, please take this cup of suffering away from me." At that moment, Jesus carried a body of flesh and blood as He was a man. However, He did set up a good example for us to follow—He obeyed God the Father completely.

Fasting

> Then Jesus was led out into the wilderness by the Holy Spirit to be tempted there by the Devil. For forty days and forty nights he ate nothing and became very hungry . . . (Matthew 4:1–2)

When we fast and pray, we may gain both devotion and concentration. The Spirit becomes stronger and the body becomes weak. To fast is a decision we make when we are aiming to get closer to God. There is no need to tell others you're fasting or to fast to please others. Matthew documented what Jesus told His disciples regarding fasting:

> And when you fast, don't make it obvious, as the hypocrites do, who try to look pale and disheveled so people will admire them for their fasting. I assure you, that is the only reward they will ever get. But when you fast, comb your hair and wash your face. Then no one will suspect you are fasting, except your Father, who knows what you do in secret. And your Father, who knows all secrets, will reward you. (Matthew 6:16–18)

Greater faith can also come from the devotion achieved by fasting.

> Afterward the disciples asked Jesus privately, "Why couldn't we cast out that demon?"

"You didn't have enough faith," Jesus told them. "I assure you, even if you had faith as small as a mustard seed you could say to this mountain, 'move from here to there,' and it would move. Nothing would be impossible. But this kind of demon won't leave unless you have prayed and fasted." (Matthew 17:19–21)

"Father, thank you for the privileges you give us when we pray."

chapter twelve

Spread the Gospel

It is the duty of every Christian to spread the Gospel, to testify how Jesus has changed our lives. This "Great Commission" comes from Jesus Himself, after His resurrection:

> Jesus came and told his disciples, "I have been given complete authority in heaven and on earth. Therefore, go and make disciples of all the nations, baptizing them in the name of the Father and the Son and the Holy Spirit. Teach these new disciples to obey all the commands I have given you. And be sure of this: I am with you always, even to the end of the age." (Matthew 28:18–20)

But how do we do it? Jesus gave the key in that scripture, when He said, "I am with you always." A Christian can only be a successful witness by employing the resources of the Word and the Spirit.

"Preach the Good News to Everyone, Everywhere"

The Resurrected Jesus urged His disciples to preach the Good News to everyone, everywhere:

> And then he told them, "Go into all the world and preach the good news to everyone, everywhere. Anyone who believes and is baptized will be saved. But anyone who refuses to believe will be condemned. These signs will accompany those who believe: They will cast out demons in my name, and they will speak new languages. They will be able to handle snakes with safety, and if they drink anything poisonous, it won't hurt them. They will be able to place their hands on the sick and heal them." (Mark 16:15–18)

Jesus told His disciples to make new disciples. He also promised them miracles would accompany those who believe. Believing is important to everyone, including the disciples of Jesus.

A successful witness must have an adequate knowledge of God's Word. As the Bread of Life, it can give us both the energy and spiritual life. We also need the Living Water of the Holy Spirit, which Jesus gives us free of charge. With the presence of the Holy Spirit we can understand the meanings of God's words. If we do not have a minimum knowledge of God's Word, the Holy Spirit will not be able to remind us in a critical moment when we are badly in need of God's help.

All of us must understand—going to church once a week is definitely insufficient to acquire a good knowledge of God's Word! Ideally, each Christian should spend at least three hours every week learn the Word. Although I have been a Christian since I was born, I only started to study the Holy Bible on a regular basis a few years ago. Within such a short period of time, I found that the Holy Bible is in fact a treasure. The more I read it the more new knowledge and interest I gain.

Giving Up Everything?

Great crowds were following Jesus. He turned around and said to them:

> "If you want to be my follower you must love me more than your own father and mother, wife and children, brothers and sisters—yes, more than your own life. Otherwise, you cannot be my disciple. And you cannot be my disciple if you do not carry your own cross and follow me." (Luke 14:25–27)

> "So no one can become my disciple without giving up everything for me." (Luke 14:33)

In about 1988, a Korean gentleman told me that his hair turned white overnight when his wife left him and joined an evangelistic team. She decided to follow Jesus and gave up her husband and their young daughter. This man felt lonely and disappointed. He has been an alcoholic ever since.

To become a disciple of Jesus and to follow Him does not necessarily mean one must leave his/her family physically. The important issue is whether one has put God in the first position within his/her heart. "For the righteous God tests the hearts and minds." (Psalm 7:9) Here are some ways one can feel that God becomes number one in his/her heart:

1. Whenever there is a disagreement between one and his/her family member(s), one should always rely on the Holy Bible and the Words of God, and
2. Whenever one is worshipping God, he/she can put aside all his/her wealth, relatives and any other possessions, so that one can feel there is no barrier between God and himself/herself.

"Carry your own cross" means that one must not do what the world or Satan tells him/her to do. Instead, he/she should only obey God's commands. All Christians should follow the steps of Jesus for his faith and obedience to God the Father completely.

It is not easy for one to overcome himself/herself by using his/her own strength. However, when one admits to God that he/she is a sinner and asks for His forgiveness, at this moment, he/she crucifies his/her "old-self" on the cross and puts an end to his/her sinful behaviors. Meantime, he/she should invite the Holy Spirit into his/her heart. He/she will then have the wisdom, strength and courage to follow the way provided by Jesus to eternal life.

True Disciples Produce Fruit

But what happens to us if we disobey Jesus and refuse to tell others of our faith? The illustration Jesus gave His Disciples applies to every believer:

> I [Jesus] am the true vine, and my Father is the gardener. He cuts off every branch that doesn't produce fruit, and he prunes the branches that do bear fruit so they will produce even more. You have already been pruned for greater fruitfulness by the message I have given you. Remain in me, and I will remain in you. For a branch cannot produce fruit if it is severed from the vine, and you cannot be fruitful apart from me.
>
> Yes, I am the vine; you are the branches. Those who remain in me, and I in them, will produce much fruit. For apart from me you can do nothing. Anyone who parts from me is thrown away like a useless branch and withers. Such branches are gathered into a pile to be burned. But if you stay joined to me and my words remain in you, you may ask any request you like, and it will be granted! My true disciples produce much fruit. This brings great glory to my Father. (John 15:1–8)

We must not be lazy in doing God's work! We must spread the Gospel or be pruned like a dead branch. Every Christian has the duty to bring in as many new believers as possible—to produce much fruit. Every Christian needs to produce fruit in order not to be cut off.

The only way we know whether a fruit will last is that the tree has a strong root and it penetrated deeply into the good soil. It needs continued patience and effort to bring the new believers into a deeper knowledge of God's words. Continued coaching may be necessary in addition to teaching and preaching. Once a new believer can stand on his/her own feet, then he/she should be encouraged to preach the Good News to others. While preaching to others, the preacher may also learn more at the same time.

But always remember that we are producing fruit under the power of the Holy Spirit, not our own power. Jesus told His disciples: "You didn't choose me. I chose you. I appointed you to go and produce fruit that will last, so that the Father will give you whatever you ask for, using my name." (John 15:16)

In Paul's second letter to the church in Thessalonica, he highlighted the issue that the call to salvation always comes from God through us: "He [God] called you to salvation when we told you the Good News; now you can share in the glory of our Lord Jesus Christ." (2 Thessalonians 2:14)

Assembling

It is important for all Christians to attend church services and gather together on a regular basis as recommended by the apostle Paul:

> "Not forsaking the assembling of ourselves together, as is the manner of some, but exhorting one another, and so much the more as you see the day approaching." (Hebrews 10:25 NKJV)

It is more important for Christians to go to church regularly than it is for students to go to school and parents to go to work regularly. By meeting other Christians, we may:

- Worship God in a way which cannot be achieved otherwise. An atmosphere of marching forward, not backwards or sideways,
- Strengthen our own faith by worshipping together,
- Learn more about God from others,
- Help and pray for others so that God will bless us,
- Bring children closer to God and prevent them from going the wrong way, and
- Receive "help" from others when we are in need.

Jesus told His disciples: "For where two or three gather together in my name, I am there among them." (Matthew 18:20)

What Should We Preach?

The guideline for preaching is to use the Holy Bible and the testimonies of the believers. The target of each preacher is to maximize the believers in Jesus so that the Master will be glorified.

Repentance

The first step is repentance. Before Jesus started to preach, John the Baptist was preparing the way for Jesus. The main effort John made was to tell people to repent and to confess their sins. At the very beginning of Jesus preaching, He started his preaching by telling people to repent: "From that time Jesus began to preach and to say, 'Repent, for the kingdom of heaven is at hand.'" (Matthew 4:17 NKJV) If there is no repentance, there is no need to confess sins. Without repentance and confession, our sins have not been washed away; instead they are being accumulated. There is no hope for eternal life. That is the reason why the Resurrected Jesus is still instructing His disciples to preach about the message of repentance. (see Luke 24:47–48 below)

Repentance is so important in the life of a Christian. Jesus emphasized the need to repent many times from the beginning to the end in the New Testament (especially in the Book of Revelation):

> I have not come to call the righteous, but sinners, to repentance. (Luke 5:32 NKJV)

> I say to you that likewise there will be more joy in heaven over one sinner who repents than over ninety-nine just persons who need no repentance. (Luke 15:7 NKJV)

> Likewise, I say to you, there is joy in the presence of the angels of God over one sinner who repents. (Luke 15:10 NKJV)

> . . . and that repentance and remission of sins should be preached in His name to all nations, beginning at Jerusalem. (Luke 24:47 NKJV)

> Remember therefore from where you have fallen; repent and do the first works, or else I will come to you quickly and remove your lampstand from its place–unless you repent. (Revelation 2:5 NKJV)

> Repent, or else I will come to you quickly and will fight against them with the sword of My mouth. (Revelation 2:16 NKJV)

> And I gave her time to repent of her sexual immorality, and she did not repent. Indeed, I will cast her into a sickbed, and those who commit adultery with her into great tribulation, unless they repent of their deeds. (Revelation 2:21– 22 NKJV)

Remember therefore how you have received and heard; hold fast and repent. Therefore if you will not watch, I will come upon you as a thief, and you will not know what hour I will come upon you. (Revelation 3:3 NKJV)

As many as I love, I rebuke and chasten. Therefore be zealous and repent. (Revelation 3:19 NKJV)

Jesus told his disciples after his resurrection: "With my authority, take this message of repentance to all the nations, beginning in Jerusalem: 'There is forgiveness of sins for all who turn to me.' You are witnesses of all these things." (Luke 24:47–48).

Why Is It So Important to Preach to the Jews?

The original mission of Jesus was to spread the Gospel to the Jews. Why have more Gentiles benefited than the Jews?

Jesus sent the twelve disciples out with these instructions: "Don't go to the Gentiles or the Samaritans, but only to the people of Israel–God's lost sheep. Go and announce to them that the Kingdom of Heaven is near. Heal the sick, raise the dead, cure those with leprosy, and cast out demons. Give as freely as you have received!

Don't take any money with you. Don't carry a traveler's bag with an extra coat and sandals or even a walking stick. Don't hesitate to accept hospitality, because those who work deserve to be fed. Whenever you enter a city or village, search for a worthy man and stay in his home until you leave for the next town. When you are invited into someone's home, give it your blessing. If it turns out to be a worthy home, let your blessing stand; if it is not, take back the blessing. If a village doesn't welcome you or listen to you, shake off the dust of that place from your feet as you leave. I assure you the wicked cities of Sodom and Gomorrah will be better off on the judgment day than that place will be." (Matthew 10:5–15)

The original mission of Jesus was to help the people of Israel—God's lost sheep—not the Gentiles. (see Matthew 15:24) However, the people of Israel refused to accept Him. It was only after His resurrection that He told apostles Peter and Paul to preach to the Gentiles (see Acts 9, 10, 11, and 13). In the Book of Acts, Luke wrote:

> Then Paul and Barnabas spoke out boldly and declared, "It was necessary that this Good News from God be given first to you Jews. But since you have rejected it and judged yourselves unworthy of eternal life–well, we will offer it to Gentiles. For this is as the Lord commanded us when he said: 'I have made you a light to the Gentiles, to bring salvation to the farthest corners of the earth.'" (Acts 13:46–47)

Today, the time has come for all the Jews to open their eyes and ears as God has removed the obstacles to seeing and hearing. Would you also preach to the Jews?

The Smallest of All Seeds

It is the Gospel that leads more people to the Kingdom of Heaven! Here is another illustration Jesus used:

> The Kingdom of Heaven is like a mustard seed planted in a field. It is the smallest of all seeds, but it becomes the largest of garden plants and grows into a tree where birds can come and find shelter in its branches. (Matthew 13:31–32)

When we repent and believe in Jesus as our Savior, we learn more and more about the Gospel, our spiritual life will grow as a tiny mustard seed grows into a large plant. As we know more about the Gospel, we spread the Gospel to non-believers, just as the mustard plant will bear new seeds.

Yeast in the Dough

Jesus also used this illustration: "The Kingdom of Heaven is like yeast used by a woman making bread. Even though she used a large amount of flour, the yeast permeated every part of the dough." (Matthew 13:33)

As a Christian learns more about the Gospel, he will change his conduct and behavior. The good conduct and behavior of one person may bring the standard of the entire group—a church, a city, a country, and even the world—to a new level of relationship with God than before, just as yeast permeates every part of the dough.

The Counselor

When we spread the Gospel, it is important for us to let the Holy Spirit take the lead. Although Christians are the children of God, we are also the servants of God when we preach the Gospel. As we are spreading the words of our Master, we need to bring along the Representative of our Master with us. In this way, new believers may build a direct relationship with God through the Holy Spirit right at the beginning. Jesus told His disciples: "But I will send you the Counselor—the Spirit of truth. He will come to you from the Father and will tell you all about me. And you must also tell others about me because you have been with me from the beginning." (John 15:26–27)

The Resurrected Jesus told His disciples: "But when the Holy Spirit has come upon you, you will receive power and will tell people about me everywhere–in Jerusalem, throughout Judea, in Samaria, and to the ends of the earth." (Acts 1:8)

It is very important that as Christians, we need to receive the power from the Holy Spirit when we preach. After all, we preach the words of God and not the words of man.

How Can They Hear?

> For "Anyone who calls on the name of the Lord will be saved." But how can they call on him to save them unless they believe in him? And how can they believe in him if they have never heard about him? And how can they hear about him unless someone tells them? And how will anyone go and tell them without being sent? That is what the Scriptures mean when they say, "How beautiful are the feet of those who bring good news!"
>
> But not everyone welcomes the Good News, for Isaiah the prophet said, "Lord, who has believed our message?" Yet faith comes from listening to this message of good news—the Good News about Christ.
>
> But what about the Jews? Have they actually heard the message? Yes, they have: "The message of God's creation has gone out to everyone, and its words to all the world." (Romans 10:13–18)

God does not force man to do anything. He always gives us a choice. However, God does tell us what is right and what is wrong. Once it's heard, the Gospel is the responsibility of those on the receiving end. They must take initiative to hear well: "Anyone who is willing to hear should listen and understand." "He who has ears to hear, let him hear!" (NKJV; see Matthew 11:15; 13:9, 43; Mark 4:9; Luke 8:8; 14:35; Hebrews 3:7, 15; Revelation 2:7, 11, 17, 29; 3:6, 13, 22; and 13:9)

Preach the Word of God

In the second letter Paul sent to the church in Corinth, he emphasized that Christians should preach about Jesus:

> We don't go around preaching about ourselves; we preach Christ Jesus, the Lord. All we say about ourselves is that we are your servants because of what Jesus has done for us. For God, who said, "Let there be light in the darkness," has made us understand that this light is the brightness of the glory of God that is seen in the face of Jesus Christ.
>
> But this precious treasure—this light and power that now shine within us—is held in perishable containers, that is, in our weak bodies. So everyone can see that our glorious power is from God and is not our own.
>
> We are pressed on every side by troubles, but we are not crushed and broken. We are perplexed, but we don't give up and quit. We are hunted down, but God never abandons us. We get knocked down, but we get up again and keep going. Through suffering, these bodies of ours constantly share in the death of Jesus so that the life of Jesus may also be seen in our bodies. (2 Corinthians 4:5–10)

In the second letter Paul wrote to Timothy in Ephesus he said:

> Preach the word of God. Be persistent, whether the time is favorable or not. Patiently correct, rebuke, and encourage your people with good teaching.
>
> For a time is coming when people will no longer listen to right teaching. They will follow their own desires and will look for teachers who will tell them whatever they want to hear. They will reject the truth and follow strange myths.

> But you should keep a clear mind in every situation. Don't be afraid of suffering for the Lord. Work at bringing others to Christ. Complete the ministry God has given you. (2 Timothy 4:2–5)

The ministry of every Christian, every preacher, and every pastor is to bring others to Christ through the use of the Word of God. Therefore, we should not preach what others like to hear. Instead, we must preach what others need to know about God.

His People, His Time, and His Preaching!

Jesus is the teacher and the believers are the students. The student should learn and do whatever the teacher has done. Jesus said: "The truth is, anyone who believes in me will do the same works I have done, and even greater works." (John 14:12)

The works should include but are not limited to:

1. preaching according to the words in the Holy Bible and personal testimonies;
2. baptizing new believers in the name of the Father, the Son; and the Holy Spirit;
3. coaching the new believers as and when needed;
4. always letting the Holy Spirit take the lead;
5. praying for the healing of the sick in the name of Jesus;
6. raising the dead in the name of Jesus; and
7. casting out demons in the name of Jesus.

Many preachers mention the Holy Spirit while they preach. However, they failed to invite Him to take an active role in their preaching. A good preacher always invites and insists the Holy Spirit to stay within him and lead the preaching throughout. He/she should let the Holy Spirit to take control regardless of any deviation against the time schedule and topics previously planned. After all, it is His people, His time and His preaching!

The apostle Paul pointed out: "Because the foolishness of God is wiser than men, and the weakness of God is stronger than men." (1 Corinthians 1:25) A servant can never be more powerful than his/her master. Christians are God's servants. Christians should make themselves available whenever being called upon, and to obey God's instructions completely. Bear in mind that Christians should live for Jesus and do everything to please God, to praise God and giving God all the Glory!

Planting Seed

As we go about witnessing to others about the power of God in our lives, we will see many different reactions to the Word of God. Jesus compares the responses from the Word of God from different people with planting seed in different types of ground:

> Later that same day, Jesus left the house and went down to the shore, where an immense crowd soon gathered. He got into a boat, where he sat and taught as the people listened on the shore. He told many stories such as this one: "A farmer went out to plant some seed. As he scattered it across his field, some seeds fell on a footpath, and the birds came and ate them. Other seeds fell on shallow soil with underlying rock. The plants sprang up quickly, but they soon wilted beneath the hot sun and died because the roots had no nourishment in the shallow soil. Other seeds fell among thorns that shot up and choked out the tender blades. But some seeds fell on fertile soil and produced a crop that was thirty, sixty, and even a hundred times as much as had been planted. Anyone who is willing to hear should listen and understand." (Matthew 13:3–9)

Jesus explained why people will react differently when we sow the seed of God's Word to them:

> Now here is the explanation of the story I told about the farmer sowing grain: "The seed that fell on the hard path represents those who hear the Good News about the Kingdom and don't understand it. Then the evil one comes and snatches the seed away from their hearts. The rocky soil represents those who hear the message and receive it with joy. But like young plants in such soil, their roots don't go very deep. At first they get along fine, but they wilt as soon as they have problems or are persecuted because they believe the word. The thorny ground represents those who hear and accept the Good News, but all too quickly the message is crowded out by the cares of this life and the lure of wealth, so no crop is produced. The good soil represents the hearts of those who truly accept God's message and produce a huge harvest–thirty, sixty, or even a hundred times as much as had been planted." (Matthew 13:18–23; see also Mark 4:14–20 and Luke 8:11–15)

Successful preaching is important to both the preacher and his audiences. In order for the preacher to preach well, he/she must do a lot of preparing to select the good soil to plant the seeds. While preaching, he/she should invite the Holy Spirit to lead. On the other hand, the audiences must be encouraged to listen in order to understand (see Matthew 13:9).

From a seed being planted in good soil to the stage of harvest involves continued care by the farmer. The same case applies to pastors treating the new believers.

"Upon This Rock I Will Build My Church"

Before Jesus was crucified, he was given high hope from the answer of one of His disciples—Peter:

> When Jesus came to the region of Caesarea Philippi, he asked his disciples, "Who do people say that the Son of Man is?"

> "Well," they replied, "some say John the Baptist, some say Elijah, and others say Jeremiah or one of the other prophets."
>
> Then he asked them, "Who do you say I am?"
>
> Simon Peter answered, "You are the Messiah, the Son of the living God."
>
> Jesus replied, "You are blessed, Simon son of John, because my Father in heaven has revealed this to you. You did not learn this from any human being. Now I say to you that you are Peter, and upon this rock I will build my church, and all the powers of hell will not conquer it." (Matthew 16:13–18)

Jesus knew the weaknesses in Peter even before he denied Him three times in the night before His crucifixion. He strengthened Peter's determination in serving God after he was resurrected:

> After breakfast Jesus said to Simon Peter, "Simon son of John, do you love me more than these?"
>
> "Yes, Lord," Peter replied, "you know I love you."
>
> "Then feed my lambs," Jesus told him.
>
> Jesus repeated the question: "Simon son of John, do you love me?"
>
> "Yes, Lord," Peter said, "you know I love you."
>
> "Then take care of my sheep," Jesus said.
>
> Once more he asked him, "Simon son of John, do you love me?"

Peter was grieved that Jesus asked the question a third time. He said, "Lord, you know everything. You know I love you."

Jesus said, "Then feed my sheep." (John 21:15–17)

In fact, Jesus taught Peter how to build His church. In the church, there are always new believers in Christ. As they are young in the knowledge of the Word of God, they require special attention. A shepherd (pastor) needs to feed the lambs (provide Biblical and spiritual knowledge to new believers) as often and as much as necessary.

As the church members have gained sufficient knowledge and experiences, they grow to adult sheep. The shepherd needs merely to take care of their other needs instead of feeding, as they can find their own food easily.

Then as the sheep grow older, they are no longer as strong as when they were young (those who become sick, weak, inactive or seldom attending church), the shepherd needs to feed them again according to what they are in need of.

Although there is no statistics regarding the number of dropouts (people who once accepted Jesus as their Savior but now don't even go to church); I believe that they are the majority. In other words, the number of people who have quit is larger than the number who attend church and worship God regularly.

Of course, attending church activities does not necessarily qualify for eternal life. We must remember "only those who endure to the end will be saved." All the pastors and servants of God are therefore encouraged to share the words Jesus spoke to Peter in the above regarding different services needed for three different categories of church members.

Harvest So Great, Workers So Few

Jesus taught His disciples how to go and preach:

> The Lord now chose seventy-two other disciples and sent them on ahead in pairs to all the towns and villages he planned to visit. These were his instructions to them: 'The harvest is so great, but the workers are so few. Pray to the Lord who is in charge of the harvest, and ask him to send out more workers for his fields. Go now, and remember that I am sending you out as lambs among wolves. Don't take along any money, or a traveler's bag, or even an extra pair of sandals. And don't stop to greet anyone on the road.
>
> Whenever you enter a home, give it your blessing. If those who live there are worthy, the blessing will stand; if they are not, the blessing will return to you. When you enter a town, don't move around from home to home. Stay in one place, eating and drinking what they provide you. Don't hesitate to accept hospitality, because those who work deserve their pay.
>
> If a town welcomes you, eat whatever is set before you and heal the sick. As you heal them, say, "The Kingdom of God is near you now." But if a town refuses to welcome you, go out into its streets and say, "We wipe the dust of your town from our feet as a public announcement of your doom." And don't forget the Kingdom of God is near!" (Luke 10:1–11)

Yes, the disciples were preaching that the Kingdom of God is near even 2,000 years ago. But God is timeless. He sees a thousand years as a day, a day as a thousand years. Peter said: "The Lord isn't really being slow about his promise to return, as some people think. No, he is being patient for your sake. He does not want anyone to perish so he is giving more time for everyone to repent." (2 Peter 3:9)

As the Good News will be preached throughout the whole world before the end will come, the project requires many workers. All Christians should join together as one large working team in spreading the Gospel!

Where to Spread the Gospel

There is no restriction as to where we should preach. "And the Good News about the Kingdom will be preached throughout the whole world, so that all nations will hear it; and then, finally, the end will come." (Matthew 24:14) Jesus preached in the temple, out in the open, on a boat, on the street, in a restaurant, and in someone's house. We should follow the pattern set up by Jesus–not limit the preaching to the inside of a church.

> And he [Jesus] ordered us to preach everywhere and to testify that Jesus is ordained of God to be the judge of all—the living and the dead. He is the one all the prophets testified about, saying that everyone who believes in him will have their sins forgiven through his name. (Acts 10:42–43, also see Mark 16:15)

When to Spread the Gospel

Although we can preach the Gospel any day of the week, one day is special. God told His selected people, the Jews, to keep the Sabbath holy. They must set aside their daily duties and any regular work. It was the day of rest for God Himself after He spent six days created the heaven, the earth, the sea and everything in them (see Genesis 2:2–3 and Exodus 20:8–11).

Keeping the Sabbath is the Fourth Commandment God gave to His selected people through Moses. It is so important that God ordered His people at least 75 times in the Old Testament to keep the Sabbath Day holy.

In the New Testament, there is also much emphasis on the Sabbath Day. Jesus said He was the Master of the Sabbath, because He was the Creator (see Matthew 12:8; Luke 6:5; Proverb 8:22–36; John 1:1–3). He told the Jews what can be done on the Sabbath Day: i.e., save lives, heal the sick and do charitable work.

Jesus always taught people on the Sabbath Day (see Mark 1:21; Luke 4:16, 31; Luke 6:6; Luke 13:10). After His resurrection, Jesus appointed Paul as one of His Apostles; and Paul, too, taught people on the Sabbath Day (see Acts 13:14; 15:21; 16:13; 17:2; 18:4).

Sabbath—the Fourth Commandment

Jesus told the Jews: "Don't misunderstand why I have come. I did not come to abolish the law of Moses or the writings of the prophets. No, I came to fulfill them. I assure you, until heaven and earth disappear, even the smallest detail of God's law will remain until its purpose is achieved." (Matthew 5:17–18)

Today, most Christians go to church on Sunday. Most of them do not know that it was man who changed the "Holy Day" from the Sabbath Day (Saturday) to the first day of the week (Sunday) in about A.D. 320. Based on the Word of God, the Sabbath Day is Saturday, and it must be kept holy and a day of rest. It is also the day God likes people to worship Him. Since the Sabbath Day was appointed by God Himself, only God has the authority to change it. But the fact is that God did not change it.

All Christians should obey God's words and commandments. Jesus said: "not all people who sound religious are really godly. They may refer to me as 'Lord,' but they still won't enter the Kingdom of Heaven. The decisive issue is whether they obey my father in heaven." (Matthew 7:21)

In order to obey God's Fourth Commandment, Christians should try their best to keep the Sabbath Day holy–to worship God and keep it as the day of rest in each week until the New Jerusalem comes from God out of heaven (see Isaiah 65:17–19, Hebrews 4:8–10, 2 Peter 3:11–13, Revelation 3:12, 21:1–2).

Man's Wisdom Leads to Death

As this God-inspired book draws to a close, you may find yourself puzzling over contradictions between God's Word and what you've always believed. I must tell you that there will always be that contradiction when we are being drawn to God. Our puny wisdom must yield to the wisdom of almighty God.

Remember, in the very beginning, God did not wish man to live on his own wisdom. God told Adam not to eat the fruit from the tree of the knowledge of good and evil. Without this knowledge, man could rely on God's wisdom to live. However, Adam and Eve did not obey God. They ate the fruit God told Adam not to eat.

Once man begins to rely on his own wisdom, he wants to stay away from God. This is the beginning of the disaster. The result is death!

But through God's love and grace, He gave us the Deliverer, the Savior and the Redeemer—Jesus. Whoever believes in Him will not perish but have eternal life. Hallelujah!

Yet man proudly depends on his own wisdom, and considers faith foolish. But look at what God thinks of man's "wisdom":

> Remember, dear brothers and sisters, that a few of you were wise in the world's eyes, or powerful, or wealthy when God called you. Instead, God deliberately chose things the world considers foolish in order to shame those who think they are wise. And he chose those who are powerless to shame those who are powerful. God chose things despised by the world, things counted as nothing at all, and used them to bring to nothing what the world considers important, so that no one can ever boast in the presence of God.
>
> God alone made it possible for you to be in Christ Jesus. For our benefit God made Christ to be wisdom itself. He is the one who made us acceptable to God. He made us pure and holy, and he gave himself to purchase our freedom. As the Scriptures say, "The

> person who wishes to boast should boast only of what the Lord has done." (1 Corinthians 1:26–31; see also John 6:63)

Shall We Pull Out the Weeds?

But if people choose to rely on their own wisdom and reject the grace of God, He will allow them to go that way. It's their choice and their judgment to face. God gives sunshine and rain to the good and the bad. God also gives freedom to man to choose. Judgment will take place only at the end of the world. If we choose Jesus as our Savior and obey the will of the Father, no judgment is pending.

> Here is another story Jesus told: "The Kingdom of Heaven is like a farmer who planted good seed in his field. But that night as everyone slept, his enemy came and planted weeds among the wheat. When the crop began to grow and produce grain, the weeds also grew. The farmer's servants came and told him, 'Sir, the field where you planted that good seed is full of weeds!'
>
> 'An enemy has done it!' the farmer exclaimed.
>
> 'Shall we pull out the weeds?' they asked.
>
> He replied, 'No, you'll hurt the wheat if you do. Let both grow together until the harvest. Then I will tell the harvesters to sort out the weeds and burn them and to put the wheat in the barn.'" (Matthew 13:24–30; see also Mark 4:26–29)

Then, leaving the crowds outside, Jesus went into the house. His disciples said, "Please explain the story of the weeds in the field."

> "All right," he said. "I, the Son of Man, am the farmer who plants the good seed. The field is the world, and the good seed represents the people of the Kingdom. The weeds are the people who belong to the evil one. The enemy who planted the weeds among

> the wheat is the Devil. The harvest is the end of the world, and the harvesters are the angels.
>
> "Just as the weeds are separated out and burned, so it will be at the end of the world. I the Son of Man, will send my angels, and they will remove from my Kingdom everything that causes sin and all who do evil, and they will throw them into the furnace and burn them. There will be weeping and gnashing of teeth. Then the godly will shine like the sun in their Father's Kingdom. Anyone who is willing to hear should listen and understand." (Matthew 13:36–43)

One More Chance

Repent, because the door may close at any time, and we don't know the time:

> Then Jesus used this illustration: "A man planted a fig tree in his garden and came again and again to see if there was any fruit on it, but he was always disappointed. Finally, he said to his gardener, 'I've waited three years, and there hasn't been a single fig! Cut it down. It's taking up space we can use for something else'
>
> The gardener answered, 'Give it one more chance. Leave it another year, and I'll give it special attention and plenty of fertilizer. If we get figs next year, fine. If not, you can cut it down.'" (Luke 13:6–9)

This may be your "one more chance." Sometimes, it appears only once in a lifetime. No one should take the risk not to accept Jesus as Savior when such a chance exists.

No One May Find God by Human Wisdom

Paul told the church in Corinth why man's wisdom cannot find salvation:

> I know very well how foolish the message of the cross sounds to those who are on the road to destruction. But we who are being saved recognize this message as the very power of God. As the Scriptures say:
>
> "I will destroy human wisdom and discard their most brilliant ideas."
>
> So where does this leave the philosophers, the scholars, and the world's brilliant debaters? God has made them all look foolish and has shown their wisdom to be useless nonsense. Since God in his wisdom saw to it that the world would never find him through human wisdom, he has used our foolish preaching to save all who believe. God's way seems foolish to the Jews because they want a sign from heaven to prove it is true. And it is foolish to the Greeks because they believe only what agrees with their own wisdom. So when we preach that Christ was crucified, the Jews are offended, and the Gentiles say it's all nonsense. But to those called by God to salvation, both Jews and Gentiles, Christ is the mighty power of God and the wonderful wisdom of God. This 'foolish' plan of God is far wiser than the wisest of human plans, and God's weakness is far stronger than the greatest of human strength. (1 Corinthians 1:18–25)

In a letter Paul sent to the church in Galatia, he warned that Christians should not deviate from the Gospel:

> Let God's curse fall on anyone, including myself, who preaches any other message than the one we told you about. Even if an

> angel comes from heaven and preaches any other message, let him be forever cursed. I will say it again: If anyone preaches any other gospel than the one you welcomed, let God's curse fall upon that person. Obviously, I'm not trying to be a people pleaser! No, I am trying to please God. If I were still trying to please people, I would not be Christ's servant. Dear brothers and sisters, I solemnly assure you that the Good News of salvation which I preach is not based on mere human reasoning or logic. For my message came by a direct revelation from Jesus Christ himself. No one else taught me. (Galatians 1:8–12)

Communion

In the evening before the crucifixion of Jesus, He told His disciples the meaning of the bread and the cup. He also told them to use it in remembrance of Him until His Return:

> On the night when he was betrayed, the Lord Jesus took a loaf of bread, and when he had given thanks, he broke it and said, "This is my body, which is given for you. Do this in remembrance of me." In the same way, he took the cup of wine after supper, saying, "This cup is the New Covenant between God and you, sealed by the shedding of my blood. Do this in remembrance of me as often as you drink it." For every time you eat this bread and drink this cup, you are announcing the Lord's death until he comes again.
>
> So if anyone eats this bread or drinks this cup of the Lord unworthily, that person is guilty of sinning against the body and the blood of the Lord. That is why you should examine yourself before eating the bread and drinking from the cup. For if you eat the bread or drink the cup unworthily, not honoring the body of Christ, you are eating and drinking God's judgment upon yourself. (1 Corinthians 11:23–29, also refer to Matthew 26:26–29, Mark 14:22–25 and Luke 22:14–20)

The frequency of the communion or the Holy Supper differs from church to church, from weekly to quarterly. The ideal frequency is once every two weeks or once every month on a fixed schedule. All church members should be notified in advance.

Before serving the Holy Supper, it is advisable to sing hymns relating to the crucifixion of Jesus and His salvation. The prayer of forgiveness of our sins should follow. Do state the use of the blood of Jesus when we ask forgiveness of our sins. We must thank God for sending us Jesus to die for our sins. We must also thank Jesus for providing us the way, the truth and the life for which cause He became a man.

"Thank you, Jesus, as we can catch men like fish now!"

Index

Old Testament

Leviticus

Numbers

1 Kings

1 Chronicles

Ezra

Job

Psalms

Psalms (cont'd)

Proverbs

Ecclesiastes

Isaiah

Isaiah (cont'd)

Isaiah (cont'd)

Jeremiah

Zechariah

Malachi

New Testament

Matthew

Matthew (cont'd)

Matthew (cont'd)

Matthew (cont'd)

Mark

Luke

Luke (cont'd)

Luke (cont'd)

Luke (cont'd)

John

John (cont'd)

Acts

Romans

Romans (cont'd)

Romans (cont'd)

1 Corinthians

1 Corinthians (cont'd)

2 Corinthians

Galatians

Ephesians

Philippians

Colossians

1 Thessalonians

2 Thessalonians

1 Timothy

2 Timothy

Titus

Hebrews

Hebrews (cont'd)

James

James (cont'd)

1 Peter

2 Peter

1 John

1 John (cont'd)

Revelation

Revelation (cont'd)

Revelation (cont'd)

Revelation (cont'd)